Golden Fire:

The Story of Cider

Ted Bruning

A Bright Pen Book

Text Copyright © Ted Bruning 2012

Cover design by James Fitt ©
Cover photograph: cider barrels at Gray's, Halstow, Devon.
By Mark Bolton www.markboltonphotography.co.uk

British Library Cataloguing Publication Data.
A catalogue record for this book is available from the British Library

ISBN 978-0-7552-1431-0

Authors OnLine Ltd
19 The Cinques
Gamlingay, Sandy
Bedfordshire SG19 3NU
England

This book is also available in e-book format, details of which are available at
www.authorsonline.co.uk

"Never to be forgotten, that first long secret drink of golden fire, juice of those valleys and of that time, wine of wild orchards, of russet summer, of plump red apples, and Rosie's burning cheeks. Never to be forgotten, or ever tasted again..."

Laurie Lee, Cider With Rosie

About the Author

TED BRUNING has been a journalist in the licensed trade and brewing industry press for over 25 years. His interest in cider was first aroused in 1996 when he compiled the third edition of the Campaign for Real Ale's *Good Cider Guide*. He subsequently launched and edited *The Cider Press,* a quarterly supplement to the Campaign's membership newspaper *What's Brewing,* and in 2009 was the major contributor to the CAMRA book *Cider.* As well as writing about the subject he has hands-on experience as a former cidermaker and the proprietor of *Cidercraft,* a specialist shop in Cambridgeshire.

Other books include *Historic English Inns* (David & Charles 1982), *Historic Pubs of London* (Prion Books 1998), *Historic Inns of England* (Prion Books 2000), *London By Pub* (Prion Books 2001), and *The Microbrewer's Handbook* (Navigator Guides 2007). Ted also has a BA (Hons) in Medieval History from University College, London.

Contents

Author's Preface 9

Introduction.. 11

1: Protocider 13

2: Cider Comes to Britain 25

3: The Yeomen of England 38

4: The National Drink?.. 52

5: So Near... 66

6: Rough v. Smooth 81

7: New Foundations.. 98

8: Rebirth... 112

9: To Market... 126

10: The Brewers' Coat-Tails....................................... 140

11: Boom and Bust 155

12: Piggies in the Middle 167

13: The Craft Revival.. 176

Postscript: A Plea for a Vintage 189

Bibliography and Further Reading 191

Author's Preface

Cider, wrote Peter Clark in *The English Alehouse*, awaits its historian; and although this book is, as far as I know, the first attempt there has been at a narrative history of cider, it still does. No work of this type can hope to be anything like a complete history without a solid foundation of local and special studies to draw on; and the problem for researchers into cider is the paucity of source material. Unregulated and untaxed for most of its history, cider has also gone officially unnoticed and unrecorded; certainly it has nothing like the wealth of court records and other primary source materials that beer and brewing have. I have therefore had to focus fairly narrowly on those aspects of cider that the available sources have revealed.

Where cider has surfaced, it has mostly been in records of a commercial and economic type – medieval account books; Tudor, Stuart, and Georgian technical manuals; late 18th-century and early 19th-century agricultural surveys. This has suited me well: my background is in trade journalism, so I am used to interpreting the world as a business. I appreciate, though, that some readers will think that my approach has been a little unbalanced, and that the romance and folklore of cider deserve rather more attention than I have given them. Fortunately, James Crowden and Fiona Mac have covered these aspects of cider far better than I could ever hope to: anybody interested in the subject should order *Cider: The Forgotten Miracle*, *Ciderland*, and *Ciderlore: Cider in the Three Counties* without delay.

Others may have hoped for more technical information to help them make cider for themselves, and a wealth of such literature is available. The

Hereford Cider Museum's website, www.cidermuseum.co.uk, lists the best of them, and by buying what books you need from the Museum you can help finance its work.

Finally, my thanks are due to Alan Stone of the Bath & West Society, Dave Matthews and Cressida Slater of the Welsh Perry & Cider Society, and Roger Jackson of Weston's Cider for their support and enthusiasm.

Introduction

Romance and alcohol go hand in hand. Jolly medieval friars and their ale. Fearless smugglers braving Atlantic storms to land their brandy casks in secluded Cornish coves. Hunting squires with their pints of port. Long John Silver and his rum. Hidden stills in remote Highland glens. The aristocratic châteaux of Bordeaux and Burgundy and their unending ranks of peerless vines.

Cider has its romance too. Not, perhaps, in its most modern manifestation – a fizzy concoction served over ice, with little character to remind you of the orchards it sprang from. But think of those gnarled orchards themselves, heavy with fruit on a misty autumn morning. Think of the toilers in those orchards, just as gnarled, and just as much part of the landscape. Think of the great oak tuns in draughty barns where the juice of the apple completes its slow, mysterious transformation over the long cold winter months. Yes, cider has its romance: as ancient as the soil in which it is rooted; as mystical as Avalon, the Celtic Isle of Apples. To subject such legendary stuff to objective enquiry seems almost blasphemous.

But cider and its sister, perry, have their history as well: a history of blunt facts, of geography, of economics, of politics. And without wishing to overturn the applecart of romance, it's a history that deserves to be told. For never in its long life has cider been as popular as it is now: no longer in the shadow of wine and beer, it has found an entirely new constituency that embraces young and old, men and women.

Paradoxically, it has been the arrival of those fizzy "over ice" brands so little redolent of apples and orchards that has effected the change. The long-established custodians of cider and its traditions had lost their way and were faltering when, in 2003, a newcomer – Magner's, from Ireland – arrived on the market. So potent was its simple idea of serving cider with a small shovelful of ice that within a couple of years it had become ubiquitous, with other makers frantically repackaging their own brands, and often reformulating them too, in hopeful imitation.

How many of those converted to cider in this way have the same sense of the history in their glasses that they would find in a single Highland malt, say, or a château-bottled claret? Few, I suspect. But it's there, all the same; and although it's the least tangible ingredient in any recipe, an appreciation of its contribution always enhances the pleasure of simply drinking.

An appreciation of the history of cider might also tempt more drinkers to try it in its purest form – not the pasteurised, carbonated cider of 4.5-5% alcohol by volume that is available everywhere, but the fresh, still cider of 6.5-7.5% that they are only likely to encounter in cider-producing regions. This is not, as many people like to think, mere rustic rocket-fuel, but a pure, natural product that was being made and appreciated by the patrician landowners of Ancient Rome and can be as subtle and as complex as any fine wine. Tasted with an open mind, an aromatic Somerset Redstreak single-varietal vintage cider from Perry Brothers, with its hint of ginger and lemon, is enough to cure the most oafish drinker of Mummerset mockery forever.

But in tracing the true story of cider, the investigator encounters one frustration after another. For cider has covered its tracks uncannily well. Even into the modern period references are scattered, fragmentary, and vague. One finds oneself looking for something one instinctively knows ought to be there but which one can barely glimpse through the undergrowth of history, or can sometimes only guess at. And not only are records maddeningly scarce, the very language is ambiguous. No wonder so many myths and legends have grown up: for so much of what we think we know about cider turns out on close inspection to be wishful thinking.

But then, if you truly love good cider and are continually frustrated at how hard it is to come by, perhaps a little wishful thinking is forgivable...

1: Protocider

What could be simpler than cider? You crush apples in a mill; you press the juice out of the resulting pulp; you leave it to ferment; and hey presto! You have cider. The Campaign for Real Ale (which promotes old-fashioned farm cider as well as cask-conditioned beer) used to have a t-shirt slogan that summed it up perfectly: "Apples – nothing else needed; nothing else wanted". Even the yeast can be supplied by nature.

Such a simple drink, devotees argue, must have been with us from time out of mind. And indeed apples are among humankind's oldest friends. Botanists until recently believed that the modern domestic apple descended from a natural hybridisation about 10,000 years ago, just after the Ice Age, of the European crab apple, *malus sylvestris*, and an Asiatic cousin, *malus pumila*, from the Caucasus. It is now argued that the different families of apple have a common ancestor but developed separately: whichever theory is right, the first humans to abandon the nomadic life and settle down to agricultural respectability seem to have appreciated their apples. Archaeologists have found carbonised pips, often in appreciable quantities, in settlements all over the Middle East and Northern Mediterranean: the earliest such find comes from Catal Huyuk in modern Turkey and dates from around 6500BC.

But if our Neolithic and Bronze Age ancestors included apples in their diet, did they also enjoy the odd beaker of cider? Despite the often-expressed belief that cider is one of the most ancient of drinks, it seems unlikely. Certainly, apple juice ferments readily enough. But getting the juice out of the apple is a complicated job calling for a level of technological development probably beyond the resources available even to the builders of Stonehenge.

We do know, though, that our distant ancestors liked a drink, and the prehistory of alcohol is almost an academic discipline on its own. There's even a strong, if disputed, school of belief that the urge to make alcohol more easily available was one of the driving forces behind humankind's transition from hunter-gatherer to farmer. The argument goes that nomadic clans first discovered drunkenness either by eating rotting fruit, which contains some alcohol (although I have yet to meet anyone brave enough to test the theory in person), or by drinking naturally-fermented sap, and decided to gain permanent access to alcohol by cultivating fruit trees and vines. And cultivation, of course, demands at least semi-permanent settlement, the theory being that while the able-bodied males of the clan continued principally as hunters, the womenfolk stayed at home to tend the trees.

Whether or not access to alcohol really was a factor, the first agriculturalists had plenty of sources of fermentable material close at hand, especially in the Middle East. The sap of the date palm is up to 70% sugar. If the trees are tapped, as archaeologists believe they were, and the sap isn't consumed immediately it will rapidly start to ferment. In fact the Hebrew word *shekhar*, one of nine used in the Bible to denote alcohol, is cognate with the Arabic *sikhar* and the Greek stem *zacchar-*, both meaning sugar; so if a narrower definition can be teased out of the Biblical contexts in which it occurs, it should mean a sweet alcoholic drink. Concentrated date palm sap, once the common sweetener of the Far East, is still called "jaggery" today, and *shekhar* also gives us, by devious etymological routes, our modern word cider.

Grapes, especially wild ones, may not have contained as much sugar as palm sap; but what sugar they did contain was just as easy to get at. Grapes can be pressed with nothing more technically advanced than a pair of feet, and the juice is just as willing to ferment as palm sap is. In fact the problem was stopping it: to remain in its unfermented state its yeasts had to be killed either by cooking it – and there is evidence of grape juice being boiled into a thick syrup to be reconstituted as required – or by chilling it in a leak-proof container in running water.

Even cereals, whose starches in their natural state are not soluble and so won't ferment, proved not all that difficult for Neolithic man to get alcohol out of. Warm, damp grain starts to sprout, activating the enzymes that convert starch to sugar. If dried, the sprouted grain becomes malt and needs only to be coarsely ground to become the fermentable base for beer. It's not hard to imagine how this process might have happened accidentally – in fact it's hard to imagine how this process might *not* have happened accidentally. A leaky granary; an apparently spoiled crop; a desperate attempt at salvage, either by spreading the damp grains in the sun or even drying them over a fire; the first suspicious nibble; and the happy discovery that the grains have become sweet, sweetness being highly prized. If the malted grains were then ground for porridge meal, and the porridge were not all consumed at once, the leftovers would start to ferment. This is not only the distant genesis of beer, it's a method of brewing still practised in parts of Africa.

Apples, however, are a different proposition, especially the small, tough apples of the ancient world. Palm sap and grapes need little by way of mechanical intervention to give up their juices, and even malted grains need only to be ground and steeped in warm water; apples, though, require not one piece of machinery but two. First the fruit has to be crushed or milled to a pulp, and then the pulp has to be pressed to squeeze out the sugary liquid. Using only the hand-querns available to Neolithic and Bronze Age households, milling anything like an appreciable volume of apples would have been a hopelessly uneconomic chore. Small batches might have been crushed as a sweetish porridge, perhaps in famine years or as a baby-food; but in nothing like the quantity required to yield enough juice to be worth fermenting. And even if those early agrarians had been able to mill apples efficiently enough to produce large amounts of pomace, they simply didn't have the technology to press it. And it's here that the story of cider is connected with olives and the extraction of their oil.

Olives first seem to have been cultivated in modern Israel, Lebanon, and Jordan; their oil was certainly being exported to Egypt from around 2000BC. By the Homeric period, cultivated olives were pretty much ubiquitous in the Mediterranean world, but the oil was still a luxury rather than the dietary commonplace it later became: in the Iliad, for instance, Patroclus uses it to anoint himself rather than to fry with. The reason for this lies in the method of extraction used. The fruit was put in a circular stone trough with a rotating upright shaft in the centre. The shaft bore an axle on which a vertical millstone was mounted, with the outward projection of the shaft forming the handle. The whole thing was operated by a slave plodding wearily round and round pushing the millstone over the fruit, with the oil and the bitter juice, *amercum*, escaping through a runnel into a collecting vat to be separated. In some cases, notably the example preserved at Pompeii, the axle projected right through the shaft and carried two facing millstones and handles, in which case two slaves had to plod wearily round and round. But even the two-man machine is small and inefficient, leaving plenty of oil still in the pomace to be extracted by a second or even third crushing. The time and effort required to operate such a device puts a natural brake on the amount of oil it can produce; hence olive oil's luxury status in Homer.

This simple machine is commonly described as an olive-press, but in fact it's nothing of the sort. It's a mill, the mechanical successor to the earliest hand-querns; and if you scale it up and substitute a horse for a slave you have exactly the sort of cider mill that remained in use until well into the last century. Examples still in perfect working order (theoretically, at least) survive on farms all over the West of England and North-West France. But it isn't a press, and if you put apples in it instead of olives you will end up with perfectly good pomace but precious little juice. For an olive is a good deal softer than an apple and surrenders its oil at the lightest touch: olive oil can even be extracted, impractically perhaps, simply by squeezing the olives in your hand. The hard cell walls of the apple demand a second process before they crack; and for that we have to wait for the arrival of the mechanical press such as the lever described by Cato in the early second century BC.

In *de Re Rustica*, Cato catalogues the buildings, slaves, and equipment needed to run a large aristocratic estate, among them the components of an industrial-scale olive press. The olives are milled and the first runnings collected as described above, but the pomace is then transferred into a willow basket that stands on a solid press-bed measuring about 6ft x 4ft. Beside the bed is a massive upright, with a horizontal beam – the lever – up to 40ft long pivoting on it. Halfway along the lever is a platen that sits comfortably on top of the basket. At the free end of the lever is a counterweight, perhaps a net filled with stones. The motive power is, again, human: a pair of ropes at the end of the beam run through pulleys attached to the rafters of the pressing shed, and a gang of slaves cautiously lowers the platen into the basket and raises it up again simply by hauling on one rope or the other. The trick is to maintain a steady, even pressure, by which means almost all the oil can be extracted.

The lever press made the production of cider on a worthwhile scale a possibility for the first time; and thanks to Pliny the Elder's *De Rerum*

Naturum we know that by the first century AD cider was indeed being made. He didn't call it cider, though: the word *cisera* wasn't coined until the Bible was translated into Latin, when it first appeared as a straightforward transliteration of the unfamiliar *shekhar*. Pliny's surviving great work includes chapters on wine-making and fruit-growing; in the former, under the heading "66 Varieties of Artificial Wine" he says: "Wine is made, too, of the pods of the Syrian carob, of pears, and of all kinds of apples", while he describes the colour of apple juice, rather oddly, as "foaming" – presumably because the juice starts fermenting and frothing almost as soon as it is pressed. And in a section headed "41 Varieties of Pear", Pliny includes the Falernian, "so called from the drink which it affords, so abundant is its juice". The inference is that its juice was commonly fermented, since Falernian is correctly a superior type of wine.

With these rather throwaway lines cider and its cousin, perry, enter history for the first time. There may well have been cider and perry long before Pliny wrote those words, but there is no evidence for them, and an understanding of the technology suggests not – or not, at least, before the invention of Cato's lever press. Cider romantics who believe that the Ancient Britons fermented the apples to which they appear to have been devoted are looking in the wrong direction: what evidence there is tells us that cider was the invention of the landed aristocracy of Rome.

Even as Pliny was writing, the lever press which had first made the production of cider in viable quantities a technological possibility was being superceded by a new invention. The lever press survives in the Mediterranean for the small-scale production of olive oil; and the Devonshire writer Hugh Stafford records makeshift lever presses being improvised by cottagers to press apples and pears in 18th-century England – although he adds: "This machine is not much used, nor is it much to be recommended". A hybrid variant, with the free end raised and lowered by a screw rather than by ropes, was reported by William Marshall as being in common use on larger farms in west Devon in the 1790s, and although it achieved an efficient extraction it took up an inordinate amount of space, required a lever as thick as the deck-beams of a man o' war, and was "altogether an uncouth, unwieldy, monstrous instrument".

Its more compact successor, the screw press, was first described by Pliny's contemporary Hero of Alexandria in his *Mechanica*; and it was so simple and economical to operate that it rapidly became the standard device for all kinds of pressing. Olives, grapes, apples, cloths, paper – anything that needed to be squeezed, in fact – could be and was processed in a screw press; and if longevity is any measure it must be one of the most successful designs in human history, for it is still in everyday use all over the world today. The commonest version uses two vertical screws standing on either side of the press-bed, with a beam between them that is lowered and raised by rotating the screws. The item to be pressed is placed on the bed with a board and perhaps a flat weight on top of it, and the beam is gradually lowered. A variant with a single central screw is almost as common, especially for smaller presses; but whether twin or single screw, this is the device that truly revolutionised the world, for Gutenberg adapted it in the 15th century to become the first moveable-type printing press. It's important to record, however, that a screw-press must have been an expensive item to build. Each screw had to be hand-cut, and the male and female threads had to correspond almost exactly. The time and skill required cannot have been negligible, and effective screw-presses must have been beyond the resources of all but the best-capitalised estates. This is a limitation that will apply from Pliny and Hero's day right through to the late Middle Ages.

But all of this rather begs a question. Why should the Romans, whose staple was wine, go to all the trouble and effort of producing a drink which Pliny himself describes as "artificial"? A clue is provided by the very nature of the books that Cato and Pliny – as well as others such as Varro and Pliny's contemporaries Columella and even Virgil – were writing. Cato's and Columella's works were manuals of estate management, while Pliny's was far more wide-ranging but was also, essentially, a handbook for businesspeople. Like the British agricultural improvers of the 16th and 17th centuries, these writers and their audience were deeply concerned with the need to make their estates as productive and profitable as possible. In Cato's day, Italy was recovering from the economic damage wrought by Hannibal's 10-year incursion; in Pliny's, Rome was emerging from a long succession of civil wars that might not have caused the material destruction of the Second Punic War but had undoubtedly had a severe impact on aristocratic fortunes. Pliny makes it clear that the aristocracy was busily engaged on maximising the revenues of their estates through experiment and innovation. Apple varieties won't grow true from seed: natural hybrids have to be grafted or budded on to rootstock, a method of cultivation known well before the Roman period. (In fact most of the hedgerow trees that we call crabs aren't true crabs at all but wildings, the feral descendants of domestic varieties). The Romans probably learnt it from the neighbouring Greek colonies of Magna Graecia or Southern Italy, and Pliny's list of 21 apple varieties is headed "Fruits Most Recently Introduced", many of which are named after the landowners who, presumably, first propagated them. In a similar vein, Columella describes his uncle's experiments with improving his flocks of sheep through cross-breeding.

The new apple varieties and more efficient production techniques described by Cato, Pliny and Columella enabled the creation of a surplus, and one of the drivers of innovation throughout human history has been the search for a way of preserving food surpluses. To subsistence farmers ever since farming began techniques including smoking, drying, pickling, salting and fermentation have literally been matters of life and death, especially in the anxious days of January and February when the surpluses of the preceding year have to be stretched until spring. In more sophisticated economies, processing fresh produce has been equally vital as a way of facilitating trade, not only by extending the life of the product but also by improving its portability and by adding value. Cheese is milk given a longer life, portability, and value by fermentation. Salami is meat given a longer life, portability, and value by salting and dry-curing. To jump forward a few centuries, whisky is beer given a longer life, portability, and value by distillation. Tellingly, Cato advises estate managers to grow apples "for preservation"; Pliny reveals that two centuries later they have followed Cato's advice by turning apples and pears into cider and perry, giving them a longer life, portability, and value by fermentation, and at the same time generating extra profit by sweating the capital and human assets they already possessed for the production of wine and olive oil.

A profitable trade in Classical Antiquity in cider and perry, especially in a perry good enough to be nicknamed "Falernian", can only be assumed, although we do know thanks to the 4th-century writer Palladius that cider and perry continued to be made and enjoyed throughout late Classical Antiquity. In *De Re Rustica*, he casually records (according to a 15th-century translation that gained wide popularity in England) "now everie wyne of pomes is made". He also gives a recipe for pear wine that involves crushing the fruit but, instead of pressing it, soaking the pulp and then wringing it in a cloth bag. But what is undeniable is that the technology necessary for the mass manufacture of cider and perry was both capital and labour intensive.

In our own time we have come to perceive the production of cider, especially in its most traditional form, as an artisanal craft practised by small farmers on a small scale. In Pliny's time it was an activity that belonged to large-scale enterprises with plenty of capital; and this is the characteristic that will persist throughout the medieval and early modern periods. But having burst upon the world in the first century AD, cider almost disappears from the records between the fall of Rome and the High Middle Ages. We catch only the odd glimpse of it, and in references that are often ambiguous; but enough to reassure us that it had not entirely died out.

The *Barzaz Breiz* or Breton Ballads were collected from oral tradition in the form of folk-songs, and published in 1839 by a French *vicomte,* Théodor Hersart de la Villemarqué. Controversy has raged over their authenticity ever since. One of them, *Le Vin des Gaulois,* purports to be a sixth-century war-song celebrating the raiding parties who made frequent incursions into neighbouring Frankish territory to steal wine, which the song says is better than Breton mead, beer, or cider (*gwin aval*). But how accurately the lyric had been transmitted over 13 centuries of repetition, and whether the *vicomte* recorded faithfully what he heard, or edited the folk-songs to make them appear more antique than they really were, or indeed made them up altogether, is still hotly debated: the latest book on the subject was published only in 1989, and comes down rather on de la Villemarqué's side.

However Gregory of Tours, in his *History of the Franks* of about the same vintage, does make one passing reference to cider alongside many mentions of wine and none of beer. There is also an apparent reference to perry in Venantius Fortunatus's *Life of St Radegund*, from about the year 600, although it is not entirely unambiguous. So virtuous was the reluctant bride of the Frankish King Clothar that she would touch no "undiluted wine or decoction of mead or fermented beer" but only "sweetened water or perry". The earlier Life of the Cornish/Breton saint, Guénolé, also has him drinking only perry, as do a handful of other early hagiographies. However the word commonly used for perry, *pyratium,* has also been interpreted as unfermented pear juice, a view perhaps supported by the context: early pears were inedibly sour, and drinking their juice must have been quite a penance. On the other hand, pear-juice spontaneously ferments as rapidly as apple-juice, so perhaps the saints' abstemious intentions were frustrated by biochemistry.

Two centuries pass before our next glimpses of Frankish cider. The Plan of

St Gall was commissioned by Adelhard, Abbot of the great monastery of Corbie, in about 820 and is a detailed blueprint for a model monastery which was never built and was perhaps never intended to be: some scholars think that it was more of a paradigm than an actual plan. As well as architect's drawings it includes instructions on the management of the proposed abbey's grounds right down to what fruit trees, and even which strains of each fruit, should be planted. And among the dozens of different trees the putative monks were to cultivate were five kinds of apple: eaters, keepers, early croppers, sweets... and bitters. The significance of this last is that bitter apples are cider apples.

Finally, not in date order but in ascending order of unambiguity, we have Charlemagne's capitulary *De Villis* of some time between 790 and 812. In many ways it's rather like the Plan of St Gall, except that it deals not with the regulation and management of an idealised monastery but of a very real set of royal estates. In it, the imperial chancery lays down minutely detailed instructions for stewards to follow regarding the equipping, manning, and management of their charges. As at St Gall, apple and pear trees are to be planted; and among the estate's labourers the steward is to ensure that there are "*siceratores, id est qui cerevisiam vel pomatium sive pyratium vel aliud quodcumque liquamen ad bibendum aptum fuerit facere sciant.*" That is, "makers of strong drink who know how to make beer, cider, perry, or other liquors." The inference that *pyratium* and *pomatium* are alcoholic cider and perry is supplied by their listing alongside beer and by the use of the word *siceratores*: the *sicera-* root is used here in its loose Biblical sense of strong drink.

Disparate, ambiguous and vague as these references may be, they share a common factor. The Breton war-band that preferred the stolen wine of the Nantais to its own *gwin aval*, if it was anything like other Celtic war-bands, was composed of young aristocrats. Gregory of Tours' one mention of cider came in the context of royal and noble feasting. Radegund, the drinker of perry, was a great queen and moved in the most elevated sections of society. And both the Plan of St Gall and the Capitulary *De Villis* dealt with planning, equipping, and managing large estates. So from its dawn in Classical Antiquity down to the early Middle Ages the character of cider did not change: it remained a minority or even a marginal drink, seldom referred to in writing. But those few references always occur in an aristocratic or landowning context, for the heavy capital investment needed to mill and press apples and pears in worthwhile quantities made cider a rarity, even perhaps a luxury, and certainly not the common beverage of the peasantry.

So marginal was cider that it even lacked a name. To Pliny the Elder it was merely wine made from apples (or pears). To the Breton warriors it was apple wine. Charlemagne's scribes did give cider and perry names of their own, true, *pomatium* and *pyratium*, but they seem never to have gained currency. Only later in the Middle Ages was the Biblical word that appears to describe palm wine, *shekhar*, rendered in Latin as *sicera* (and in Basque as *sagadoa* – another indicator that cider is not an ancient drink, for it has no word of its own even in the most ancient of European languages), adapted to give us the Old French *chistre*, the Norman French *cidre*, and the English "cider".

But if it was a minority product, nameless and rarely recorded, its production still seems to have become widespread. It is always dangerous to try to extrapolate backwards from the modern situation, especially over such a long period, but cidermaking is common throughout what were once Frankish lands and even beyond. All of us who have been on holiday in Normandy, or have even just passed through, will be aware of its cider: Normandy was a fully-integrated part of the Frankish empire until 911, when Charles the Simple ceded the region to an especially persistent army of Norse raiders led by Rolf the Ganger. Brittany, although never as fully-integrated into the Empire as Normandy had been, was also under Frankish influence and is another noted cider-producing region.

Less well-known, in this country at least, is the cider tradition of Central Germany, also known as Franken or Franconia, with Frankfurt-am-Main as its principal city. Cider is also made in quantity both on a craft scale and by large commercial concerns along the Moselle, in Hesse, and in the Saarland. It has not one but three names in German: *Apfelwein*, *Most*, and *Viez*; and there is a *Viez* tourist route stretching from Saarburg to the border with Luxembourg, which also produces cider under the name *Viez*. The words *Most* and *Viez* are both Latin-derived: *mustum* is simply the Latin for fruit-juice, while *Viez* comes from *vice* meaning substitute (as in the English vicar and vice-captain), which takes us right back to Pliny and his "artificial wines". Although it's hard to pin down in the absence of written records, these Latin derivations seem to point us back to the Franks and the two great manuals of estate management, the Plan of St Gall and *De Villis*. If the Emperor himself and the leading churchman of his day were advocates of fruit husbandry and cidermaking, it seems safe to assume that nobles throughout the huge and sprawling Frankish Empire ordered their own estates along similar lines; and this brings us back again to Cato, Pliny, and the question of technology.

It's often said that where the grape stops, the apple begins. This may be true today, if to an ever lessening extent; it certainly wasn't true in the temperate period of the early Middle Ages before the advent of the Little Ice Age in the early 14th century. In the 13th century, towards the end of the Little Climatic Optimum, there were vineyards as far north as Lincoln, Leeds, and even the Scottish Borders. And as the Christian church spread northwards following the collapse of the Western Roman Empire in the late 5th century, first converting Rome's barbarian successor states and then expanding beyond the empire's former boundaries, it brought viticulture and winemaking with it. For wine was, and is, essential to climax of the Mass, the Consecration; and as every priest said, and says, Mass every day, then wherever there are priests there must be wine. To the monks who followed in the wake of the first missionaries, planting vineyards was a statement of intent as well as a doctrinal necessity: Christianity was here to stay, and the Church was putting down roots both physical and metaphorical. Thus we learn from the chronicler Aimoin (c960-1010) that vines grew in abundance at the great monastery of Jumièges in Normandy, where a charter of 1472 records a large vineyard as still being in use; more monastic vineyards are attested at Caen and Lisieux, and indeed winemaking persisted in Normandy until the late 18th century when the vineyard at Argance near Caen finally gave up the struggle. As for Germany, it can scarcely be coincidence that the *Viez* regions and the winemaking regions are virtually coterminous.

The connection with cider is a technological one. If Cato's lever press made the extraction of juice from apples possible, Hero of Alexandria's screw press made it cost-effective. We have already noted the dimensions of Cato's lever-press: the cost of the beams alone, not to mention the size of the building needed to accommodate it, made it a major item of capital expenditure. The screw-press, however, is far more compact and less wasteful of materials, the cost of cutting the screws notwithstanding. It can also, unlike the lever press, be worked by a single operative. Grapes can be crushed by treading, extracting "free-run" juice without the need of a mechanical press, but a mechanical press can extract far more juice. Such a large capital investment needs to be justified, though, by being worked as hard as possible; and the grape-harvest can last for as little as a month or less. By planting early and late cropping varieties of apple and pear, the press can be put to work for two months either side of the grape-harvest. Thus winemaking makes cidermaking technically possible, while cidermaking makes winemaking economically viable. So it is not, as is often claimed, to the dim, weird, distant Celts that we owe our cider but to the drive for the efficient management of large seigneurial estates transmitted from the Romans to the Franks and then to the various Medieval kingdoms that carved up Charlemagne's legacy.

2: Cider Comes to Britain

Did the Anglo-Saxons make cider? They could have: the technology existed a mere 30 miles across the sea in the Frankish empire, as we have seen, and there were close trading and political links between the Franks and the Saxon kingdom of Kent from an early date. But that doesn't mean they actually did; and a big linguistic problem stands between us and any certainty on the subject.

To make cider, the Saxons would have had to possess the technology to make wine: in particular, efficient mechanical pressing equipment. They were already familiar with wine when they started their conquest of what was to become England, because they had been in contact with Roman society – first as raiders, then as mercenaries and settlers – for more than a century. As raiders, wine must have been part of their plunder. As mercenaries, it could have been part of their pay. As settlers, they would have found it in daily use among their Romano-British neighbours. And after they rebelled in about 450 and started their conquest in earnest, they seem to have come across untended vineyards in the territories taken from the defeated British, for there are references both to wild vines – *wilde wingearde* – and, in charters, to *wintreows* or "wine-trees" as boundary markers, suggesting overgrown and abandoned vines.

Familiarity with the product, however, doesn't imply the knowledge necessary to make it. Only after King Aethelbert of Kent nailed his colours to the Frankish mast in 597 by agreeing to convert to Christianity can we say for certain that the technology necessary for winemaking became available. For one of Aethelbert's first acts after the conversion was to give Augustine enough land to found a monastery. Over the next century monasteries spread across the whole of England: in 664 Whitby Abbey in North Yorkshire hosted the Synod that united the Celtic and Saxon churches, and the Venerable Bede's monastery of Jarrow, 400 miles from Canterbury, was established by 680. Between Canterbury and Jarrow there lay many dozens of minsters and abbeys, some with only half-a-dozen brothers, some with over 100. And as we have already discovered, where there are Christians there is Mass, and where there is Mass there must be wine.

Viticulture was soon an established and even commonplace feature of Anglo-Saxon life. In the 730s Bede records: "*On sumum stowum wingeardas growath*" – "in some places vineyards grow". In the mid-10th century King Eadwig gave a vineyard to Glastonbury Abbey; his successor Edgar gave one at Watchet to Abingdon Abbey *cum vinitoribus* – with vine-dressers – and in 990 a Bedfordshire widow named Aelfgifu left the produce of her vineyard to the Abbey of St Albans. Vineyards are mentioned in lawcodes including Alfred the Great's. Westminster Abbey owned vineyards at Staines, and wine both imported and domestic is mentioned in letters, leechdoms, and a host of other writings. Clearly, Anglo-Saxon landowners both secular and religious were active in viticulture, although wine was definitely a high-status drink for the rich, as Aelfric's late 10th-century *Colloquy* makes clear: Teacher: What do you drink? Pupil: Ale if I have it, otherwise water. Teacher: Don't you drink wine? Pupil: No, I am not rich enough. And wine is not for the young and foolish but for the old and wise.

What is much harder to establish, though, is whether the Saxons' grapes shared the wine press with apples. Wine production, as we have seen, doesn't actually require a press, but cider production most certainly does; and presses are not mentioned at all in the literature save for a single depiction of one in an illuminated 11th-century Book of Genesis. In *Anglo-Saxon Food And Drink* (Anglo-Saxon Books, 2006) Ann Hagen reports some 50 wine compound words, of which 35 relate to vine growing and wine production – *wincole, winseax, winbeam* – but no compound suggesting a wine press. The Saxons were certainly familiar enough with apples, which are mentioned frequently in leechdoms and feature in many place-names and also as boundary markers in charters. Apples were evidently valued, too: their abundance was prayed for at the coronation of Aethelred the Unready. But familiarity with apples need not imply familiarity with cider. The Saxons don't even seem to have had a word for it: *aeppel win* appears infrequently, but as a gloss for *ydromellum* or strong mead; and anyway *aeppel* does not necessarily translate as apple, but as a generic term for almost any fruit – a *brambel aeppel*, for instance, is a blackberry. Indeed this generic usage persisted in many languages until the early modern period, when new and exotic fruits and vegetables were commonly dubbed "apples" – hence the French *pomme de terre*, the Italian *pomodoro* (tomato), the Dutch and Flemish *sinaasappel* (orange), and our very own pineapple.

And then there is the problem word, *beor*. It and its compounds – among others *beorsetle*, meaning a drinking bench, *beor sele*, meaning a *beor* hall, *beorbydene*, meaning a *beor* barrel, and *beorscype*, meaning a drinking bout – occur frequently in Old English literature of all kinds: leechdoms, glosses, laws, sermons, penitentials, and poems including the oldest of them all, Beowulf. Some rents were even paid in it: for instance, in the mid-9th century Bishop Cuthwulf leased a piece of land for an annual rent of 15 sesters of *beor*, or about 25 gallons. The context generally indicates a highly-prized drink, socially and gastronomically a step up from *ealu* (ale) and on a par with *medu* (mead) if not perhaps *win*. It has generally – and not unreasonably, you might think – been translated simply as beer; but Ann Hagen makes a strong case for identifying it as cider.

Her argument is based on many factors, not least that while we know the meanings of *ealu*, *medu*, *win*, *morath* (mulberry wine), and *piment* (spiced wine), we don't know the meaning of *beor*; and cider is the only candidate. It is occasionally contextually associated with *ofetes wos* (fruit juice) or is *gewrungen* (pressed). It is also regarded as stronger than other drinks – in one leechdom, pregnant women are advised to avoid it – and is often described as being sweet. Her interpretation is reinforced by the fact that the Old Norman for cider is *bère*, both *beor* and *bère* deriving from *bjorr*, an Old Norse word for strong drink, rather than bere or barley (the Normans, it should be remembered, were originally Vikings themselves).

But there are problems. One is that the word is so frequently interchangeable with others, especially in poetry. Anglo-Saxon poets had a maddening habit of side-stepping a word's meaning in favour of its music. Often the poet's choice of word is determined by the requirements of scansion, a taste for alliteration, or the avoidance of repetition: in *Beowulf*, for instance, the hero is taunted by Unferth, who is *beore druncen* at a *beorescype* in King Hrothgar's *meoduhalle* where many a *medoful* (mead-cup) has been drained. Context, in this case, doesn't supply an unambiguous meaning.

Another problem is that *beor* is almost always used in contexts that imply both sweetness and strength. Its sweetness is attested by its frequent use as a gloss for such Latin terms as *mulsum*, which we know to have been based on honey; and as evidence of its strength Hagen quotes a leechdom that gives the weight of *beor* as considerably less than that of water, alcohol being 20% lighter than water. But with pure cider, you can't have sweetness and strength together. Hagen claims that cider yeasts will work up to some 18% alcohol by volume; cidermakers of my acquaintance will allow about 14%, but to achieve that strength the juice has to have considerable amounts of extra sugar added. In a hot, dry growing season pure apple juice will contain enough sugar to yield a cider of about 8.5% ABV; 6-7.5% is more usual. So cider is not, typically, stronger than wine, as Hagen claims; at best it is as strong as the most alcoholic of beers. And at that strength it cannot be sweet: cider yeasts are voracious, and fruit sugars are easily digestible, so a strong cider will have fermented out to near-complete dryness. Naturally sweet ciders are generally very low in alcohol – modern French examples are often below 3% – because they are made by adding lime to precipitate the nutrients the yeast requires, and by frequent racking from one vessel to another to inhibit the build-up of an active yeast population.

There are, however, methods by which a drink that was both strong and sweet could have been made using the technology available at the time, which might give us a clue as to the true nature of *beor*.

Perhaps the most straightforward is ice-distilling which, unlike the more usual method of distilling by evaporation, is simplicity itself: you merely leave a tub of alcoholic liquor outdoors in the middle of winter and periodically scoop out the ice. Alcohol freezes at a much lower temperature than water, so by removing the ice you are increasing the concentration and thus the strength of the liquor. This was once a common practice among cidermakers in New England, who called the resulting spirit applejack; and if your base liquor is sweet your end result will be sweeter still, as well as stronger. There is no reason why Norse and Anglo-Saxon brewers, winemakers, or cidermakers should not have ice-distilled their products – it could even have been an accidental discovery, like that of malt – but on the other hand there is absolutely no evidence that they did.

Another method of making super-strength cider possible using early Medieval technology might have been to add extra fermentable material, either honey or fruit concentrate, to the must before fermentation. This would certainly boost the alcohol content, although the end result would still technically be dry. However it would *taste* sweet, because apple concentrate is made by boiling the juice down, during which some of the sugar is caramelised. The Norfolk cidermaker Robbie Crone tried this, using only naturally-occurring yeast, and produced a cider of about 14% alcohol with the character of a fortified wine: the caramelisation creates a vinous, toffee-ish flavour with a slightly burnt note, rather like Madeira. The addition of honey would have a similar effect, although the flavour would be rich and round rather than sweet. And if *beor* was indeed cider boosted with sufficient quantities of honey it would have been a prohibitively expensive luxury for aristocrats and warriors only, just as the literary context suggests.

(A variant of this method known in the 17th and 18th centuries was simply to concentrate the apple-juice by boiling, reducing it to as little as half its original volume, and then ferment the result. It appears to have been common practice in Devon and was much derided by writers from other regions: the Herefordshire poet John Phillips wrote in 1708:

"...Nor let the crude humours dance

In heated brass, steaming with fire intense,

Altho' *Devonia* much commends the use

Of strengthening *Vulcan*...

Thy wines sufficient, other aids refuse."

But this method requires a heroic amount of fuel, and strong cider made from concentrated juice, if it existed in the Anglo-Saxon period, would have been an expensive luxury. But it is dangerous to extrapolate from one age to another, and there is not a shred of evidence to suggest that *beor* was a cider made in this way).

Unsupported theorising about ice-distilling and the use of honey or concentrate aside, there remains one method of making super-strength liquor that was perfectly familiar to brewers from the art's very beginning, and that is simply to use a greater quantity of malt in the mash. The yeast will give up the struggle before all the sugars have been converted into alcohol, yielding an ale of 7%-9% alcohol by volume with plenty of residual sweetness. But extra-strong ale or beer is expensive to brew because of the amount of malt required and can only have been the preserve of the better-off, making it surely the likeliest candidate for *beor*. Hagen does note, when making her case for *beor* as cider, that there are no references to *beor mealt* as there are to *ealu mealt*. But if *beor* was simply very strong ale, it would have been brewed with normal *ealu mealt* – just lots of it.

There is, however, a reference to "*beor aut ofetes wos*", that is "*beor*, or fruit juice", which has to be explained. In Classical Latin, of course, "*aut*" means "or" as in "either ... or", the mnemonic being "*aut* roast beef *aut* roast mutton, *vel* half-a-crown *vel* 2/6"; but maybe one shouldn't credit an Old English monk with the Classical education to depend on such fine distinctions. Perhaps, then, *beor* is a generic term, analogous to the modern word "spirits", for any particularly strong, sweet drink, be it ice-distilled liquor, cider fermented with added concentrate or honey, or ale brewed with a higher than usual proportion of malt. The case for Anglo-Saxon cider, though, is further weakened by the rarity with which apples and vines are recorded as being grown side by side, as one would expect if considerable quantities of cider were being made on wine presses. The *Gerefa*, an 11th-century book of estate management, advises the reeve to establish orchards in winter and vineyards in the spring. But that is about it. So the evidence we have doesn't prove conclusively that cider was made at all before the Conquest.

It is the Normans who are generally credited with introducing widespread cider production as well as two new apple varieties, the costard and the pearmain, to England. The actual evidence, though, is not entirely supportive. If anything, the invaders seem to have been as keen on their wine as the native aristocracy they displaced. Domesday Book is not always crystal-clear, but it appears to list between 40 and 50 vineyards 20 years after the Conquest, mostly in the South-East. Many of them must have been inherited from the previous owners, but some are described as newly planted. The list under-represents the true extent of winemaking in Norman England since those listed are manorial rather than monastic: Domesday was principally a record of taxable property, and as monasteries were tax-exempt their vineyards would have gone unrecorded. So plenty of wine was being made in the England in the late 11th century; and the adventurers who had accompanied William on his expedition and had been rewarded with grants of land – as many Flemings, Bretons, and North Frenchmen as true Normans – seem to have been wine-bibbers rather than cider drinkers. On the other hand, the earliest English rendition of the Biblical *sicera* that I am aware of is "siþere", with the hard "c" of the Latin written instead as a "th". This comes from about 1320 (see below), and appears to me to be close to the way a Norman would have pronounced the Old French *cistre*, dropping the "s" of the central consonant as in *"château"* for *"castel"*.

Nevertheless, the 120 years following the Conquest have left us not a single record of cider. Only one orchard is mentioned in Domesday, one of 10 acres at Nottingham given to William Britto by the King; and William of Malmesbury, in about 1120, writes of both orchards and vineyards at Thorney in the Isle of Ely, which he says is so thickly planted with apples and vines that it is like an earthly paradise. These are the earliest notices of medieval orchards, some monastic, some manorial, others on burgage plots in towns. Nearly 300 such references dating from 1200-1450 were recorded by the community archaeologist Rebecca Roseff (www.historyatthecidermuseum.org.uk/orchards, 2007) in a search of The National Archive and Access to Archives (A2A) websites, where the archives of County Record Offices are stored. The number of references, Roseff found, increased as time went on, perhaps reflecting more assiduous record-keeping as much as an actual growth in the number of orchards. The size of orchards ranges from the humble to the grand: an early notice, from about 1200, records an orchard attached to a house in Gloucester; another, from 1203, refers to an orchard at Stowe Priory in Staffordshire; a third, from 1216, mentions the manor of Marney's Orchard in Cornwall. Monastic orchards at Canterbury, Kirkstead, Dunster, Coventry, Gloucester and Bristol are well-attested in the archives. Other references, reflecting Anglo-Saxon charters, use orchards as boundary markers in title deeds. But what Roseff didn't find was many mentions of cider: her search revealed just 11 unequivocal records and is worth quoting in full.

- In Staffordshire in 1200, a house called Pressurhus with outbuildings including a cider mill (*molendina ad poma*).
- In Hampshire in 1270, a quitclaim (a deed rather like a modern conveyance) including a tun of cider and a quarter of corn per year.
- In Sussex in 1275, the sale of cider by Battle Abbey.
- In Yorkshire in 1275, a reference to cidermaking at Richmond.
- In Warwickshire in 1276, purchase of cider for 20s at Wootton Wawen.
- In Cornwall in 1341, cider mentioned on a list of victuals purchased.
- In Sussex in 1349, an expenses claim put in by Roger Daber, reeve of Surrey and Sussex, for buying 52½ barrels of cider and hauling them

to Shoreham to be shipped to Calais, presumably for the garrison. The cider cost £34 6s 8d and the total cost was £44 19s 6d.

- In Devon in 1358, sale of cider at Sampford Peverel.
- In Devon in 1383, reference to collecting apples, carrying them to a presser to be milled and pressed, and bringing home two barrels of "ciser".
- In Devon in 1452, reference to cider at Kingskerswell manor.
- In Gloucestershire between 1475 and 1485, references to a cider mill at Rodley.

The earliest of these records comes not from the Norman period but from the Plantagenet. And indeed the earliest unequivocal record of cider in England is also Plantagenet, predating the Staffordshire "pressurhus" by only 16 years. It comes in the pipe roll – the king's record of income and expenditure – for 1184. William FitzRobert, Earl of Gloucester, had died without a male heir the previous year, and among the revenues of his vacant estates accruing to the king were the proceeds of sales of meat, grain, wool, cheese, wine... and cider.

Henry II, the first Plantagenet, succeeded the luckless King Stephen, last of the Normans, in 1154 and brought with him as his wife's dowry the enormous Angevin lands of South-West France, notably Bordeaux and Gascony. These were already important wine-producing regions, and a big trade soon sprang up between Bordeaux and London. Perhaps the trade was not only in wine, but also in the technology used for making it on a near-industrial scale – notably the screw press which is indispensable for making cider in worthwhile quantities. A charter of 1230 granting Bishop Jocelyn of Bath the lease of a cider press hints that this may be so; and the written evidence seems to reinforce the idea that widespread cidermaking was not after all introduced by the Normans, as is so widely supposed, but by the Plantagenets more than a century later. King John, the third Planategenet, died of dysentery in 1216 having famously surfeited, according to the contemporary chronicler Roger of Wendover, on "peaches and new cider".

Cider production might have been further stimulated by the beginning of the Hundred Years' War in 1337 when the Angevin patrimony and its vineyards were frequently the scenes of sieges, battles, and *chevauchées* – the highly destructive long-distance raids conducted by mounted flying columns. Between the beginning of the war and 1340 supplies of wine from the Dordogne valley and Entre-Deux-Mers dried up entirely, a pattern of disruption that was to be repeated over and over again; did the French-speaking aristocracy of England turn to cider to make good the shortfall?

There's little actual written evidence to support the supposition; Roseff suspects, though, that many references to cider might be obscured because it was often simply recorded as wine. In support of her suggestion is an often-quoted reference from Norfolk in 1204, where Robert de Evermere of Runham paid a quantity of pearmains and four tuns (*modios*) of the wine made from them annually as rent – a rent which continued unchanged until 1326. (This, incidentally, is the first mention of the supposedly Norman pearmain; the costard was first documented even later than that, in 1296 in Oxford, where it was on sale at 100 fruits a shilling. And the early pearmain may not even have been an apple at all: it derives from the Old French *permain*, meaning a pear. Only much later does the word pop up again as a type, or rather a group of types, of apple; so one of the earliest documented records of cider in Medieval England might not have referred to cider at all, but perry).

There are, of course, many other references to cider in the medieval period. Although cider has not attracted the attention of workers in local studies to the extent that brewing has, it was researched in the early years of the last century by the prolific economic and social historian Louis Francis Salzman, who was also president of the Sussex Archaeological Society and a keen chronicler of the county. In *Industries of the Middle Ages* (1913), he records the 12th-century historian and journalist Gerald de Barri alleging cider's use by the monks of Canterbury instead of Kentish ale as an instance of their luxury. In 1212, says Salzman, the sale of cider was a source of income for Battle Abbey, some of it coming from the monastery's estate at Wye, Kent, which was still producing a good deal of cider during the 14th century. Cider was imported from Normandy to Winchelsea in 1270, he says, while at Pagham a mill and press were wrongfully seized by the escheator's officer in 1275, and at the same place in 1313 the archbishop's bailiff had to account for 12 shillings spent on buying four cider casks, repairing a press, and hiring men to make the cider. In the county rolls of 1341 no fewer than 80 parishes in West Sussex were reported as paying their tithes in cider, amounting to £5 in Eastbourne and 10 marks (£6 13s 4d) at Wisborough. In Wisborough in 1385, William Threle granted gardens and orchards to

John Pakenham, reserving to himself the produce of half the trees whether for eating or for cider (*mangable et ciserable*) at an annual rent of a pipe of cider and a quarter of store apples (*hordapplen*); he also retained the right of access to the "wringehouse," and the right to use the press for his fruit. Peter Clark, in *The English Ale House* (Longman, 1983) cites research showing that the manor of Alciston in Sussex produced some 500 gallons a year throughout the later Middle Ages. It was also a Sussex priest and religious poet, William of Shoreham, who in about 1320 injuncted baptism "ine wine... inne siþere, ne inne pereye, ne ine þing þat never water nes". The text, though, doesn't necessarily imply that baptism in cider was actually practised in 14th-century Sussex: it merely expounds on the doctrine of true baptism. Interestingly, though, William doesn't include ale – which was, after all, mostly water, in his list of proscribed baptismal liquids. Further afield, Clark notes that the manorial orchards at Banham, Norfolk, yielded enough apples in 1281 to make three casks of cider worth 10 shillings each.

Alicia Amherst's *History of Gardening in England*, published in 1895, reveals more instances of seigneurial cidermaking, both lay and monastic. In 1285-6 the bailiff's accounts for the Earl of Devon's Exminster manor lists cidermaking as a regular source of revenue, while at Plympton in the same year a small surplus is recorded as remaining from the previous season. In 1352 the Almoner of Winchester Abbey mournfully records in his accounts: "*et de cisera nihil, quia non fuerunt poma hoc anno*" – "and of cider none, because there were no apples this year". And well might he have been mournful, for cider sales could be a useful source of income: in 1388, for instance, the garden accounts of Abingdon Abbey include 13s 4d "*de cicera vendita*".

The rather wobbly Latin forms *cisera* and *cicera* are clearly variants of *sicera*, the original transliteration of the Hebrew *shekhar*. But why *sicera* should have been applied to cider at all, when the Biblical context suggests something rather different, is yet another puzzle. Perhaps the scribe who first translated it used the same reasoning as Ann Hagen: he had a good enough rendering of all the other Biblical words for alcoholic drinks, but there was no apparent mention of cider. Ergo, *sicera* must mean cider. William of Shoreham's rendition, siþere, is the earliest use of the English word rather than a French or Latin equivalent that I have come across; a century later the translator of the famous "cider Bible" in the chained library at Hereford Cathedral, renders Luke 1:15, the coming of John the Baptist, as: "For he shall be great in the sight of the Lord and shall drink neither wine nor sidir" – "sidir" glossing our old friend *sicera*. Chaucer makes the same observation of Samson in The Monk's Tale, written a few years previously, but spells the word "ciser". The late appearance of an English rendition of *sicera*, though, is significant: it suggests that it is of the same etymological vintage as other Norman and Old French borrow-words exclusive to the baronial dining-table. The English-speaking peasantry raised cows, calves, sheep, and swine, which by the time they had been cooked and served to the French-speaking gentry had become beef, veal, mutton, and pork. So cidermaking still seems to have been a seigneurial rather than a peasant activity: a medieval baron might raise a goblet of cider, but his tenants drank ale. Why should this be, when apples were so widely and freely available?

The lack of that one essential and expensive piece of capital equipment, an effective press, would have prevented the vast majority of people from making their own cider. They could mill the fruit using a giant pestle and mortar made of a tub and a bat, perhaps nail-studded, like the ones seen by William Marshall in west Devon in the 1790s (several stone versions dating from the 16th century are preserved in the Cider Museum at Valognes, Normandy). These devices were laborious – Marshall's were operated by six or seven men at a time – but they were feasible. But as for pressing – even a crude home-made contrivance such as the improvised lever press described by the Devon landowner and cidermaker Hugh Stafford in his *Treatise* of 1753 (if we may, for the moment, anachronistically assume that it was known three or four centuries earlier) can scarcely have produced worthwhile quantities without huge effort.

All a brewster or ale-wife needed, by contrast, was a tub for mashing the ale (it might perhaps double as a wash-tub), a single cask to decant it into for fermentation, and a very few specialised utensils. But ale had other advantages too, notably in the necessary investment in labour. Barley for malting (or other grains: medieval brewsters also used wheat, rye, and oats) was harvested as part of the village's normal activity and did not therefore entail any additional labour. Once malted it could be stored almost indefinitely, and the brewster merely had to take a sufficient quantity for a single mash to the mill (a seigneurial monopoly which she had to pay to use) to be ground. The brewing process itself consisted of mashing the malt grist in hot (not boiling) water until the sugars had been extracted, perhaps throwing in a few herbs for flavour, and then adding a cup of bread yeast. In two or three days the ale would be ready to drink or sell, and in two or three days more it would all be gone. The same grist was mashed twice more for successively weaker brews, making the brewing even more economical.

To be fair, it is possible to make a weak alcoholic beverage from apples in exactly the same way as the medieval brewster made her ale, dispensing with the press by soaking chopped or ground apples in hot water to dissolve the fruit sugars and fermenting the result. The *dépense* or maceration method, as it is known, is frequently recommended to modern home winemakers who have no mill or press; but the labour involved in crushing enough apples to get a worthwhile quantity of pomace would still have been considerable. Worse, the extraction is so inefficient that additional sugar is needed to generate a significant amount of alcohol, and sweeteners of any kind were at a premium until the early 19th century when the French discovered how to refine beet sugar. And speculation aside, there is no record of anyone making cider in this way in the medieval period and therefore no reason to suppose that they did.

The requirement for capital equipment was not the only factor militating against small-scale cidermaking: the labour required was another, and perhaps just as great. First, apples had to be picked just at the time when the village was busiest, with haymaking in June and July, the grain harvest and the gleaning, winnowing, and threshing in August and September, and ploughing and sowing winter wheat in October and November. And collecting apples, whether by shaking the trees with a panking pole or simply waiting for the fruit to fall, is a laborious business. Even with access to an orchard it takes a surprising amount of time and effort; if the only apples the peasant could get were crabs and wildings gathered from hedgerow and woodland, the process would demand an even greater investment in labour just when all hands were needed in the fields. Second, while grain can be stored for malting and milling as required, apples have to be milled within a few weeks of being picked; so the whole year's crop has to be processed more or less in one go. This requirement carries with it a further demand on capital, for as well as the work involved in harvesting, milling, and pressing, cidermaking demands sufficient tankage for the primary fermentation of the entire output, and the same capacity again for the slow secondary fermentation. Investments of both capital and labour on this scale, I suggest, might have been within the resources of the lord of a reasonably prosperous manor, but were simply beyond the reach of his subsistence-farming tenants. They are also reflected in the price of cider: 2½d-4d a gallon, reckoned by Roseff on the basis of the Shoreham figures, compared to ¾d-1½d a gallon for ale.

But then, at the very apogee of the High Middle Ages, a change came that would start the slow process of democratising cider; and that change came in the awful shape of the Black Death.

3: The Yeomen of England

The bubonic plague that arrived in Europe, probably from China or India, in the 1340s was without doubt the single greatest cataclysm ever to hit the West, killing perhaps a third of the entire population and therefore more destructive even than World War II. Worse, it followed several famine years earlier in the century, probably linked to the transition from Climatic Optimum to Little Ice Age, which had already seen the desertion of much marginal land for lack of hands to work it.

Terrifying and devastating though the Black Death was, the labour shortage it created worked to the advantage of the survivors. Almost overnight, the great open fields of Eastern and Southern England became choked with weeds as the untended strips of the victims fell rapidly into decay. In many cases there was no-one to work them, so they remained vacant and neglected for years; but in many others, more ambitious tenants took them over. It was these more ambitious tenants who founded what would become a whole new social class: the yeomen of England.

The concentration of holdings in fewer hands was only one aspect of a profound change in the nature of farming in England that was, if not triggered, at least vastly accelerated by the Black Death. The most significant in a general sense were a large rise in wages that lasted until the early 16th century and greatly increased mobility of labour. Both were the result of desperate competition among landlords to attract workers. Despite Edward III's efforts to stop them, peasants left their villages in unprecedented numbers to look for the best payers – again, leaving untenanted holdings for their more far-sighted neighbours to acquire, and incidentally founding what would become another new social class: that of landless day-labourers.

Coupled with this diversification into two classes of yeoman farmer and landless labourer was another development that can be traced to the years before the plague but accelerated dramatically afterwards. Central to the traditional account of the medieval English village – at least, of the lowland village – are its common pasture and its three huge open fields or *champions*, each for different crops and divided into long strips each ploughed, sown, and harvested by a different tenant. By the early 14th century this pattern was beginning to break down. Its theoretical advantage, which presumably went back to the time when newly-conquered land was shared out between the first Anglo-Saxon settlers, was that each family got an equal proportion of the good land and the bad. But it was defective in so many ways. It was cumbersome in that a single family might hold several strips in different parts of the fields and have to spend as much time migrating between them as actually working them. It was restrictive in that although each strip was individually worked, the whole field had to be ploughed, sown, harrowed and harvested by all the villagers at the same time. And it was inflexible in that all the tenants had to farm their strips in the same way: there was no prospect of diversifying into soft fruit or poultry or livestock if your strips were part of a huge field devoted to cereals or legumes. The solutions that were increasingly adopted towards the end of the medieval period were engrossment and enclosure.

Engrossment was simply the consolidation of scattered strips into single parcels. It had to be done by agreement, and with the consent of the lord; and the attraction of farming a single piece of land seems to have won out in many districts over the risk of getting second-rate land as your share. Already in the early 14th century a significant number of villages were opting to abandon the strip-farmed open field system and divide their arable into separate holdings or closes; and with more and more strips vacant after the Black Death, engrossment was widely adopted throughout the lowlands. Enclosure was altogether more radical and was less usually consensual since it involved the landlord evicting the villagers from the common pasture and either leasing it back to them in parcels or, where the shortage of labour persisted, turning it into a sheep ranch. In fact few of Britain's 2,000-odd deserted villages were lost as an immediate consequence of the Black Death, but many of them became so depopulated through the combined effects of the disease itself and the subsequent migration of labour that they were no longer worth cultivating, and so were turned over to stock breeding.

By 1500, something like 45% of English villages had been subjected to engrossment and enclosure, and their landscape had changed from a vista of vast unfenced open fields to a patchwork of separate farms, each surrounded by its own hedges and ditches. The new farms varied greatly in size from smallholdings of 20-30 acres to substantial affairs of 80 acres or more, depending on the energy, ambition, far-sightedness or just plain luck of their occupants. And those same qualities determined what went on behind the hedges, too, for this new breed of yeoman farmers was no longer bound by what their neighbours did: for the first time they were truly independent and could plant what they wanted, when, and where.

The effect of this change was truly revolutionary. The population gradually recovered from the Black Death and went on to double between 1400 and 1700; but with independent entrepreneurs guiding the nation's ploughs, food production was able to keep pace with population growth. There were many other side effects, too, notably the gradual transition from a barter economy of labour service and food rents to an almost exclusively cash economy. But the side-effect that we are interested in is that the creation of an entirely new class of independent farmers was eventually to propel cider from its former status as an incidental, albeit highly valued, by-product of seigneurial estate management towards a new status as the drink of choice of almost a third of England, produced on an artisanal scale on hundreds if not thousands of farms.

The yeomen of England, newly elevated to independence from the semi-servile state of villeinage, found themselves subject to exactly the same pressures that had affected Cato, Pliny, the Carolingian stewards addressed by *de Villis*, and their own seigneurial landlords – namely, the need to work their farms at full speed all year round. Independent they may be, but they were still tenants with rent and taxes to pay, and even an 80-acre holding had to be worked hard to produce enough revenue to meet all the farmer's obligations. One of the options not available to previous generations was to specialise; and it's at this point that the two main apple-growing regions, the Eastern and Western counties, begin to emerge – if for very different reasons.

In the Eastern counties, the spread of fruit-growing was dictated by the size and rate of expansion of the growers' principal market – London. As the most populous city in Christendom, medieval London had a voracious appetite for foodstuffs of all kind; as the home, for at least part of the year, of the richest and most powerful people in the country, it had an equally impressive appetite for luxury foodstuffs. As early as the 1180s William Fitzstephen, Thomas Becket's secretary and biographer, noted in his Description Of London that all the suburban houses had gardens with fruit trees, a practice that seems to have been common across the country: Norwich was renowned for its orchards, and Rebecca Roseff records orchards on burgage plots in towns including Bridgnorth, Chester, Tarporley, Bristol, Castor, Tavistock and others. But London and the Thames Valley, home to maybe 20% of the country's entire population, were the main markets for produce of all kinds. Many of the great men in the land maintained their own, quite considerable, kitchen gardens at their London homes: the garden at the Bishop of Ely's palace in Holborn was as famous as the renowned gardens of Ely Cathedral itself; the Earl of Lincoln's kitchen garden, also in Holborn, was even bigger. Some idea of the value of the London fruit market in the 14th and 15th centuries may be supplied by the accounts of these two gardens: in 1300 the Earl of Lincoln's gardens sold apples and pears worth £9, compared to £4 for all its other produce put together; while between 1380 and 1480 the diocese of Ely let its gardens out for a yearly rent of £3, implying that the tenant was making several times that sum. At one point the Earl of Essex even turned a large part of Smithfield into a market garden. Most of the produce that fed London, though, came from the surrounding countryside, and from the 14th century onwards, as London continued to swell, the acreage put to fruit and vegetables in Middlesex, Essex, Surrey and in particular Kent grew in proportion.

The expansion of market gardening and fruit growing, at a time when a more commercial attitude to agriculture was beginning to succeed subsistence farming, brought with it new interest in improved orcharding techniques and fruit varieties. The 15th-century poet John Lydgate, a near-contemporary of Chaucer's, speaks of new apple varieties including the Pomewater, Ricardon, Blaundrelle and Queening, while John Gower in his *Confessio Amantis* records what appears to be a high-tannin cider apple, remarking that love is "like unto the bitter-swete, for though it think a man first swete, he shall well telen at last that it be sower." Perhaps Mercutio was also thinking of the cider-apple, nearly two centuries on, when he said: "Thy wit is a very bitter sweeting, it is a most sharp sauce." (*Romeo & Juliet*, Act II Scene 4).

The growth of one new industry soon attracted the attention of another –

publishing. Throughout the 15th and 16th centuries a quickening stream of manuals, handbooks and treatises, some of them in verse, were issued by the book publishers to satisfy the fruit-growers' demand for knowledge and information. Some of this material would already have been familiar to classical scholars: *De Re Rustica* by the late Roman writer Palladius seems to have been separately translated twice in the first 20 years of the 15th century, by a monk of Westminster called Nicholas Bollard and another of Colchester whose name is unrecorded. Palladius was also widely translated across Europe. The section on grafting and planting was re-used a few years later by Robert Salle, whose somewhat questionable tips included grafting onto elm or alder stock to guarantee red apples, or injecting the stock with dye to produce the same result. Another tract of roughly the same date, and re-using the same material, is known as the Porkington Treatise.

A more original work – very original, in fact, since it is the first English-language gardening manual we know of – is *The Feate Of Gardening*, a 196-line poem by "Mayster Ion Gardener". The earliest manuscript comes from about 1440; but judging from the copying errors it contains, the poem itself seems to be older and may have originally been in Kentish dialect. Nothing is known of "Ion Gardener", which was surely a pseudonym; but his advice is so thoroughly practical that he may very well have been a market gardener of the emergent yeoman class, among whom a good standard of literacy was becoming more and more widespread. The poem's eight sections include "Of Settyng and Reryng of Trees", "Of Graffyng of Trees", and "Of Cuttyng and Settyng of Vynes". It advises stocks to be planted in January and grafting – apple on to apple, but pear on to hawthorn – to be carried out between September and April as follows:

"Wyth a saw thou schalt the tre kytte
And with a knyfe smowth make hytte
Klene atweyne the stok of the tre
Whereyn that thy graffe schall be.
Make thy kyttyng of thy graffe
Bytwyne the newe and the olde staff."

Clay had to be smeared on the stock "to kepe the rayne owte," and moss bound over the clay using "a wyth of haseltree rynde".

Gardener's short treatise, practical and sound though it may have been, can hardly have gained wide currency, since it exists only as a single manuscript given to Trinity College, Cambridge, as part of a collection of miscellany in 1738. But the expansion of the printing industry in the 16th century led to a brisk trade in practical manuals devoted to market gardening and plant husbandry of all sorts, many of them basically herbals, but many with sections devoted to fruit growing. One stimulus for the publication of so many treatises on various aspects of estate management – taking us back, once again, to Cato, Pliny, and *de Villis* – might have been the rapid decline in viticulture following the climate change of the early 14th century, with growers turning to hardier fruits to replace their now unproductive vines. Another was the Dissolution of the Monasteries in the 1530s, when the confiscated estates of some 600 suppressed abbeys, convents, and priories were put on the market. Most of the purchasers were great magnates; but in most cases the 15,000 separate manors and farms the monasteries had owned were then let on to hard-headed entrepreneurs eager for technical information to help them maximise their revenues. Sir Anthony Fitzherbert's *Book of Husbandry*, first published in 1523, went to a second edition only two years later followed by others in 1534 and 1548. William Turner's *Libellus de Re Herbaria Nova* was published in 1538, with an expanded edition in 1562. Then came Thomas Tusser's celebrated *A Hundred Good Points of Husbandry* in 1557, expanded to Five Hundred Good Points in 1562, which went through many editions; Thomas Hill's *The Art of Gardening* in 1563, reissued with a new section entitled *A Treatise on the Art of Grafting and Planting of Trees* in 1577; Leonard Mascall's *A Booke of the Art and Maner, Howe to Plante and Graft All sorts of Trees* in 1572; and John Gerard's *Catalogus Arborum* in 1597.

By this time there was very serious interest in commercial fruit-growing – serious enough for the Fruiterer to the King, Richard Harris, to forestall the Dutch and French nurserymen who sold their own grafts in London markets by investing in a substantial nursery on royal land at Teynham, Kent, in 1533 – fittingly, only a few miles from the village of Brogdale, where today the Horticultural Trust is the home of the National Fruit Collection. Here Harris specialised in grafting imported varieties for sale to fruit-growers and market gardeners, as described in an anonymous pamphlet of 1609, *The Husbandman's Fruitful Orchard*:

"One Richard Harris of London, borne in Ireland Fruiterer to King Henry the eight fetched out of Fraunce great store of graftes especially pippins, before which time there were no pippins in England. He fetched also out of the Lowe Countries, cherrie grafts and peare graftes of diuers sorts. Then (he) tooke a peese of ground belonging to the king in the Parrish of Tenham in Kent being about the quantitie of seaven score acres whereof he made an orchard, planting therein all those foraigne grafts. Which orchard is and hath been from time to time, the chiefe mother of all other orchards for those kinds of fruit in Kent and diuers other places. And afore that these said grafts were fetched out of Fraunce and the Lowe Countries although that there was some store of fruite in England, yet there wanted both rare fruite and lasting fine fruite. The Dutch and French finding it to be so scarce especially in these counties neere London, commonly plyed Billingsgate and diuers other places, with such kinde of fruit, but now (thankes bee to God) diuers gentlemen and others taking delight in grafting , have planted many orchards fetching their grafts out of that orchard which Harris planted , called New Garden."

Harris's royal master also took an interest in fruit-growing, not only planting a considerable orchard of his own at Hampton Court but also, at the end of his reign, passing a protective Act making malicious damage to fruit trees a serious offence punishable by a fine, with punitive compensation to the owner of the trees of three times the trees' value. One wonders how valuable a trade fruit-growing had become, if sabotaging competitors' orchards was a common enough practice to warrant separate legislation?

That landowners from the crown down made good use of the advice these treatises contained may be judged from Ralph Holinshed's *Chronicle*, published in 1577, in which he attests: "Even as it fareth with our gardens, so doth it with our orchards, which were never furnished with so good fruit nor with such variety as at this present. For, beside that we have most delicate apples, plums, pears, walnuts, filberts, etc, and those of sundry sorts, planted within forty years past, in comparison of which most of the old trees are nothing worth, so have we no less store of strange fruit, as apricots, almonds, peaches, figs, corn-trees in noblemen's orchards. I have seen capers, oranges, and lemons, and heard of wild olives growing here, beside other strange trees, brought from far, whose names I know not. So that England for these commodities was never better furnished."

Frustratingly, the treatises don't reckon cidermaking very highly among the arts of market gardening and orcharding. The exception is Gerard, who recognises the value of cidermaking as a supplemental activity and recommends secondary planting of fruit trees in pastures and hedges. "I have seen in the pastures and hedgerows about the grounds of a worshipful gentleman dwelling two miles from Hereford ... so many trees of all sorts that the servants drink for the most part no other drink but that which is made of apples, the quantity of which is such that ... the parson hath for tythe many hogsheads of cider, (and) the hogs are fed with the fallings of them, which are so many that they make choice of those apples they do eat, and will not taste of any but the best," says Gerard. "An example doubtless to be followed of gentlemen that have land and living; but Envy saith, the poor will break down our hedges and we shall have the least part of the fruit. But forward, in the name of God! Graff, set, plant, and nourish up trees in every corner of your ground: the labour is small, the cost is nothing, the commodity is great. Yourselves shall have plenty; the poor shall have somewhat in time of want."

Note that Gerard speaks of Hereford, where cidermaking had evidently become well established. The record for the Eastern Counties is sparser; but given that one of the earliest mentions of cider (or possibly perry) in England came from Norfolk, it seems scarcely credible that cidermaking had died out. In the 19th century Norfolk emerged as an important cidermaking centre; nevertheless, the documentary evidence of continuity in the intervening centuries is slim and relates to the South-East rather than East Anglia. William Harrison, in his *Description of Britain* published as a preface to Holinshed's Chronicle, rather flatteringly observes: "In some places of England there is a kind of drink made of apples which they call cider or pomage, but that of pears is called perry, and both are ground and pressed in presses made for the nonce. Certes these two are very common in Sussex, Kent, Worcester, and other steeds where these sorts of fruit do abound, howbeit they are not their only drink at all times, but referred unto the delicate sorts of drink, as metheglin is in Wales, whereof the Welshmen make no less account (and not without cause, if it be well handled) than the Greeks did of their ambrosia or nectar, which for the pleasantness thereof was supposed to be such as the gods themselves did delight in."

Nearly a century later John Beale, in a postscript to Evelyn's *Silva,* mentions rather less flatteringly that he has often had cider from Kent and Essex, but that it was not as good as the cider of Herefordshire. Kent also gives us our first record, from 1585, of the tradition of "wassailing". On Twelfth Night the young men of the town of Fordham would go from orchard to orchard waking up the trees for the New Year by singing a wassailing carol and, if their ritual was anything like later wassailing traditions, pouring a libation on the roots and placing a sop or a cake in the lower boughs. But it doesn't unambiguously give us a record of cidermaking: we don't know that the bumper crop that the ceremony was intended to guarantee was used to make cider, and not only orchards but also beehives and livestock were wassailed at different places and times. A century later, Aubrey records draught oxen being "wassailed" as well as orchards, and in fact it's only comparatively recently that wassailing has become specific to cider orchards. There is, however, a reference to old, decayed cider orchards in the Home Counties in John Norden's *Surveior's Dialogue* (1610), in which he complains that they are not being replanted.

That cider went so unremarked in Eastern England is surprising, because everything was in place for the foundation of a successful trade. There was a ready and rapidly expanding market close at hand (London's population doubled to more than 250,000 in the 16th century); there was an entrepreneurial class of independent yeoman farmers producing, according to Harrison, a very superior cider; there was an abundance of fruit – A2A has references to nearly 500 orchards in the East and South-East in the 15th-16th centuries; and there was, at last, widespread application and therefore availability of the appropriate technology.

Throughout the later Middle Ages, lowland farmers increasingly started cultivating industrial crops such as saffron, hemp and flax to supplement their arable. One of these was linseed, whose oil was in common use as wood varnish, as a medium for paint, as lamp oil, and in making oilcloth to cover windows. Extracting the oil from the seed required a screw press; and the manufacture of linseed oil (and its valuable by-product, oilcake) was only one of a growing number of applications for the screw press. For instance, in well-to-do households bedsheets and table-cloths were smoothed in small screw presses mounted on the cabinet in which the draperies were stored – hence the use of the word press to mean a chest of drawers or cupboard. William Caxton adapted existing screw presses to make his first moveable-type printing press in 1476; before that, they had been used since at least 1300 to block-print religious pictures and playing cards. The paper he printed on also required a screw press: indeed paper was made in almost exactly the same way as cider – short billets of wood, their bark stripped off, were thoroughly soaked, ground into pulp in mills, and then pressed dry. The first paper mill in England was recorded by Caxton's successor, Wynken de Worde, in 1494 in Hertfordshire.

Two explanations suggest themselves for cider's low profile in Eastern England. One is that the London market – the city had 250,000 inhabitants by the end of the 16th century – was simply so voracious that there was rarely much surplus fruit to make any great quantity of cider with. This might account for John Norden's lament: presumably the old cider trees were being replaced by table varieties. Another is that cidermaking, by its very nature, went largely unremarked. Most records of medieval village life come from manorial court rolls, and much of what we know of medieval brewing is extrapolated from the endless fines that were levied on ale-wives or brewsters. But if cidermaking was mainly a seigneurial activity it would have incurred no fines – the Lord of the Manor was hardly going to fine himself! There would no official tax records, either, for in the Tudor and early Stuart periods cider was untaxed. What records we have, therefore, are either anecdotal or come from surviving private account-books.

If the 15th and 16th century records for cider in the East and South-East are disappointingly quiet, there is more solid evidence of cidermaking in the West and South-West. The last four references revealed by Roseff's search of the County Records are all from the South-West: in Devon in 1358, sale of cider at Sampford Peverel; in Devon in 1383, reference to collecting apples, carrying them to a presser to be milled and pressed, and bringing home two barrels of "ciser"; in Devon in 1452, reference to cider at Kingskerswell manor; and in Gloucestershire between 1475 and 1485, reference to a cider mill at Rodley. The second of the references she collected is particularly interesting, seeming to suggest the contract-pressing of apples on a commercial footing. She also found four records of orchards in 15th-century Herefordshire: three leases dating from 1413, 1428, and 1445, and King's Orchard in Hereford as a place-name in 1413, while the bailiff's accounts for Eton Tregoz between 1445 and 1465 record the receipt of 5s a year from the sale of "pressed fruit", implying that cider or perry or perhaps both were being made there. There is also, after a fashion, archaeological evidence: Roger French (*The History and Virtues of Cyder*, Robert Hale, 1982) records the existence of a substantial number of cider cellars, either adapted by the widening of existing cellar doors or purpose-built, at late 16th and early 17th-century farms and manors across the Western counties and the Welsh border country. The cellars were necessary to keep the cider cool during its long, slow, secondary fermentation; the width of the doors are testament to the size of the vats used – a Herefordshire hogshead, says French, was 110 gallons compared to the standard 36-gallon beer-barrel.

The development of orcharding in the more hilly and rainy conditions west of the Axe-Tees line followed a different pattern from the expansion of market gardening in the Eastern counties, which may explain why cidermaking appears to have been so much more widespread. In the East, with its comparatively flat landscapes, light soils, and moderate rainfall, intensive arable soon became the dominant form of agriculture, with market gardens clustering particularly around London and other high-value specialist crops such as hops and saffron being introduced on the more suitable soils. Top fruit, stone fruit, and soft fruit of all sorts were also grown intensively. To the west of the Axe-Tees line, though, a combination of more rugged terrain, heavier soils, and higher rainfall militated against intensive farming of any kind, except in pockets such as the Vale of Evesham and central and southern Herefordshire (which boasts all of the Grade I and much of the Grade II land in the West Midlands). Here the practice of open-field farming had never been as common as in the East. There were, of course, suitable localities where it was the norm; but in general the pattern of agriculture in the West and South-West tended towards discrete farms, often scattered rather than in tightly-nucleated settlements, and with mixed uses including stockrearing. The gradual enclosure of common lands made this tendency even more evident.

All these conditions favoured orcharding over arable. Fruit trees are perfectly happy and manageable on land too sloping to be cultivated, while the hills shelter them from the early frosts that in the more exposed East all too often nip the fruit in the bud. They thrive on soils too heavy to be easily broken by horse-drawn ploughs, and plentiful rain in spring only goes to swell the fruit. Most importantly, and unlike wheat or barley, they are generous, willingly sharing their space with sheep or cattle which enjoy their shade while obligingly manuring their roots and keeping down the brambles that would otherwise hinder the harvest. Economically, the cider that came from these orchards was always secondary to the livestock – Somerset and Gloucester are as famous for their cheese as for their cider; the Cotswolds were always wool country above all else; and Herefords are an iconic if sadly dwindling breed of cattle. But as a secondary crop cider and perry added considerable value to a farm especially where, after the haymaking in July or August, there was no grain harvest to divert the farmer's attention from gathering and processing his apples.

During the 16th century, orcharding became as prevalent in the Western counties as it already was in the East, and was practised by gentry both great and middling. An inventory of the property of Edward Stafford, Duke of Buckingham, executed for treason in 1521, described his newly laid-out grounds at Thornbury, Gloucestershire, as including "a large and goodly orchard, full of young graffes well laden with fruit". In the same county we find Justice Shallow entertaining Falstaff: "Nay, you shall see my orchard where, in an arbour, we will eat a last year's pippin of my own graffing, with a dish of caraways." (Henry IV Part II; Act 5, Scene III). Worcester, according to tradition, owes its coat of arms – argent, a fess sable, three pears sable – to its perry pear orchards. The story goes that the city fathers, in order to entertain Elizabeth I on her procession of 1575, transplanted a tree of black pears in full fruit (the royal visitation occurred in August) from Whiteladies House nearby to Foregate, a sight that so delighted the Virgin Queen that she ordered black pears to be shown on the city's arms. Doubters point out that the city's arms were only granted in 1634; but Michael Drayton in his *Polyolbion* published 20 years earlier evokes the bowmen of Worcester at Agincourt deploying under a banner depicting "a pear tree laden with its fruit". His description is more suggestive of the county of Worcestershire's arms, granted only in 1947, which do indeed show a tree laden with black pears, than of the city's; but at least it demonstrates that Worcester was closely identified with its local pear variety – a very hard one, suitable only for slow cooking or milling for perry – well before the official grant of arms.

But if mastering orcharding techniques, competing to raise exotic fruits, and keeping up with or, in some cases, contributing to the latest literature had by now become an accepted gentlemanly pursuit, cidermaking by the 16th century seems not to have been entirely the preserve of the well-capitalised landowner. The community website of the Devon village of Witheridge records an alehouse keeper, Raphe Poole, being fined in 1561 for selling cider by false measure; and Peter Clark, in *The English Alehouse*, cites a history of the Malvern Hills that reports local cottagers making perry from crab-pears growing wild in the woods in the 1580s. If these are indeed early signs that cidermaking was breaking out of the manorial straitjacket and was being taken up among the less wealthy, then the question of technology arises again.

The Malvern cottagers may have been making their perry by maceration or *dépense*. But the improvised press described by Hugh Stafford has already been referred to; and now that we are a century or so closer to his description of it, it might be timely to go into more detail. To make a crude lever press, said Stafford, a large hole needed to be cut right through the thickness of a substantial tree, about 6ft up the trunk. Into this hole a 12ft pole or beam had to be inserted. Under the beam, and near the trunk, a trestle was placed with a shallow trough on it. On the trough (which, naturally, had to have a spout leading to a collecting vessel) was placed the "cheese", the term still used today for pomace wrapped in coarse cloth. On the cheese was placed a plank, and one or possibly two stout rustics would then get a good hold of the free end of the beam and pull down with all their weight. One of the drawbacks of this system, Stafford observed, was that the receiving vessel was more than likely to be upset during the process; another was its inefficiency, for he notes that the pomace could not be wrung anything like dry by such a contraption. A third, of which he says nothing, is the concomitant damage to a perfectly healthy tree. But unless screw presses had come down in price – and the cutting of screws was not to be mechanised until the late 18th century, so it still had to be done by hand – then a makeshift lever press was probably all the cottagers of Malvern had.

They were almost certainly not much better equipped for the previous step in the manufacturing process, the milling or pulping of their pears. As previously mentioned, in the cider museum at Valognes, Normandy, you can see examples from the 16th century of the *auge et pil*, the poor man's cider mill. Basically, it's just a giant pestle and mortar, with the *auge* or mortar made of stone and the *pil* of wood. In French, the milling process is referred to as *pilage* to this day; and there are many hobby cidermakers who will confess rather ruefully to having relied on a galvanised bucket and a length of 4x4 to pulp their apples before investing in a small scratter mill of their own. I say ruefully because although *pilage* or, in English, "beetle and tub", works perfectly well on a small scale – and is indeed the method of milling recommended by Gervase Markham in *The English Husbandman* (1613) – it is an incredibly laborious business. It takes an age to get a respectable quantity of pulp, and by the end of it even a strong man will be quite exhausted. Anyone who has tried it and has then bought a scratter mill will wonder why they ever delayed the purchase.

The labour involved in working a beetle and tub and making and operating a crude lever press – not to say the collection of sufficient crabs in the first place – suggests a co-operative effort between neighbours. Perhaps to the perrymakers of Malvern, their labours were not a serious business or a part of their livelihoods at all, but were just one of the communal pleasures of village life, a social activity with the prospect of a divvy-up of the product in a few months' time. A hobby, in fact. But it is also an indication that the pleasures of cider and perry were becoming more widely appreciated, and that cider was no longer peculiar to the rich man's table.

In the 17th and 18th centuries, cider production and consumption were to expand dramatically among both rich and poor. But the driving forces behind the expansion – members of the same landed classes whose commercial ambitions underlay what we have come to call the agricultural revolution – were not consciously aiming at a mass market. Their vision, made explicit in both word and deed, was to challenge the trade in imported wine and to establish fine cider as the drink of choice of the nation's affluent.

4: The National Drink?

The late Tudor and Stuart periods saw an immense expansion in English shipping as foreign trade expanded both in volume and in range. The establishment of the American colonies and the Navigation Acts ensuring that all transatlantic cargoes were carried by English ships; the nascent slave trade and the capture of Jamaica in 1655; intermittent naval warfare with Spain, and constant privateering; the opening up of the oriental spice trade and the defeat between 1651 and 1674 of the Dutch – allies in religion but deadly rivals in commerce: these created vast fleets, both naval and merchant. Sir John Hawkins estimated in 1584 that "the substance of this realm hath trebled in value" since the accession of Elizabeth I in 1558; exports trebled again between 1638 and 1688; and customs receipts on foreign trade multiplied tenfold over the course of the 17th century.

The great increase in foreign trade, especially with West Africa and the Americas, favoured the West Country ports of Bristol, Plymouth, and Exeter and created a generation of seagoing Devonian gentry whose names – Hawkins, Grenville, Drake, Raleigh – still resonate today. And being Devonian gentry with considerable estates they were not only consumers but also producers of cider, a commodity which now formed a useful and indeed life-saving addition to their ships' stores.

Cider as a supplement to ship's rations probably first won favour for its keeping qualities. A sealed cask of cider or perry at its full strength of 6.5-8.5% alcohol by volume will not only keep but will go on improving for months or even years, but even after broaching will keep for two or three months or so before turning to vinegar. Strong hopped ale has similar durability until the cask is opened, upon which it will spoil within days. Men used to drinking several pints of small beer a day while ashore needed a ration of alcohol to make life bearable while at sea: and until it was superseded by rum, cider supplied the need admirably. But it had an additional benefit, too.

Physicians in the 17th century did not know that scurvy was caused by vitamin C deficiency. But they were aware of its terrible consequences, especially on the much longer sea voyages that were now becoming commonplace: in 1605, on the very first expedition of the newly-formed East India Company's flotilla, 114 of the 425 sailors died of it. The antiscorbutic properties of fresh fruit were known at the time: the one ship in the Company flotilla that carried fresh lemons suffered no cases of scurvy; and in his Utopian novel *New Atlantis*, published in 1624, Francis Bacon has the stricken seamen treated on their arrival at the mystical island of Bensalem with oranges.

This passage from *New Atlantis* has been taken by some modern writers to imply that Bacon regarded cider as an antiscorbutic. The full text reveals that he didn't: "We had also drink of three sorts, all wholesome and good: wine of the grape; a drink of grain, such as is with us our ale, but more clear; and a kind of cider made of a fruit of that country, a wonderful pleasing and refreshing drink. Besides, there were brought in to us great store of those scarlet oranges for our sick; which (they said) were an assured remedy for sickness taken at sea." But even if there is no documentary evidence that seafarers were aware of the antiscorbutic properties of cider at that early date, ship owners and sea captains must have known from their everyday experience that crews well supplied with cider were rarely afflicted with scurvy; and as Roger French has shown, cider in its natural, unpasteurised state does actually contain enough vitamin C to prevent the sickness.

Whatever the state of medical knowledge, though, there is ample evidence to show that cider was routinely taken to sea. Tristram Risdon's *Chorographical Survey of Devon* (1605) notes that cider "is found a drink very useful for those that navigate long voyages, whereof one tun serveth instead of three of beer, and is found more wholesome in hot climates." Francis Bacon, again, observes in a letter to the Duke of Buckingham that "cider and perry are notable beverages in sea voyages". Cider is "very wholesome for man's body, especially at the sea," says Gervase Markham in *The English Husbandman* (1613). John Parkinson in his *Paradisi in Sole Paradisus*

Terrestris (1629) says: "In the West Country of England great quantities are made, yea, many hogsheads and tuns full, especially to be carried to sea in long voyages, and is found by experience to be of excellent use to be mixed with water for beverage." Perry, he adds, "which is the juice of pears pressed out, is a drink much esteemed as well as cyder, to be both drunk at home and carried to sea, and found to be of good use in long voyages". Thomas Westcote in his *View of Devon* (1630) calls cider "a drink both pleasant and healthy, much desired of seamen for long southern voyages as more fit to make beverage than beer, and much cheaper and easier to be had than wine." And finally James Crowden, the poet of cider, records in his *Cider: The Forgotten Miracle* (Cider Press, 1999) that group of settlers heading from Exmouth for Newfoundland in 1620 to exploit the cod fishery took a good deal of "sider" with them, and that Ben Franklin recommended cider as an antidote to the seaman's diet of salt cod.

It would be stretching the evidence to say that Devon cider found a new mass-market because of its value as ships' stores; but this is the first hard evidence we have of a substantial and growing commercial market for cider. The undoubted but unquantifiable demand from shipowners was matched by a fortuitous increase in supply thanks to the final collapse of domestic viticulture, the result of climate change. The early years of the century saw a succession of severe winters that virtually wiped out the country's remaining vineyards; thereafter the climate generally worsened, with "frost fairs" on the Thames a not uncommon diversion, and re-establishing viticulture on a worthwhile scale defeated all those who attempted it.

With both demand and supply expanding, contemporaries recorded a visible increase in cidermaking in Devon at the time. John Hooker's *Synopsis Chorographica* (1600) refers to the "abundance of fruit and cider" in the county; Risdon says that "many copyholders may pay their lord's rent with their cyder only"; and Westcote adds that "of late years there has been an enlargement of Devon orchards". This expansion was not confined to Devon, either: in 1601 a Shrewsbury chronicler, quoted by Peter Clark in *The English Alehouse*, observed how Worcestershire and Gloucestershire were "refreshed with great store of cider and perry". And, indeed, cider seems at this period to have been moving beyond its original territory as a luxury adornment to the rich man's table, not only as an item in ship's stores but as a normal part of the dietary repertoire of ordinary workers, certainly in the west and south-west.

We have already met the 16th-century Malvern cottagers making perry out of crab pears scrumped wild in the woods, and Gerard's Herefordshire gentleman whose orchards were so bountiful that his servants drank "no other drink but that which is made of apples", in which he also paid his tithes. This observation of Gerard's, in particular, suggests a second possible cause of the increase in cider production and consumption from the 17th century on, in addition to sales to shipowners. We know that in the 18th and 19th centuries farmworkers in cider-producing regions were paid part of their wages in cider – is Gerard hinting that the practice had its roots in the late 16th? It would be tempting to build a temporal bridge to a still earlier time, and link "truck" back to the rations of bread, cheese, and ale doled out to feudal peasants performing their customary labour service on the lord's demesne. It seems unlikely, though, that serfs would receive anything so high-status as part of their subsistence. But at the dawn of the 17th century we discover the hitherto-unreported practice of making "small cider" for farm workers, many of whom "lived in" alongside the household servants and for whom board as well as lodging was part of the remuneration package.

Water was often poured into the trough at the milling stage, but in comparatively small quantities and more as an emollient and lubricant than to stretch the fermentable material (although it was thought at the time that water did, in fact, help the fermentation process get started). However, we have heard Parkinson state that cider taken to sea might have water added – presumably to make it weaker and therefore less prejudicial to the good order of the ship. Commonly, though, the cider was not simply watered down; rather, the pomace was rehydrated after the first pressing and was then simply pressed again – a process identical to the brewer's practice of getting three progressively weaker mashes out of the same grist. Gervase Markham in *A Way To Get Wealth* (1623) describes it thus: "Now after you have pressed all, you shall save that which is within the hair-cloth bag, and putting it into several vessels, pour a pretty quantity of water there unto, and after it hath stood a day or two and hath been well stirred together, presse it over again, for this will make a small perry or cider." From the farmer's point of view the second pressing avoided wasting the pomace's remaining value and at the same time provided his workers and servants with a drink that was alcoholic, but not too alcoholic. It was known at the time as "beverage" – according to Roger French, a general term signifying watered-down wine or beer. Later it became known as "ciderkin".

During the course of the 17th century, cider's availability as an everyday drink for common people spread slowly beyond its heartlands. Peter Clark notes that retailers of cider were recorded in Oxfordshire and Nottinghamshire in the early part of the century and says that from the middle of the century it also started appearing on the inventories of alehouse keepers, who had previously dealt only in ale. By the time of the Restoration it was being widely traded: Sir Paul Neile in his contribution to *Pomona* (of which much more below) refers to a Herefordshire maker despatching both cask and bottled cider in a barque to London, presumably down the Wye and the Bristol Channel, round Land's End, along the south coast, through the Straits, and into the Thames – a journey of seven weeks. Production figures are impossible even to guess at, although John Evelyn claimed in the 1660s that Herefordshire was "one entire orchard" producing 50,000 hogsheads a year; and by the time the Civil War had to be funded, cider was an important enough commodity to be included in the list of goods to be assessed for excise duty. This was first imposed by Parliament in 1643, which strongly suggests that cider was also being made in appreciable quantities in the eastern and south-eastern counties that the Roundheads controlled; but having been given the idea, the King soon followed suit. The rates of duty levied are suggestive, for they favoured cider over beer. Beer was taxed at two shillings per 36-gallon barrel while the duty on cider was only two shillings a hogshead, which could be anything from 60 to 100 gallons or even more. The preferential rate is an indicator that cider was still in the main produced by landed gentlemen who had greater lobbying power than the common brewers. The tax was not repealed at the Restoration – in fact it was increased to 2/6 and lasted until 1830; but it is unclear how effectively it was collected.

Paying for war damage and restoring the profitability of damaged estates was one of the stimuli behind a new school of improving literature that began to appear even before the war ended and continued throughout the Commonwealth and after the Restoration. But for the first time, growing fruit and making cider was also strongly suggested as a means by which cottagers and smallholders might increase the income from their meagre patches of land; and given the spirit of the times it comes as no surprise to find that there was also a strong religious ethic underlying the urge to make the most of the earth's fruitfulness. But a powerful sense of mission is only one factor that distinguishes the improving literature of the mid- and late-17th century from the agricultural tracts of Tudor times. Another is that many of the 17th-century writers were connected, a côterie, albeit one so broad that it embraced both Puritan divines and Royalist landowners, who had these things in common: the benefit of generations of experience in every aspect of cidermaking from orchard husbandry to fermentation; a spirit of rational enquiry tied to a dedication to constant experiment and improvement; a huge pride in – and enjoyment of – their cider; and a zealous belief that it deserved to be, and could become, England's national drink.

The central figure in this circle was Samuel Hartlib, a German scholar and polymath who arrived in Charles I's London as a refugee from the 30 Years' War. His experience of the ravages of civil war, and the deep understanding of estate management revealed in his book, *Samuel Hartlib, his Legacy, or an Enlargement of the Discourse of Husbandry used in Brabant and Flanders*, published in 1645, attracted the attention of the Parliamentary authorities, who awarded him a pension of £100 a year. Hartlib's *Legacy* advocated intensive horticulture and an increase in market gardens, nurseries, and orchards, not so much as a way of restoring the fortunes of the landed gentry but as a way of maximising the revenue of peasant smallholdings. Hartlib advocated paying close attention to the selection and propagation of the most productive plant varieties, including cider apples, which he claimed were badly neglected in England. "We have not nurseries sufficient in this land of apples, pears, cherries, vines, chestnuts, almonds, &c: but gentlemen are necessitated to send to London some hundred miles for them," he wrote; adding however, that there were "many gallant orchards" in Kent, around London, and in Gloucestershire, Herefordshire, and Worcestershire, and that in Kent and Surrey plums "pay no small part of the rent."

A prolific correspondent, Hartlib established a range of contacts in Interregnum England that included the poet Milton, who dedicated his *Tractate on Education* to him; the young Christopher Wren, who designed a transparent glass beehive to illustrate Hartlib's 1655 book *The Reformed Commonwealth of Bees*; and John Evelyn, a Royalist writer who was later to become a founder member of the Royal Society, a courtier of Charles II's, and a diarist contemporary with, but very different in tone from, Samuel Pepys. Evelyn met Hartlib in November 1655 and recorded the meeting in his diary, describing him as "a public spirited and ingenious person, who had propagated many usefull things and arts... This gentleman was master of innumerable curiosities, and very communicative."

Two improving ciderists, similar in some ways but very different in others, who attracted Hartlib's patronage were Ralph Austen and John Beale.

Austen was a Staffordshire man, a rigorous Puritan, and a soldier in the Parliamentary army who may have taken part in the siege of Oxford that effectively ended the first Civil War in 1646. Afterwards he settled in the city and established a small nursery there, although he also described himself as a proctor of the University, where he spied on the diehard Royalist dons in what had been Charles I's wartime capital. In 1653 he wrote his *Treatise on Fruit Trees*, a work that was not only practical but was also shot through with Biblical references. He and his contemporary Adolphus Speed (*Adam out of Eden*, 1659) worked on the twin principles that efficient work was both Godly and profitable. A pamphlet of Austen's, *The Spiritual Use of an Orchard*, compares every aspect of nursery work – planting, grafting, transplanting, harvesting – to a stage in the Christian life, while Speed, although equally zealous in inspiration, also argued that intensive horticulture could improve the annual value of a piece of land tenfold – an attractive proposition to smallholders who were being excluded from their accustomed commons by enclosure.

Anyone attempting to profit from *Adam out of Eden*, however, was likely to be disappointed, since it was fatally undermined by errors and superstitions copied verbatim from much earlier sources. Austen was more rigorous: not only is the *Treatise* a sound practical manual, it also devotes much space to debunking the sort of horticultural myths common in the 15th century and evidently still current. His "errors discovered" included the belief that if you engraved an inscription on a peachstone and planted it, the same inscription would appear on the stones of the ripe fruit. Others were: "to have all stone fruit taste as ye shall think good, lay the stones to soak in such liquor as ye would have them taste of," and "to have red apples, put the grafts into pikes' blood." "These things," he says simply, "cannot be."

Austen and Hartlib corresponded frequently during the book's production, and in dedicating the *Treatise* to Hartlib Austen was doubtless hoping to attract the patronage of his sponsors in Parliament; but without success. So he continued as a nurseryman in Oxford, and in 1655 attempted to enclose 40 acres of Shotover Forest for an orchard. However despite appealing to the Commonwealth authorities for financial help, or to be awarded Royalist assets seized by the Committees of Sequestration, he failed to raise the money to buy out the commoners and instead, in 1659, opened what must have been England's first dedicated cider factory on land leased between Queen Street and Shoe Lane in Oxford. Sadly, it proved a dead end: in 1676 Austen died childless, with no-one to carry on the business.

Hartlib's other cidermaking protégé was, like Ralph Austen, a deeply religious man; but there the similarities end. No Puritan, Beale was the high-church rector of Yeovil and a Royalist with top-ranking connections. One of his cousins, for instance, Viscount Scudamore of Holme Lacy in Herefordshire (Beale's native county), had been Charles I's ambassador to France and was to make a single but very great contribution to the development of 17th-century cidermaking – the propagation of the Redstreak apple. The Redstreak, a near-dwarf tree that grew a large, purplish fruit with red-streaked flesh, is variously described either as a cutting he brought back from France or a wilding he discovered growing on his Herefordshire estate. Whichever version is accurate, Scudamore's Redstreak very quickly became the leading variety of the region, growing quickly, cropping heavily, and yielding a cider whose superior qualities were disputed by very few.

Although a Herefordshire man by birth, Beale was also well-connected in Somerset, where the influential Phelips family of Montacute were also cousins and actually found him his living. So Beale had a foot in both of the main cidermaking camps, and probably helped bring together the *Pomona* circle. Hartlib helped Beale publish his *Herefordshire Orchards* in 1657 – Beale appears to have known Herefordshire and its cidermaking gentry so intimately that one wonders how often he visited his parish in Somerset – and is also credited with introducing him to John Evelyn. The introduction was to prove significant, for both men joined the Royal Society as founder members in 1662 and when Evelyn was asked by the Commissioners of the Navy to produce his great work on forestry, *Sylva* (1664), he turned to Beale for help with the production of its annexe, *Pomona*.

Even in the context of the vast amount of improving literature that was published in the 17th century, *Sylva* stands out, gaining enormous credibility through its quasi-official status and running to three editions in Evelyn's long lifetime (he died in 1706) with a fourth not long after. *Pomona*, as it were, rode on its coat-tails. It was not an official publication of the Royal Society's; but being published as an appendix to *Sylva* gave the appearance of one. Evelyn himself wrote the Preface and credited Beale for much of the main body of the work; *Aphorisms upon Cider*, which follows the main body, is a series of papers on various aspects of arboriculture and cidermaking by other authorities including Sir Paul Neile, a researcher in optics, courtier of Charles I's, and founder member of the Royal Society; John Newburgh of Dorset; and Captain Silas Taylor, a former officer in Cromwell's army who had served on the Herefordshire Committee of Sequestration and dealt leniently with Scudamore.

Although Beale's main contribution is at bottom a practical dissertation on all the processes of growing apples and making cider – and only one of many on the market – Evelyn's Preface is more of a political, economic, and indeed moral manifesto, and an extreme one at that. The men behind *Pomona* had an agenda, and this was their way of progressing it. They had seen the court of Charles II turn into, according to Andrew Barr in *Drink: A Social History* (Pimlico Books, 1995), "a satellite of Versailles", with a king dependent on Louis XIV for secret subventions, a cadre of courtiers (including Evelyn) who had spent many years in exile in France, and a vogue amounting almost to mania for all things French – art, dress, manners, food, and drink. (Pepys in 1663 records drinking "a sort of French wine called Ho Bryan, that hath a good and most particular taste". This was in fact Haut Brion, the first Bordeaux wine to be marketed under the name of its parent château, as a consequence of which Francophile courtiers would pay seven shillings a bottle for it – four times the price of other French wines). The ciderists had also seen cider gaining in importance as a marketable commodity and envisioned turning the Western Counties into England's Burgundy and Bordeaux, with the cider they made and sold enjoying equal status with imported wine.

Evelyn's thesis was that cider was a far better drink in every way than either beer or wine, and that determined measures should be adopted to advance its manufacture. Hops, he said, were wasteful, "seldom succeeding more than once in three years yet requiring constant charge and culture"; and as for brewing with barley, why, "the nation drinks its very bread-corn!" He went on to argue that as peoples of all countries preferred their indigenous beverages to foreign introductions, so the people of England should naturally favour their native wine – ie cider – over French, Rhenish, Sack, Canary and Malaga, an opinion he substantiated by reporting a wager between a Herefordshire cidermaker and a London vintner, taking the form of a series of comparative blind tastings won hands down by cider made, of course, from Scudamore's Redstreak.

Evelyn urged the King himself to take the lead in ensuring the necessary increase in the nation's supply of cider by planting fruit trees on all his manors and estates. Noblemen and citizens would surely follow the royal example, he argued; but if their tenants objected to making such a long-term commitment (it takes a modern cider apple tree five years to bear; in the 17th century it took the fastest grower – again, the Redstreak – more like 10 or 12), then their landlords must force them to by inserting suitable covenants in leases. Landlords would be better off in terms of the rent they could charge by £5 for every 20 trees by doing so, he said. Parliament should pass an Act, too, requiring a given density of cider trees to be planted on all enclosed land on pain of a forfeit to be spent on poor relief; commons and wasteland must also be planted up with the profits going to the poor "which would afford them a most incredible relief". And planting fruit trees in "hedgerows, champion-grounds, land-divisions, mounds and headlands ("where the plough not coming, 'tis ever abandoned to weeds and briars") would "add considerably to these advantages without detriment to any man". The Preface finally proposed that while all these thousands of trees were coming to fruition, the Royal Society would provide training to all who needed it in turning the fruit into cider.

Well, the law Evelyn called for was never passed; the commons and wastelands were never planted for the poor; leases were never altered to force short-term tenants into long-term investments (although tenants were commonly obliged to replace dead trees); and as far as we know the King never roused himself to set his people a good example. For the truth about the men behind *Pomona* was that although some of them were in one sense or another courtiers, they were all actually slightly suspect. Beale had been a close associate of Hartlib, a Parliament pensioner who was snubbed by all after the Restoration. Taylor, of course, had been an out-and-out rebel, if a kindly one; and Evelyn himself (whose ancestral home in Surrey was deep in Parliament-held territory) had prudently set off on a four-year grand tour of France and Italy shortly after the outbreak of hostilities in 1642. And although after the Restoration Evelyn was often with the King, and was sometimes found useful work to do (such as his *Fumifugium*, a report on air pollution in the Capital, and his work on the creation of the Royal Hospitals), he remained on the fringes of power, an observer rather than an actor. (Sir Kenelm Digby, a leading ciderist although not a contributor to *Pomona*, was even more suspect as a Roman Catholic and the son of Sir Everard Digby, a leader of the 1605 Gunpowder Plot). Not for nothing was

Pomona dedicated to Thomas Wriothesley, Earl of Southampton and, as Lord High Treasurer, the most powerful ally Evelyn could hope to attract. But both Wriothesley and his royal master – and, for that matter, *Pomona's* intended audience – had experienced the effects of unrestrained enthusiasm all too recently. They might be receptive to money-making ideas, but had no appetite for the enforced planting of apple trees backed up by the threat of a fine.

To be fair, though, the Aphorisms appended to *Pomona* hardly live up to the emotion of the Preface, or support its radical agenda. Sometimes they flatly contradict it: in the first few lines of the very first chapter Beale (whom we suppose to have composed most of the main body of the work) states his intention as "relieving the want of wine by a succedaneum of cider" – hardly consistent with the Preface's outright attack on wine as a foreign and inferior substitute for the real thing. And Sir Paul Neile, in his contribution, openly admits that he actually prefers cider made from eaters such as "golden pepins, Kentish pepins, and pearmains". But although a Yorkshireman by birth, Neile was then living at White Waltham in Berkshire, where the grower's main business was supplying the London trade with table fruit. The ciders he had daily access to were by-products of this trade; and as we have seen in Norden's *Surveior's Discourse*, the region's old cider orchards were not being replanted.

Often the worthies who contributed the Aphorisms disagreed with each other. John Newburgh recommends tumping the apples on a bed of reeds for up to six weeks before milling them; Dr Smith says they should go straight from tree to mill. Neile goes into enormous detail on the correct way of bottling cider so that it "frets" or sparkles; Taylor dismisses his entire argument in a paragraph. Their failure to show a united front seems to embarrass Evelyn; in an "Animadversion" or miniature preface he even apologises. "If some of the following discourses seem less constant, or upon occasion repugnant to one another, they are to be considered as relating to the several gusts and guises of persons and countries, and not be looked on as recommended, much less imposed," he says. A far cry from the admonitory and prescriptive tone of the Preface!

Nevertheless, the contributed papers open a fascinating window on the wide range of habits and practices of the day. Of bottling, discussed at length in the Aphorisms, we will speak later. From Newburgh we learn that it was common in Devon to boil the juice before fermenting it, presumably to concentrate the sugars and thus generate more alcohol (although of course the boiling would also have killed the natural yeast, so the must would have had to have been pitched like beer); that the cider merchants of Dorset (interesting to note that merchants or wholesalers were already operating in the 1660s) liked to buy liquor that was encrusted with a "leathercoat", which they believed improved the cider's keeping qualities and which they even reinforced with a few handfuls of wheatbran. From Beale we learn that all sorts of additives including mustard, spices, and fruit were routinely added to cider to help preserve it or to ameliorate its tannic harshness (cider with raspberries being "an excellent women's wine", says Captain Taylor). Neile describes the process of keeving, or racking the cider off its lees to inhibit fermentation and thus ensure a much sweeter end product (although he didn't quite understand how the process works). And both he and Newburgh advocate reserving the unpressed first weeping from the stack of cheeses to ferment separately, a practice which Newburgh says was favoured in Devon, and which in Jersey added five shillings to the price of a hogshead.

(This practice is analogous to the way the Hungarians make Tokay wine today. The outward-facing grapes that have had the most sunshine will be much riper than the rest of their respective bunches, and when the fruit is collected in baskets or *puttonyos* they will begin to weep slightly under the weight of the other berries. This first running is so intensely sweet that it will scarcely ferment; its wine, Escenzia, is so rare, so expensive, and so exquisite, that in Hapsburg days it was reserved entirely for the use of the Emperor. Neile said that the French made wine in this way, the best wine coming from the unpressed first runnings or sweatings, a pink wine from a second, very light, pressing, and a "harsh" red wine from the final pressing).

Pomona may have fallen short of Evelyn's hopes in that the measures advocated in the Preface never came to pass. But other factors were at work that ensured growing popularity for the best-quality cider; principally, the return to traditional hostility with France after more than a century of comparative peace. This had started with Charles I's abortive expeditions of 1627-29 in support of the Huguenots against Louis XIII, in which the young Scudamore actually took part, and continued sporadically until the reign of William III when war with France became practically institutionalised. The upshot was a series of embargoes on French imports in 1649-57, 1678-85, and 1689-1713. Indeed, Evelyn specifically mentions its availability in times of interrupted trade as an advantage of cider over wine.

Portugal was the immediate beneficiary of the embargoes (Charles II was married to a Portuguese princess, Catherine of Braganza); but domestic cidermakers also saw their produce gaining ever wider acceptance both among the upper classes in its pure, undiluted form and, as a cheaper and less alcoholic second pressing, among the farm labourers of the West Country.

The propagandists were naturally encouraged to further efforts. Foremost among them was John Worlidge, a prolific author on agricultural improvement in general whose *Systema Agriculturae* ran to five editions in his lifetime. Among his other works were *Systema Horticulturae* and *Apiarium, or a Discourse of Bees*; but his best-known book was and remains *Vinetum Britannicum* (1676), basically an enlargement of *Pomona*, which ran to three editions. Worlidge, who lived in Petersfield in Hampshire, was also an inventor: his horse-drawn seed-drill predated Jethro Tull's more famous version by 20 years; and for the cidermaker he invented the "ingenio", the first scratter mill, a hopper that fed the apples into a chamber containing two rollers turned by a hand-crank. Its advantages over the traditional horse-powered circular trough were that it was cheaper to buy, took up less space, and could be fitted with a water-powered belt-drive.

Like Evelyn, Worlidge's thesis was that cider was the equal of wine and was indeed the true wine of Britain, and should therefore be Britain's national drink. He repeated the story, with variations, of the tasting challenge between a cidermaker and a wine merchant, and proclaimed: "There is not a drink known to us generally palatable as cider: for you may make it sute with almost any humorous drinker: it may be made luscious by an addition of a quantity of sweet apples in the first operation, pleasant being made with Pippins or Gennet-Moyles only: racy, poignant, oyly, spicy with the Redstreaks and other sorts of fruits, even as the operator pleases. And it satisfies thirst, if not too stale, more than any other usual drink whatsoever."

He also pushed the economic advantages of planting fruit trees, "it being one of the best and most advantageous pieces of improvement of our country farms yet known". Redstreaks could fetch up to eight shillings a bushel, he said, while the cider made from them sold at £8 a hogshead or, if well-matured, even £20. But he stressed, following Austen and Speed, that growers didn't have to be big landowners to benefit: "That which most tempts the rustick to the propagation of this fruit for the making of this liquor is the facile and cheap way of raising and preparing of it, for in such years as corn is dear, the best cider may be made at a far easier rate than ordinary ale; the thoughts whereof add much to the exhilarating virtue of this drink, and will I hope be a good inducement to the farther improvement of it."

But successful and widely-read though they were, the works of Evelyn, Beale, Austen, Worlidge, and others such as Timothy Nourse, William Worth, and Richard Haines have to be seen in context. These were only a few among a multitude of writers on agriculture during a genuinely revolutionary period in farming practices. New patterns of land-holding, new crops, new techniques of improving the soil, new machinery and indeed a new near-industrial ethos, driven by a fortunate marriage of economic need and rational enquiry, meant that by the end of the 17th century England was able to feed itself despite the growth of the population from four to nearly six million, and that it continued to be able to feed itself during the even greater increase of the 18th. But the most powerful transformation was occurring not in the rugged west, but in the more fertile, populous, and better-connected east. If we are to look for the reason why cider never became England's national drink, as its proponents desired, and continued to come a poor third to beer and wine, we need to look no further than the diffuse structure of the cider industry itself compared to the intensification of farming on the other, more economically developed, side of the Axe-Tees line.

5: So Near...

As the 17th century drew to a close, cidermaking appeared to have reached an apogee of popularity and respectability. True, the radical agenda proposed by Evelyn had not been fulfilled. But the more pragmatic, commercial approach of the rest of the *Pomona* circle and of John Worlidge and other improving writers had made a deep impact on the landowning gentry. Touring Herefordshire in 1696 the diarist Celia Fiennes observed that apples and pears grew everywhere; not just in orchards but "even in their cornfields and hedgerows", just as the improvers recommended. Hereford itself, she noted, was a prosperous city with well-paved streets "handsome as to breadth and length."

And the message was spreading far beyond the Western counties of England, too. In 1682 an Irish clergyman noted that the farmers of Portadown were getting 30 shillings a barrel for their cider, and many of them were making 20 or 30 barrels a year. In Suffolk in 1728 a Jerseyman who had migrated to Suffolk found his vines wouldn't grow and replaced them with cider apples from his native soil. His name was Clement Chevallier, and the location of his endeavours was Aspall Hall near Debden. His direct descendants are still producing cider there today, using locally-grown cider apples as well as the table and cooking fruit more common in the region; which makes Aspall Cyder not only Britain's oldest-attested cidermaker but also its longest-established family-controlled company. And in Bloxholme, Lincolnshire, in 1755 Thomas Hitt, gardener to Lord Manners, recorded in his *Treatise of Fruit Trees* that cider varieties including Stire, Redstreak, and Woodcock were being grown in the pastures and wheatfields of his master's estate.

For the gentry, though, it was not only production in commercial quantity that mattered; it was also the quality of the product. What they sought, in Sir Paul Neile's words, was a cider that was "pleasant"; ie, that was free from the harsh, tannic, and even acetic notes that one finds in some modern farmhouse ciders. Although they didn't – and indeed couldn't possibly – understand the biochemistry, they had discovered from their own experience that frequent racking from one cask to another preserved at least some of the sweetness of the unfermented juice by inhibiting the build-up of the yeast population and slowing the rate of fermentation. They had also found that slowing the fermentation both by racking and by keeping the temperature down helped prompt the malo-lactic fermentation during which malic acid is transformed into the mellower lactic acid.

Racking reduces the rate of attenuation (the conversion of sugar into alcohol) and therefore reduces the alcoholic strength of the final product. But Roger French estimates, using measurements of gravity made by Thomas Andrew Knight for his *Pomona Herefordiensis* (published in 10 parts between 1808 and 1810), that the first-pressed cider enjoyed in country mansions was as strong as table wine – which, when French was writing, ranged from 9%-11% ABV. No modern cider apple would reliably produce enough sugar to generate such a volume year after year. What would have boosted the gravity of the juice, though, was the routine practice of heaping the picked or fallen fruit either outdoors ("tumping") or in drying-lofts for long periods before pressing. This had two effects: saccharification, or the conversion of unfermentable starch into sugar, continues for some time after apple and tree have parted company; and partial dehydration concentrates the sugars and makes the resulting juice sweeter still. Hugh Stafford was a great advocate of tumping: windfalls he said, should be heaped for 10 days; picked apples for two weeks; and late varieties for up to six weeks. Beale, in *Pomona*, had noted some varieties being tumped from harvest until Christmas. The tumps should be made in the orchard rather than in a barn or apple loft, says Stafford, to let the fresh air keep the apples cool and, presumably, to prevent mould and mildew that might spoil the juice from developing. The degree of concentration that can be achieved by tumping is far from negligible: Captain Taylor reckoned that it took 20 bushels of freshly-picked apples to fill a hogshead, compared to 30 bushels if they had been properly tumped. It would also soften them, making them easier to mill. Counteracting the effects of tumping, the frequency of racking recommended by Neile and Stafford will inhibit the development of the yeast population, slowing the fermentation and leaving a considerable quantity of residual sugar and therefore a lower alcoholic content. Knight does not specify whether the juices he tested were from apples that had been tumped, although given the high readings it seems likely. It would be interesting to know how far the effects of tumping and continual racking cancel each other out; but even without conducting the experiment it seems quite possible that the lower end of French's estimate of the alcoholic strength of fine table cider in the 17th and 18th centuries is not far out. Robert Hogg, a key figure in the late 19th century when tumping and racking were not so religiously practiced, observed that cider's strength ranged between 5% and 10% ABV, which overlaps with French.

Alcoholic strength notwithstanding, the best ciders of the day were certainly prized as highly, and praised as lavishly, as fine wine. The very glasses from which the wealthy drank their cider bears witness to the esteem in which it was held: this was a golden age in English decorative glassware, and the Cider Museum in Hereford has a fine collection of elegantly sculpted crystal chalices with marvellously delicate air-twist or white-twist stems. And cider was even considered a fit subject, not only for technical tracts, but also for poetry on an epic scale.

Cider: a Poem in Two Books, published in 1708, was more than 1,400 lines of blank verse written by John Phillips, previously known for a patriotic minor epic about the Battle of Blenheim. Phillips was born in 1676 Bampton, Oxfordshire, where his father was vicar. But the family came from Herefordshire and had many connections among the cidermaking gentry there, so the choice of cider as the subject for his magnum opus probably seemed natural enough to the tubercular young classical scholar. And the interesting thing is that educated society – with the notable exception of Alexander Pope – accepted it as natural too, and took to it enthusiastically. The poem remained in print throughout the century, and when Phillips succumbed to tuberculosis the year following its publication he was considered worthy of a memorial plaque in Poet's Corner in Westminster Abbey. And despite Phillips's short career and slender output, Dr Johnson even included a biographical essay about him in his *Lives of the English Poets*.

In truth, though, the poem was not really about cider at all. True, it included all the standard advice about selecting the right site and soil for an orchard, choosing the best varieties, planting, grafting, harvesting, milling, pressing, blending and so on; but the cider-related matter was only a part of what was really a wide-ranging, even encyclopaedic, celebration of the poet's ancestral county, its folklore, its history, its landed families – even its women. And it was a virtuoso display both of classical erudition and technical ability: Phillips quite deliberately cast his great work as a blend of Virgil – nodding, as he passed, to Horace, Lucretius, Catullus and Ovid – and Milton, the first poet since the Elizabethan dramatists to use blank verse. As an earnest and accomplished acolyte (despite Milton's having been a diehard republican, while Phillips was an equally ardent royalist), Phillips did capture something of the addictive flow of the master. But his devotion to Virgil sometimes caught him out. The poem contains many near-verbatim translations of passages from the *Georgics*; so planters are advised to leave their orchards open to the warm west wind, which may have been benign in Classical Italy but was not so kind in the lee of the Black Mountains! Indeed Dr Johnson called Phillips "a man who writes books from books"; and given the delicate state of his health it is unlikely that he was personally acquainted with the operation of the panking pole, or did more than adapt the writings of the improvers to suit a more scholastic purpose.

But if *Cider's* advice was not to be followed too closely, its very success did prove one thing: that the best ciders of the day were well-known and much appreciated among the upper classes. It was the delight of gentlemen in cider-producing regions to regale visitors with their finest vintages – "to treat thy neighbours with mellifluous cups", in Phillips's words; and not just in their natural state, either, for they devoted great efforts both to creating sparkling bottled ciders and to distilling cider brandy. Both processes had made great strides in the 17th century; and as dedicated improvers, the cider-producing gentry adopted them with enthusiasm.

Wine had been distilled on the Continent since at least the late 11th century, when Marcus Graecus published the earliest known recipe for "aqua ardens" in his *Liber ignium ad comburendos hostes*. These early distillates were seen as a medicine rather than a beverage: Arnaud de Villeneuve in his 13th-century treatise *De Vinis* says: "Some people call it eau de vie, and this name is remarkably suitable, since it is really a water of immortality. It prolongs life, clears ill-humours, revives the heart, and maintains youth." It was also, according to the 14th-century French writer Raymond Lulli, a psychotropic: in the first recorded reference to what is now called Dutch courage, he praised "the marvellous use and commodity of burning waters even in wars, a little before the joining of battle, to stir and encourage the soldiers' minds."

By the 15th century people had evidently begun to drink spirits for pleasure as well as health. Whisky was being made in Scotland in 1494, when James IV granted Friar John Cor "eight bolls of malt" for aqua vitae; and many German cities tried to ban them altogether. The English, however, were some way behind their European (and Scottish) cousins: in 1525, a translation of a German work was published in London under the title of *The Vertuose Boke of Distyllacyon of the Waters of all maner of Herbes for the help and profit of surgeons, physicians, apothecaries, and all manner of people*, was still only recommending the medicinal qualities of spirits. "Aqua Vitae," says the *Vertuose Boke*, "purifyeth the wits of melancholy and of all uncleanliness, when it is drunk by reason and measure; that is to understand five or six drops in the morning, fasting, with a spoonful of wine."

But by 1559, when Peter Morwyng published his *Treasure of Evonymous*, there were a number of distillers in London producing *marc* from wine-lees and spoiled wine, a practice Morwyng endorses. "Burning-water, or Aqua Vitae," he writes, "is drawn oute of wyne, but, wyth us, out of the wyne lees only. And peradventure it is never a whit the worse that it is drawne oute of lees." The speed with which the popularity of spirits spread in England is evidenced by the many reprints of the *Treasure of Evonymous* and another treatise on the same subject by Conrad Gesner, translated by George Baker under the title of *The Newe Jewell of Health*. Soldiers returning from Elizabeth I's Dutch war of 1585, where they had first encountered gin, made spirits more popular still.

Distilling on a domestic scale evidently became popular quite rapidly: Gervase Markham in *The English Housewife* (1615) gives recipes for herbal distillates with a preposterous number of ingredients, mainly medicinal in purpose, on the clear assumption that any well-to-do household would possess a still. (Although he also described Aqua Composita, distilled from "the best ale that can be brewed," Imperial Water distilled from Gascon wine, and Cinnamon Water distilled from sack, all clearly intended as beverages rather than doses). But not until 1639, when the Distillers Company was chartered, do we hear of distillation on a large scale, and already it was clear, from the terms of the Company's charter, that native spirits were pretty rough stuff: "No Afterworts or Wash (made by Brewers, etc) called Blew John," said the regulations, "nor musty unsavoury or unwholesome tills, nor dregs of beer; nor unwholesome or adulterated wines or Lees; nor unwholesome sugar-waters; musty unsavoury or unwholesome returned beer; nor rotten corrupt or unsavoury fruits, druggs, spices, herbs, seeds; nor any other ill-conditioned materials of what kind soever, shall henceforth be distilled, extracted or drawn into small spirits, or low wines, or be any other ways used, directly or indirectly, by any of the Members of this Company, or their successors at any time hereafter forever." This roster of abuses was almost certainly exaggerated; but it does make the case that spirits can be obtained from almost any fermented base.

By the time Evelyn's *Pomona* was published, it seems evident that many cidermakers were distilling their produce for their own enjoyment pretty much as a matter of course: both Newburgh and Dr Smith mention it in their papers – as indeed does Worlidge in *Vinetum Britannicum* – but in passing and without comment. And the probate inventory of the Spread Eagle in Midhurst, East Sussex, taken in 1673, includes a small pewter still – and this being cider country, it is not merely possible but probable that the innkeeper, Henry Courtney, had been making cider brandy for his guests. But only in 1684, with the publication of Richard Haines's *Aphorisms upon The New Way of Improving Cyder, or Making Cyder-Royal* was distilling cider brandy as a commercial venture seriously proposed.

A prosperous farmer from the Sussex Weald, Haines was also a devout Baptist whose first published works were Gospel commentaries. His piety was doubtless also the spur for his keen interest in poor-law reform, and in many books and tracts he sought to promote the creation of almshouses on the Dutch model where paupers could be employed weaving linen and producing other manufactures to reduce the country's dependence on imports.

An instinctive protectionist, Haines argued that a growing trade gap, especially in new luxury products such as coffee, chocolate, and brandy, was the source of the economic slump of the 1670s. The total annual value of these he put at two or three million pounds. On the other hand, he said, English manufactures had decreased. His remedies were both to stimulate and protect the manufacture of English goods and to ban imports that he saw as superfluous such as "that outlandish, robbing, and (by reason of its abuse) Man-killing Liquor, called BRANDY" (brandy referring then to all distilled spirits, including gin). In this he echoed a petition put to Parliament in 1673 praying that brandy, coffee, tea and chocolate might be prohibited.

According to the petition: "Before brandy, which is now sold in every little alehouse, came into England in such quantities as it now doth, we drank good strong beer and ale, and all laborious people, their bodies requiring, after hard labour, some strong drink to refresh them did therefore every morning and evening used to drink a pot of ale or a flagon of strong beer, which greatly promoted the consumption of our own grain, and did them no great prejudice; it hindered not their work, neither did it take away their senses nor cost them much money, whereas the prohibition of brandy would prevent the destruction of His Majesty's subjects, many of whom have been killed by drinking thereof, it not agreeing with their constitution."

Excise figures from the time hardly support Haines's complaints. In 1684, the year that his *Aphorisms* was published, excise was paid on just over half a million gallons of English-distilled spirits, compared to some 350,000 gallons of imports. Imports were fast catching up, though: 10 years later, despite William III's 1689 Act encouraging the distillation of surplus grain and embargo on French brandy, production of English spirits amounted to 800,000 gallons compared to 1,250,000 gallons imported mostly from Holland, Spain, Portugal and the Canaries. Haines's appeal to national interest echoed Worlidge's, and although it jumped the gun somewhat it was not without justification. The lengthy subtitle of *Aphorisms* sums up his argument: "For the Good of those Kingdoms and Nations That are Beholden to Others, and Pay Dear for Wine, Shewing That Simple Cyder, frequently Sold for Thirty Shillings per Hogshead (vis Three half-pence a Quart) may be made as Strong, Wholesome, and Pleasing as French wine usually sold for Twelve-pence a Quart; Without Adding anything to it, but what is of the Juice of Apples; and for One Penny or Three-half-pence a Quart more Charge, may be made as good as Canary commonly sold for two Shillings. As also, how one Acre of Land worth now Twenty Shillings, may be made worth Eight or Ten Pound per Annum." To drive home the message, it is dedicated to "All Kings Princes and States, who have no wines of their own Production," including the "Kings of the two Northern Crowns" and the States General of the United Provinces.

The drink Haines sought to promote was not actually plain cider brandy, but a blend of cider and cider brandy that he called "cyder-royal", the exact equivalent of the *pommeau* sold in Normandy today. He made it by adding to a hogshead of cider the distillate of a second hogshead and leaving the two to marry for two or three months, to produce a beverage not only "stronger and more palatable" than straight cider, "but also more wholesome, no longer being cold, sickly, and apt to generate wind." It was as strong and as pleasant as French wine, he said, adding: "Being the product of our own soil, it must needs suit our constitutions better than outlandish liquors. It can be recommended as an appetizer and tonic, and even excessive indulgence has no harmful effects." In this he may have been overegging his pudding more than somewhat, but he was not without supporters: William Worth, writing in the Britannian Magazine in 1691, averred that brandy made from cider or perry was "little inferiour to that of France", and as late as 1747 Edward Cave, founder of the *Gentleman's Magazine*, writing under his usual pen-name Sylvanus Urban, was still urging his readers to make cyder-royal.

But Haines's advocacy came too late, and England never developed a tradition of cider brandy production as Normandy and Brittany did, competition from east of the Axe-Tees line being to blame. William III, who came to power only four years after the publication of Haines's *Aphorisms*, and his successor Queen Anne deregulated distilling almost completely in a series of measures aimed at hitting French imports while finding a way of soaking up the huge surplus of East Anglian grain caused by agricultural improvement and a new wave of engrossment and enclosure. Gin was soon cheaper than beer, and production ballooned from its 1694 level to more than 6,000,000 gallons by 1736, when the entire population was only 6,200,000, and more than 8,000,000 gallons by 1743. The sheer size of the gin industry is best understood by estimating the amount of wash – the basic unhopped malt liquor that went into the still – the distillers brewed. It took 8-10 gallons of wash to make a gallon of spirit; so in 1743 the mainly London-based distillers brewed at least 64,000,000 gallons of wash, the equivalent of 1,70,000 beer barrels – significantly more, in fact, than the output of the city's beer brewers. Indeed, it could be argued that the gin-distillers of late Stuart London pioneered the mass-production technology that made possible the industrial-scale porter brewing of the mid-18th century. And it is even possible that skills learnt in cidermaking helped usher the distillers into the new age of mass production. Few of the 750-odd common brewers of the late 17th century could have required or manufactured fermenting vessels much bigger than the eastern hogshead of 60-65 gallons; in the western cidermaking regions, though, hogsheads of 100 gallons or more were everyday items, and tuns and pipes of up to 400 gallons cannot have been uncommon. If the coopering skills required to construct the enormous vessels required by the distillers were anywhere, they were surely in the cider industry.

In the face of such powerful competition, commercial cider distilling as advocated by Haines never even made the starting blocks; and there is little evidence, anyway, that the cidermakers of the period ever considered cider brandy as more than a purely domestic pleasure other than a passing reference in William Ellis's *The Compleat Planter and Cyderist* (1756) to "many hogsheads of perry carried by wagons to Worcester to the distillers to draw a spirit from it, which is sold for 10 shillings per hogshead" and a tax of four shillings a hogshead imposed in 1759. And even if they had tried to create a market for cider brandy in the Western counties, they would have run into stiff competition from imported rum. Following Cromwell's capture of Jamaica in 1655, distillation was taken up by the colonists of mainland America and rum quickly became their principal export. Caribbean and American rum was soon flooding into the western ports of Bristol and Plymouth in quantities and at prices the cidermakers could never have hoped to match.

It is certain, though, that cidermakers large and small continued to make cider brandy for their own pleasure throughout the 18th century. William Ellis records the distillation of cider lees as still commonplace in Herefordshire, and the agricultural writer William Marshall in his *Rural Economy of the West of England*, published in 1796, records "the housewives of Devon" distilling a *marc* of cider lees, "of course illegally" using a porridge pot with a tin head and a condensing pipe passing through a hogshead of cold water, "this liquor being passed twice through this imperfect apparatus." But any lingering prospect of the commercial distillation of cider was killed off after 1823 – perversely, you might think – by legislation intended to bring the whisky distillers of the Scottish Highlands out into the open where they could be effectively regulated. A much relaxed and simplified tax regime succeeded, eventually, in turning Scotland's moonshining into a respectable and prosperous industry; but the other side of the legislative coin was the introduction of a minimum 40-gallon still capacity, as well as right of entry for excise officers and a strict inspection régime. This proved too much for the cider distillers of the western counties, whose much smaller home stills were mostly banished to the lumber-room or scrap-heap – although Hogg does refer to distillation in the 1880s, and there were continuous rumours right up to the mid-20th century of farmers using the small patent stills intended for making veterinary doses to distil their own brandy.

In commercial terms, then, cider brandy production turned out to be a blind alley. The failure of English cider brandy or cyder-royal to establish a niche lay in the nature of the cidermaking industry itself. For the truth is that it wasn't really an industry at all, and the likes of Newburgh and Neile weren't entrepreneurs in the modern sense. For them it was a branch of estate management, all part of being a country gentleman. And even if they had been more enterprising, the chances are that they still would have failed. For the grain that went to make gin wasn't a by-product of mixed farming: it was intensively grown on vast estates in the most populous and easily cultivable part of the country, and the best served with mass communications such as navigable rivers and canals. And the distilleries that made the gin weren't small affairs housed in the corner of a barn: they were full-blown capitalist industries, and perhaps the first genuinely mass-producing factories in British and indeed world history.

Bottling, however, proved to be an innovation with a bright commercial future; although not perhaps in the way that the cidermaking gentry had envisaged.

Bottles first came to England as purely decorative tableware into which wine was decanted from the cask before being brought to the table by, appropriately enough, the butler. The glass may have been beautiful, but it was also fragile – far too fragile to be used as anything more than ornament. Then in 1615 the national timber shortage, when even the staves of exported barrels had to be reimported, prompted a ban on the use of charcoal in iron smelting and glass manufacture, and the glass industry had to use coal to fire its furnaces instead. The higher temperatures of coal-fired furnaces, and the experimental addition of manganese and iron to the molten glass, created a product thick and strong enough to be portable and to withstand (sometimes) the pressure created when the contents started spontaneously to referment, as often happened. The invention is credited variously to Sir Robert Mansell, Treasurer to the Navy 1604-18, who ran a glassworks in the 1620s, and Sir Kenelm Digby, scholar, rake, adventurer, and minor courtier who owned a glassworks in the Forest of Dean coalfield in the 1630s. Whichever of them deserves the credit, it must have been Digby who brought the possibilities of the new, stronger bottle to the attention of the *Pomona* ciderists, for he was well-known to John Evelyn, who mentions meeting him several times in his *Diary,* and was a fellow founder of the Royal Society. Experiments with bottling beer had been going on for some time – Hugh Plat recommends it in *Delights for Ladies* (1609), as does Gervase Markham in *The English Housewife,* – and the ciderists were interested in any innovation that promised to allow them to store and mature their best vintages for far longer than the two years or so that it would age in cask. What they discovered was that the spontaneous refermentation which they had actually been trying to avoid in cask cider was very desirable in the bottle, producing a mellow or "pleasant" cider with a light sparkle or "fret".

Two distinct methods of bottling emerged from the ciderists' experiments. Sir Paul Neile favoured straining the fresh-pressed juice off its "gross lees" before allowing it to ferment, and then racking it frequently – every day, if necessary – until it cleared naturally, before bottling it with a piece of white sugar the size of a nutmeg in each bottle to mature over the winter. With almost the entire fermentation taking place in the bottle, temperature control was crucial: if the weather was frosty, the bottles had to be laid on a layer of hay, and covered with more hay; on mild days it could be left to stand on the stone floor of the cellar; in unseasonably warm weather, the bottles should be part-buried in sand – which would not only insulate them, but would also catch most of the shards if they exploded. A laborious business, made more so by the necessity of periodically venting the bottles to allow excess CO_2 to escape. Captain Taylor, on the other hand, favoured fermenting the cider in cask over the winter and bottling it in spring, storing it in a water-filled cistern to keep it cool. "This makes it drink quick and lively," he rhapsodised; "it comes into the glass not pale or troubled but bright yellow, with a speedy vanishing nittiness, which evaporates with a sparkling and a whizzing noise; and than this I never tasted wine nor cider that pleased better."

It was Taylor's method, being considerably less labour-intensive, that became the industry norm. But it seems to have been Neile's method that made its way across the Channel to the Champagne region of France.

It is often said that the French, and in particular Dom Pérignon, cellarer of the Abbey of Hautvilliers near Epernay from 1688-1715, simply copied English cidermakers in evolving naturally sparkling wine; but it's a myth. Dom Pérignon's greatest contributions to modern Champagne lay in the fields of viticulture and vinification rather than packaging, and in fact by the time he arrived at Hautvilliers Champagne had already evolved from a still white table wine into a sparkling bottled wine. Like other wines, it was commonly exported to England in barrel, and bottled over here. But Champagne is a northern and therefore temperate region with a consequently late grape harvest, and by the time the previous year's vintage arrived in England in spring it had generally not finished fermenting. Bottling it in the new strong bottles cut down on explosions; and when the winemakers of Champagne decided to start bottling it themselves it was Neile's method, or something like it, that they adopted. The full *méthode champenoise* with its *pupîtres* and its *dégorgement* was developed over the course of more than a hundred years in France, not in England, achieving its present level of sophistication in the early 19th century; so it's perhaps an overstatement to say that the English "invented" Champagne. The one thing of which there can be no doubt, however, is that the bottle-glass that made Champagne possible was the bottle-glass perfected by Mansell and/or Digby.

Although the Champagne region is in Eastern France, its winemakers possessed the same advantages over the cidermakers as the gin-distillers did. They were intensive and efficient producers, producing the volumes needed to satisfy a mass-market combined with the cost-base required to make the trade profitable. This came with the bonus of big export markets close at hand, for the Champagne region is as close to South-eastern England, logistically speaking, as the cider-making counties. It became fashionable as the drink of the better-off from as early as the late 17th century, demonstrating that the English aristocracy and middle classes preferred fine wine over fine cider, however acceptable the latter might be as a curiosity or occasional substitute. The constant interruptions in the wine trade caused exasperation – "If I have the spleen, it is because the town of London affords not one drop of wine," complained Sir William Congreve in 1706 – but didn't persuade the higher echelons of society to grace their tables with fine English ciders instead. The earnest and repeated plea of the ciderists that, really, their cider was as good as any imported wine simply reinforces the impression that their target market didn't think so; and after 1703 when the Treaty of Methuen gave Portuguese wine preferential treatment, imports from Portugal began steadily to expand – all the more rapidly after 1730, when the Portuguese started fortifying their export wines to create the Port we know today. The 18th century was an era of heavy drinking, and a capacity to drink several bottles of Port a day was much admired. But the gentry's taste was for strong, sweet, red wines – even

Bordeaux vintners adulterated their wines to taste like Port, during the intervals of peace when its import was permitted – not the more subtle, delicate ciders and perries being produced in the Western counties. As late as 1756, William Ellis was still pressing the patriotic case for cider over wine; but as he himself admitted: "The common notion is that cyder is a weak, windy, insipid liquor, a drink more fit for women than men; a notion that has done infinite damage to this nation, and which took its rise and long continuance from the weak, sweet Herefordshire and London-made ciders that indeed please the palate for summer drinking, but yet is very unfit for winter. And it is upon this account that the consumption of vast quantities of this excellent liquor has been discouraged and the importation of foreign wines encouraged."

The failure of the ciderists to establish their product as the national drink might be attributable in some part to their inability to produce a drink that appealed to the palate of port-swilling London clubmen and their bourgeois imitators; but it lay ultimately in the fact that they were small producers, not even focused primarily on cider, located in a region that was, by comparison with their competitors' home territories, remote and rugged. But if that seems a gloomy assessment of the cidermakers' situation, it may not have appeared so at the time. The evangelists of cider – Evelyn, Worlidge, Haines, Ellis – may have represented a very small minority. Most cider-producing landowners seem to have been perfectly happy with their lot, with no ambition to establish the western counties as England's Bordeaux and Burgundy. Their "failure" to establish cider and cider brandy as rivals to wine and gin does not seem to have appeared as a failure to them. Certainly the stream of published material continued unabated throughout the 18th century: Timothy Nourse's *Campania Felix* in 1700; Sir John More's *England's Interest, or the Gentleman and Farmer Joined* in 1712; Moses Cook's *Art of Making Cyder* in 1724; Batty Langley's *Pomona* in 1729; Hugh Stafford's *Treatise* in 1753; Thomas Chapman's *Cyder Maker's Instructor* and Ellis's *Compleat Planter and Cyderist* both in 1756; Thomas Hale's *Compleat Body of Husbandry* in 1758; JN Morse's *On Grafting, Planting, and Making Cyder* and *Characteristic Account of 29 Sorts of Apple*, both in 1796; Charles Dunster's *On Apple Trees* in 1799 – the continuing popularity of this kind of literature, repetitive as much of it was, shows that throughout the 18th century landowners and large farmers maintained a lively interest in a profitable trade.

These gentry were not without influence, either. In 1763, following the end of the ruinously expensive Seven Years' War, Lord Bute's administration raised the excise on cider for sale from seven shillings a hogshead to ten and sought to enforce its previously patchy collection. It also tried to levy an additional tax on cider made for domestic consumption, empowering excise officers to enter private homes to collect the tax of five shillings a head on all adults living in a house where cider was made – a provision that a political earthquake.

Bute, a Scottish Tory – a descendant of the Stuarts, in fact – had been George III's tutor and was the experienced young king's political favourite. By appointing him Prime Minister in 1762, the King thoroughly antagonised the largely Whig landowning class; and the invasion of privacy implicit in the tax provided them with the perfect opportunity for an ambush. There were demonstrations in cidermaking regions, including a funeral march through the streets of Exeter, whose City Corporation financed the gathering and publication of a petition against the tax; Bute, whose portrayal as a Scot and an interloper did him no good, was everywhere hanged in effigy; excise officers were physically obstructed; and a veritable torrent of pamphlets with titles like *Address to Honest English Hearts*, *Plain Reasons for Repeal*, and *Case with Respect to the New Excise Duty* cascaded into the coffee-houses of London. A satirical ballad published by "a cyder merchant of the South Hams" strikes a note that wouldn't be out of place in a modern tabloid:

"Ah, hapless old England! No longer be merry
Since Bute has thus tax'd your beer, cider, and perry.
Look sullen and sad, for now this is done
No doubt in short time they'll tax laughter and fun."

Bute clearly underestimated the political power of the Whig gentry; but had he been a keener student of the history of his adopted nation he would have known that the introduction of excise in 1643 had contained precisely the same provision levying tax on private brewing and empowering excisemen to enter private houses – and had met with precisely the same response. This time, though, the opposition was even more formidable, being led by William Pitt the Elder: the campaign gave us his most memorable political dictum, if not the most memorable political dictum in our history – that "an Englishman's home is his castle". In the spring of that year, Bute's administration duly fell. The tax on cider for domestic consumption, and in particular the invasive power given to the officers who were supposed to collect it, was repealed after only three years, although the excise duty on cider for sale remained in force until 1830 when it was raising a mere £260,000 a year compared to the yield from beer duty of £3,200,000.

The defeat of Bute's cider tax was pretty much the last hurrah, though, for gentrified cidermaking as practised by Neile, Newburgh, Stafford and the like. By the end of the 18th century cider as a luxury product, carefully made from the first runnings of the concentrated juice of partly-dried apples, frequently racked to preserve its "pleasantness", and put into bottles that had to be moved according to the weather and vented from time to time, had almost had its day. As a commercial commodity handled (and generally diluted and otherwise adulterated) by a national network of merchants and wholesalers, cider had to be processed quickly and cost-effectively. And in a 20-year period of continuous and intense warfare followed by protracted economic hardship, growers and makers had to look hard at defending their revenues. Even if fine cider could fetch handsome prices, it could never reach a mass market; and by the end of the 18th century it was clear that the future lay with a product of admittedly poorer quality but with much wider appeal.

6: Rough v. Smooth

Roger French, in *The History and Virtues of Cyder*, emphasised the distinction between the fine ciders made by the gentry and the rough or common version made for the mass market by adopting the conceit of spelling the former with a "y" and the latter with an "i"; and you will still find plenty of people who think the variants have or had different meanings. In fact they were completely interchangeable in those orthographically more relaxed days: both occur in *Pomona*, and I have even seen one 18th-century frontispiece where the word is spelt "sider". The long "y" was the more usual variant in the 18th century but gradually died out in the 19th as spelling became more standardised; the stories you will hear of "cyder" being the real thing and "cider" being mere scrumpy are just that: stories.

Orthography notwithstanding, French's distinction is entirely justified and was specifically made by Hugh Stafford in his *Treatise* of 1753, where he described in great detail the different ways of making "rough" cider for the market and fine or "smooth" cider "fit for a gentleman". And having been involved in the management of cidermaking for 20 years, he said, both for connoisseurs and for the market, he was speaking with some authority. (He spells both fine and rough versions with a "y", incidentally).

The differences between common and fine cider lay first in the selection of apple varieties used, and then in the treatment of the juice during fermentation. Much of *Pomona* is concerned with the qualities of cider made from different varieties: the virtues of the Pearmain, Pepin, Gennet Moyle, Eliot, Green Fillet, various Musts and so on are rehearsed at length although Beale concludes: "after many years' trial of those and many other varieties, the Red-Strake carried the common fame." The inference is that the gentry of the ciderists' acquaintance favoured single-varietal ciders and were engaged in an almost alchemical pursuit of the best; rarely is blending to capture the best characteristics of different types even mentioned. Stafford does not explicitly state that common cider was made by blending the juice of whatever apples came to hand. But the tradition that comes down to us is one of blending: modern cidermakers regard their blending skills as highly as the brandy distillers of Cognac do, and single-varietal ciders are a very recent introduction (or rather reintroduction) to the market. It's therefore reasonable to assume on almost every ground – cost, consistency, reliability of supply, ease of handling – that the common ciders of the 18th century were blends of the miscellaneous pressings supplied to merchants by legions of small producers.

Equally marked was the difference in the way the juices were processed. To make fine cider, said Stafford, the first runnings from the press should be strained straight into an open vessel or "keeve" and left until a head or cap of pulp started to form. (The last runnings could be held back to make an inferior cider). It should then be "pricked", or drawn off via a tap about four inches from the bottom of the keeve, into closed casks, leaving both cap and dregs behind. It should be racked into a clean cask as soon as white froth showed at the bung-hole; and it must be repeatedly racked thereafter "until the cyder is as sweet as you desire and ceases hissing". Finally it should be fined using either isinglass or eggwhite. The resulting drink would be "soft and mellow and perfectly sweet".

Common cider, by contrast, needed no such care and attention, even though "the loss of one or two rackings is attended with a disagreeable coarseness, harshness, bitterness, fetidness, and sometimes with all these faults". It didn't need to be strained or keeved but could be filled into closed casks straight from the press, and racked only infrequently. This is, essentially, how modern farm cider is made; and if today's artisanal makers take issue with the allegation of coarseness, harshness, bitterness, and fetidness, it's worth noting that many common cider drinkers in the 18th century liked their drink infused with aromatic herbs such as clary, a variety of sage.

As well as making fine cider for the gentry and common cider for the market, Stafford made "water-cyder" (also called "ciderkin", "ciderlet" or "zeyder") by soaking his pressed cheeses and then pressing them again; this, he said, would produce "an agreeable liquor for common use which, when well managed, retains its virtues for several months and will even intoxicate if drunk too plentifully". This was commonly given to farm labourers and estate workers, and it was often suffused with spices to give it some flavour. Or, as John Phillips put it:

"Thou, more wise, shall steep
Thy husks in water, and again employ
The ponderous engine; water will imbibe
The small remains of spirit, and acquire
A vinous flavour; this the peasants blithe
Will quaff, and whistle as thy tinkling team
They drive..."

One wonders whether the 10 hogsheads of cider provided for the townsfolk of Leominster by Sir Michael Newton in 1732 as part of the entertainment to mark the birth of his son (along with 30 cases of wine, an ox-roast, and 20 shillings put behind the bar of every public house in town) were fine cider, common cider, or water-cyder?

If cider brandy was never distilled on a commercial scale, and naturally sparkling bottled cider never really challenged the aristocratic taste for imported wine, common cider did achieve considerable distribution from the Restoration onwards, first in its home districts and then beyond. Daniel Defoe, visiting Herefordshire in 1725, remarked that: "We could get no beer or ale in their publick houses, only cyder; and that so very good, so fine, and so cheap that we never found fault with the exchange." He went on to record: "Great quantities of this cyder are sent to London, even by land carriage, tho' so very remote, which is an evidence of the goodness of it, beyond contradiction." Land carriage, however, was not the favoured option: navigable rivers, coastal shipping, and, later in the 18th century, canals made bulk transport cheaper, easier, and usually quicker. Already in *Pomona* itself we have encountered an acquaintance of Sir Paul Neile's sending a considerable quantity of cider to London on a rather extended waterborne journey via the Wye, the Bristol Channel, the English Channel, and the Thames; Newburgh's Dorset merchants were presumably also using coastal freighters; and in the 1680s Charles Davenant, the Commissioner of Excise, observed that Lechlade, at the head of the newly navigable Thames, was the port of embarkation for cider destined for London (Peter Clark, *The English Alehouse*).

Thanks to Cromwell's capture of Jamaica and defeat of the Dutch, London at the Restoration was beginning its transformation from a provincial backwater (by comparison with Paris, say, or Venice) into the mercantile, financial, and commercial capital of the West. These days we tend to home in on the poverty, the slums, the highwaymen, the footpads, the gin fever, and all the other afflictions the city undoubtedly suffered in the 18th century; but at the time it was regarded as a city of opportunity and wealth, and migrants – refugees, almost – flocked in from the countryside where the latest and final wave of enclosure was in brutal progress. Collectively, Londoners had a greater disposable income in the 18th century than any other comparable group of English men and women at any preceding period of history. And, as migrants do, the new Londoners brought many of the customs, habits and tastes of their native shires with them – customs, habits, and tastes that an increasingly sophisticated retail trade was eager to supply. Peter Clark makes an inventory of the provincial beers that were finding a ready market in the affluent taverns and alehouses of the capital in the late 17th and 18th centuries: beers from Dorchester, Burton, Lichfield, Derby, Yorkshire, Nottingham, Norfolk, and Devon were among 23 different types listed by contemporary writers in the 1720s. And to migrants from Herefordshire, Gloucestershire, and the West Country, the availability of cider must have come as a welcome taste of home.

In such a populous and concentrated market, the sales potential of regional specialities extended far beyond their original immigrant constituencies. Consumers exposed, many of them for the first time, to all sorts of novelties – tea, coffee, and chocolate from distant lands as well as liquors from different parts of Britain – became experimenters, accustomed to and insistent upon a much wider choice of goods than they could ever have known at home; and the urban retail trade was only too willing and able to satisfy them. The rate of throughput achievable in a metropolitan tavern or alehouse made it both possible and profitable to stock a range of products of unprecedented breadth; and as ranges broadened, the traditional lines of demarcation between different sorts of victuallers – tavern keepers, innkeepers, alehouse keepers – began to blur. In the early 18th century there were still specialist outlets such as dram shops that sold gin and little if anything else; but otherwise even the coffee-houses were becoming indistinguishable from taverns and alehouses. The blanket term "public house" is late Stuart in origin and was evidently in common use by Defoe's time, and reflects the fact that, within limits, pretty much all licensed outlets now stocked all licensable commodities (wine excepted – it was too expensive for most alehouse customers). As part of the city publican's standard repertoire, therefore, cider could be said to have arrived in the mainstream: not as the national drink, nor in quite the form that the *Pomona* ciderists and their contemporaries relished it; but it has been a permanent feature in British pubs ever since.

By the end of the century cider was to be found on sale not only in the capital's taverns but in inns almost everywhere. The travel diaries of John Byng, Viscount Torrington, in the 1780s and early '90s were illustrated with a selection of the itemised bills he paid in inns all over the north of England. These were printed by local stationers and there is, in all of them, a space for "cyder and perry". Byng himself never actually bought any, which leads one to wonder whether the quality of late 18th-century cider was everything that Evelyn or Worlidge might have hoped for. But whatever its quality, the liquor that Byng spurned was almost certainly bottled.

Large-scale bottling at this period was still at a primitive stage. Bottles were individually blown and filled, making the whole process a labour-intensive and therefore relatively expensive one, low wages notwithstanding. Indeed bottle production was not fully mechanised until 1903, and hand-filling was still commonplace for many decades after. But for the cider merchants bottling made widespread distribution possible, since few retailers outside the western counties can have had the consumer demand to make draught cider a viable proposition. (Some bottled cider was even exported by London and Bristol merchants to the expanding empire in India and the Caribbean). And as we have seen, the cidermakers of the 18th century were still, at heart, farmers who had not mutated into specialised industrial concerns as brewers had. Cider was just one of many products of their estates, and they were certainly not interested in distributing and marketing it. By the late 17th century these functions had already fallen into the hands of merchants or dealers who were more than just wholesalers but were closer to the *negoçiants* of the French wine trade. As well as transporting and marketing the cider, they often actually made it, buying raw juice from individual growers and blending and fermenting it to their own requirements and standards – standards that were often highly dubious.

Adulteration had long been an issue in the liquor industry: in *Pomona* Evelyn had excoriated London vintners for the "sophistications, transformations, transmutations, adulterations, bastardisings, brewing, tricking, and compassing" they practised in an effort to make a little good wine go a very long way. It was still an issue for Hugh Stafford nearly a century later, when he recorded some of the methods and ingredients used by dealers to extend the life of stale cider or disguise off-flavours in badly-made cider. These included boiling a mixture of honey, water, and sound cider until it was reduced by a third and then stirring a gallon into each hogshead of stale cider, presumably to encourage a mild refermentation; hanging bags of spices in hogsheads of oxidised cider; and using various compounds of burnt alum, orris root, mastic, ginger, lime, chalk, plaster, wheat bran and bean flour to treat various bacterial disorders such as acetification and "rope". Dealers coloured cider with coarse sugars, boiled molasses, parched wheat (which also produced a slight refermentation to make a flat cider "brisk"), and even the juice of rotten apples. They also distilled the "ciderkin" fermented from rehydrated pomace to add strength and body to thin or weak ciders. But, Stafford added primly, "such as are intended or are fit for a gentleman's use do not require these brewings and adulterations". And in fact, common cider was not only much adulterated, it was also used as an adulterant. Defoe, writing from Honiton in Devon, noted: "From this place they send 20,000 hogsheads every year to London, and which is still worse, that it is for the most part bought by the merchants to mix with their wines, which if true is not much to the reputation of the London vintners."

The abuses perpetrated by cider merchants, and the failings of the producers that lay at the root of the problem, were best summed up by Robert Hogg in the 1880s: "The farmers (of the 18th century) grew rich, their farms kept increasing in size, and the attention given to their orchards became less and less until at last they begun to be looked upon sometimes as a nuisance. This neglect, as years went on, became disastrous; failing trees had their places supplied by any worthless varieties at hand; little care was given to the management of the fruit or to the making of the liquor, beyond the two or three hogsheads required for the household use. Then, year by year, enormous quantities of cider and perry of a very indifferent quality were produced and, as the natural consequence of this deterioration, they could only be sold at prices less and less worthy of consideration.

"The quantity produced was far too great to be consumed locally, and hence arose the need of the cider merchants, 'cider-men', or 'buyers of sale liquors', as they were called at the end of the last century, who bought up everything by wholesale, and almost at their own prices. There can be no question but that, with some honourable exceptions, these middlemen have done more damage to the just reputation of cider and perry than all other causes put together. In ordinary seasons many thousands of hogsheads passed through their hands and were submitted to various processes calculated rather to destroy than to regulate proper fermentation. The liquor was fined, flavoured and fortified to suit, in their estimation, the public taste. It was then sent to London and Bristol, (in those days the two great centres of trade,) the best in bottles to (mis)represent pure wholesome cider in the home market, whilst the greater part of it found its way, it is said, to the Continent, to return again to this country, in the shape of cheap Hamburgh Ports and Sherries; or, more probably, it was manipulated at home for these purposes. Not a little of this nefarious traffic, it is to be feared, goes on at the present day."

Adulteration was one thing: it was common in all branches of food processing, and perhaps consumers took it for granted. Outright poisoning, though, was quite another.

Devonshire colic had first been recorded in 1707 in a dissertation on arthritis by an Exeter doctor named William Musgrave. "In Devonshire there is a colic arising from the rough and acid cider, drank there in too great a quantity," he wrote. "That the cider is the cause is manifest from hence: that this colic infests those who use themselves to that liquor, and in proportion as they make use of it." Phillips, although a Herefordshire rather than a Devonshire man, recorded its symptoms in *Cyder*, published the following year: "Oft... with pungent colic pangs he'll roar/and toss and turn, and curse th'unwholesome draught". Other than that it seems to have gone unremarked – perhaps because it was so common that it was taken for granted – until 1739, when another Devon doctor, John Huxham, described it in more detail. Symptoms included: "Excessive tormenting pain in the stomach and epigastric region... weak pulse and coldish sweats ... the tongue coated with a greenish or brown mucus and the breath most offensive. An enormous vomiting, for the most part green bile... so very acrid it was tinged with blood." In addition there were severe cramps, muscular and skeletal pains, vomiting, intractable constipation, and even paralysis; but although it was distressing and disabling, it was rarely fatal. In his description of the disease Huxham recalled an apparent epidemic of it in 1724, which had been a bumper year for cider apples. In addition, he noted that it occurred in autumn, when the first of the early cider was ready for drinking but was still rough and acid; he therefore attributed the illness to the overconsumption of acid cider.

And there it might have remained had not an eminent Devon-born physician, George Baker, taken it up again nearly 30 years later. Originally from Modbury, Baker was now resident in London where he was not only a Fellow of the Royal Society but was also physician to the Queen's Household and a close friend of society figures such as Oliver Goldsmith and Sir Joshua Reynolds. He was researching lead poisoning generally, especially as it affected miners in Derbyshire and the unfortunate customers of vintners who used lead as an adulterant, when he noticed its similarity to the disease afflicting his native county. In 1767 he read a paper to the College of Physicians, *An Essay Concerning the Cause of the Endemical Colic of Devonshire,* that comprehensively demolished excess acidity as the cause. Drawing on his knowledge of lead poisoning, statistics gathered from Devon hospitals, and analyses carried out by a newly-qualified and ambitious Scottish chemist, William Saunders, establishing the presence of lead in samples of Devon cider, Baker discovered that outbreaks were not confined to autumn but occurred year-round; and that well-to-do drinkers of fine cider were as badly affected as the common sort who made do with rough. So faulty had been Musgrave and Huxham's observations that they had even failed to spot that the symptoms – especially intractable constipation where one would have expected unstoppable diarrhoea – were not consistent with excess acid. They were, however, entirely consistent with the lead poisoning with which Baker was already familiar. He blamed the local habit of using lead – still widely mined on Dartmoor, despite the exhaustion of tin reserves that had once outstripped Cornwall's – as a convenient all-purpose sealant and liner. The gaps between the stones making up the mill troughs were filled with it; press-beds were lined with it; cisterns and pipes were made of it. As shot, it was even used to clean the insides of bottles. Colic, he added, was eight times as common in Devon, where lead was freely used, as in Herefordshire, where it wasn't.

Soon after it was read to the Royal Society, the paper was published in Devon where initial responses were favourable, even somewhat relieved that the cause of what was, after all, a very nasty affliction, had been tracked down. Then an anonymous pamphlet was published denying that lead was ever used in cidermaking in Devon. Immediately afterwards came a weightier pamphlet from Francis Geach, the surgeon at the Royal Hospital, Plymouth, denouncing Baker's paper and restating Huxham's original theory that acidity was the cause of the colic. Included in Geach's publication was an essay by Thomas Alcock, the former Vicar of Runcorn in Cheshire, who had retired to Plymouth and now dabbled in cidermaking. Alcock had been one of the pamphleteers involved in the campaign against Bute's cider tax and was just as quick to leap to the cidermakers' defence in face of this new threat. He repeated the claim that no lead was used in Devonian cidermills and presses, and asserted that the local custom of planting trees so close together so the fruit couldn't ripen properly was the cause of them offending acidity.

From his lofty social eminence, Baker could afford simply to ignore Geach and Alcock's attempt to refute his paper; but to Saunders, controversy could only mean publicity, which might advance his ambitions. In a pamphlet of his own he denounced Geach's paper as "a dull, uninstructive repetition of a vain, unsubstantial theory" and added that he had documentary proof of 30 lead-lined mills and presses in three parishes alone. Geach fired a return broadside in 1768, publishing work by a Bristol chemist, William Cookworthy, who claimed to have repeated Saunders's analyses and found no lead; and Alcock rejoined the fray in 1769 with a new, longer edition of his original pamphlet. By then, though, Saunders had moved on and the argument petered out. With hindsight it's curious that Geach and Alcock, who were perhaps oversensitive to any new threat to their county's livelihood following Bute's tax, should have chosen the tack they did: better, surely, to admit that the colic had an easily-remedied cause such as lead in the mills rather than a less tractable one such as badly planted orchards? Nevertheless, it seems that the use of lead as a sealant and liner was gradually and quietly abandoned: the agricultural writer and researcher William Marshall, in *The Rural Economy of the West of England* (1796), found no presses where lead was still in use, although he was told of one, and in the earlier *Rural Economy of Gloucestershire* (1785) had found a lead-clamped cider press at Newnham. Marshall, however, was a lead sceptic and blamed colic on the widespread distillation of cider lees on makeshift domestic stills frequently lined with tin.

The row is chiefly remembered now because of the scientific and methodological significance of Baker's original paper; how much long-term damage it did to the cider industry in Devon, if any, is debateable. But even without allegations of taint, there were enough geographic, demographic, and structural factors constraining the growth of common cider to ensure that, like fine bottled cider and cider brandy, it was never able to challenge the dominance of its chief competitor – in this case, beer.

By the end of the 17th century, the British brewing industry was just beginning to see the rise of the "common brewer" – that is, brewers producing beer for surrounding pubs; according to Dr Ian Hornsey (*A History of Beer & Brewing*, Royal Society of Chemistry 2003), there were at this time about 750 common brewers and 40,000 "brewing victuallers", or pubs that still brewed their own beer. National production was divided evenly between the two sectors, with London's common brewers producing around 1,500,000 barrels a year (a 36-gallon barrel being the industry's standard unit of account). Definitive figures are impossible to come by, but the national output of beer seems, by extrapolation, to have been around 9,000,000 barrels.

Production figures for cider are even harder to estimate, but by the end of the 17th century it was said that 10,000 hogsheads of cider – the equivalent of 30,000 brewer's barrels – were exported each year from Worcestershire alone, while Herefordshire produced 50,000 hogsheads or around 150,000 barrels. Defoe records 20,000 hogsheads or 60,000 barrels being exported from South-East Devon in 1725. Guessing the total output of Devon, Somerset and Gloucestershire as equal to that of Herefordshire and that of the lesser counties – Dorset, Cornwall, Monmouthshire, Shropshire, Norfolk, and Suffolk – to be equal to that of Worcestershire, we arrive at a total of 660,000 barrels. These figures are, of course, extremely rough; but it's not unreasonable to assume that at the beginning of the 18th century Britain's brewers were outproducing cidermakers by a factor of 10:1. The gulf was only to widen as the century wore on.

While the brewing industry was rapidly concentrating, specialising, and becoming more ruthlessly capitalistic, cidermaking by and large remained fragmented and unfocussed. Farmers and landed gentry continued to make cider for their own tables and workforces and for local publicans, selling surpluses on to merchants for wider distribution. Profitable it may have been, but it was an aside to their core activities; and whenever grain prices rose the temptation to grub up orchards in favour of arable was almost irresistible. Re-establishing the lost orchards if grain prices fell, though, was a much harder step: the costs were high and new plantings would not bear for 10 years or more. Throughout the century, common brewers progressively replaced brewing victuallers and started to build up tied estates, often by allowing retail customers generous credit and then, when they fell into debt, seizing their pubs in settlement. Many familiar brewing names, Whitbread and Courage among them, were already firmly established as major industrial concerns by the end of the 18th century; by contrast, there wasn't a single dedicated cidermaking business until the late 19th.

That cidermaking remained much closer than brewing to its agricultural roots also made it more sensitive to changes in the price of its raw materials. For the big brewers of the North and East of England, arising in the new industrial cities and alongside the growing network of canals and navigable rivers, raw materials became a progressively lower proportion of overall costs; fluctuations in hop and barley prices therefore became a less and less significant factor in determining wholesale prices. This stabilising element was not built into the structure of the cidermaking industry. Roger French, expanding a point made anecdotally by Marshall in *The Rural Economy of Western England*, demonstrates that while the overall price of cider remained flat, even stagnant, throughout the 18th century (while all other costs including rents were steadily rising) they could and did fluctuate wildly from year to year according to the quality and quantity of the crop. The degree of price fluctuation possible in a single decade was demonstrated by the agricultural historian William Curtler drawing on records from Aspall Hall in Suffolk: in 1742 apples fetched 10d a bushel; in 1745 a shilling; but in 1746 only 4d. This unpredictability was a further disincentive to specialisation and added to the temptation to grub up. It also slowed the pace of replanting so that orchards tended to become less and less productive, driving the smaller producers out of the market: if, as it was observed at the beginning of the century, a couple of productive trees could pay a cottager's rent, they certainly couldn't by the end of it.

Geographically and demographically, too, brewers had the advantage, enjoying more and more concentrated and rapidly increasing customer bases served by extensive and developing transport links. An industry that was both expanding and concentrating at the same time could afford to invest in new technologies such as steam power, temperature control, and cheap glassware that cut their costs, increased their production capacity, and allowed them to innovate. Porter, the first beer in the world to be produced on a genuinely industrial scale, became popular from the 1720s on, and from the early 19th century was generally succeeded by brighter, paler beers made from barley cheaply and reliably malted over coke and served in cheap and attractive glassware. Cidermakers, with their rural bases, inflexible production, poor communications, and low populations, could afford neither to mechanise nor to innovate; even in the expanding western cities cider was gradually eclipsed by beer, and substantial brewers such as George's of Bristol were able to carve out solid market positions.

Cider's handicap when it came to competing with beer was partly cultural, too: it remained a "foreign" drink not only in the North and East, where the working classes continued to favour beer and gin while the gentry stuck with wine and brandy, but also in western cities where population growth was in large part fuelled by immigration from beer-drinking regions such as Ireland, further reinforcing the position of brewers such as George's.

By the end of the 18th century, then, cidermaking had failed to evolve as an industry in the way that brewing had, and remained a branch of a fragmented and low-intensity mixed agricultural economy. But if the dreams of the *Pomona* ciderists remained unfulfilled, the cidermakers of a century later could be relatively satisfied with a product that had gained national acceptance and distribution and from which they were able to derive reasonable profits in good years.

Unfortunately, though, cidermaking's failure to evolve presented a particular problem that was only just becoming clear. Cider apple varieties are clones, and have to be propagated by grafting or budding because they won't grow true from seed. What this means is that they can't develop resistance to a host of pests ranging from mildews to mites. Eventually, then, varieties become disease-prone and start to fail; and if, thanks to a lack of investment, they are not being replaced with newly-developed varieties, they will simply die out. This appears to have happened to Lord Scudamore's redoubtable Redstreak towards the end of the 18th century. In *The Management of Orchards and Fruit Liquor in Herefordshire* (published as part of *The Rural Economy of Gloucestershire* in 1785), Marshall reported: "Artificial propagation cannot preserve the varieties in perpetuity. All the old types that raised the fame of the liquors of this country, are so far in decline as to be deemed irrecoverable. The redstreak is given up ... the stocks canker and are unproductive."

Unlike his great contemporary and rival Arthur Young, Marshall made a point of settling and farming in the regions he was researching, often for some years; so his severely critical verdict on the cider-growing regions where he spent much of the 1780s and '90s was informed by a great depth of personal experience. Here he found an industry, if indeed it could be called an industry, that had fallen far short of the ambitions of the 17th-century ciderists and was in many important respects moribund. In the earlier of his two treatises, he criticised the cidermakers for technical failings in every stage of their enterprises from orcharding to fermentation. For the "cidermen" or dealers, on the other hand, Marshall actually (and almost alone) had a measure of praise. They were mostly local, from Bristol, Gloucester, Hereford, Worcester, Upton, and Ledbury, but "of late years the London dealers have found their way into it and in a plentiful year buy up great quantities." The growers insisted on pressing their crop themselves to reduce the expense of transport, but lagged so far behind as not even to have discovered the use of the thermometer. The cidermen, on the other hand, were "far advanced in the ordering of the liquor" and often supervised the pressing of the apples, buying the juice straight from the press and fermenting it according to their own practices and precepts.

For the growers, though, his scorn knew no bounds. As he observed: "The management of orchards and their produce, though it enters into the practice of almost every occupier of land, is far from being properly understood. The primary object of farmers, in general, has been that of supplying their own immoderate consumption. The market for sale liquor has hitherto been confined. In a plentiful year it has barely paid for the slavery of making it."

Of the condition of many of the orchards of Herefordshire and Gloucestershire he was equally scathing. "Lower boughs are seen dangling, as bell ropes, perhaps to the ground, while the upper part of their heads are loaded with wood as impervious to the sun and air as the heads of pollard oaks or neglected gooseberry bushes; with, perhaps, an additional burden of mistletoe and moss to bear," he wrote. "Indolence and false economy are, no doubt, the principles on which this slovenly conduct is pursued. The improvident occupiers of those neglected orchards, unmindful of the damage they annually sustain by the encumbrance of the trees, refuse to bestow a little leisure time, or lay out a few shillings, to render them productive.

"What avails the number of trees, if they are not productive? It is healthy bearing trees that fill the drink house and send a surplus to market. Their encumbrance on the soil is nearly the same whether they are barren or fruitful; and it may be a moot point, whether even many of those which are productive much more than pay for their encumbrance: how ridiculous, then, to spare any reasonable expense in preferring them in a state of health and productiveness or to suffer those to encumber the soil which are past recovery?"

The results of underinvestment extended to the antiquated design and poor standard of manufacture of the mills and presses and to the fermentation of the must and the quality of the finished product. "Farmers, in general, considering fruit liquor as the beverage of their servants and workpeople, have no stimulus toward excellency in the art," wrote Marshall. "If it has body enough to keep, no matter for the richness and flavour. The rougher it is, the further it will go.

"The cider which is drank in this and all the cider countries with so much avidity and in such quantity is a very different liquor to that which is drank in the rest of the kingdom. A palate accustomed to sweet cider would judge the rough cider of the farmhouses to be a mixture of vinegar and water, with a little dissolved alum to give it a roughness. Men in general, however, whose palates are used to rough cider, consider the sweet sort as an effeminate beverage."

Worse still, in the eyes of one who was such a rigorous investigator of all he saw, was the unquestioning pursuit of traditional practices and the adherence of each cidermaker to his own preferred methods. "Although farmers in general, more particularly the lower class, are very deficient in the management of their liquors, there are men, especially among the more substantial yeomanry and the principal farmers who ferment their own liquors for sale, that are far advanced on the line of right management", said Marshall. "Unfortunately, however, these men, priding themselves on the superiority of their liquor (more perhaps than on any other produce of their estates) become jealous of their art and are not sufficiently communicative with each other. Hence the difference in their several practices, and hence the present imperfection of the art."

So much for the collaborative approach of the *Pomona* ciderists, so eager to share their knowledge with each other and the world. And so much, too, for the ceaseless pursuit by Scudamore's generation for new and better varieties. "There has, no doubt, been a period when the improvement of the apple and the pear was attended to in this country," Marshall mourned. "And should not the same spirit of improvement revive, it is probable that the country will, in a course of years, be left destitute of valuable kinds of the two species of fruit which, though they may in some degree be deemed objects of luxury, long custom seems to have ranked amongst the necessities of life."

The 1790s found Marshall in west Devon, where he was kinder about orcharding practices, especially the selection of sheltered slopes unsuitable for other purposes but protected from frost and gale. The trees here he found much shorter than elsewhere – not much bigger than a modern bush variety – whether through training or the use of dwarf stock he never found out; and as a consequence could be much more densely planted and more easily harvested. He heartily approved the practice of mulching the trees with cut bramble and furze and weeds from the arable fields and declared that the climate produced potentially better cider than either Herefordshire or Gloucestershire.

Of the west Devonian cidermaking techniques he was less laudatory. Most of the district's farms, he found, were too small to have proper mills and here the *auge et pil* method of crushing was still widely practiced. It was called "pounding", and the sheds in which it was carried on were therefore known as pound houses. Some farmers used what he referred to as a hand-mill, presumably a form of scratter-mill like Woridge's *Ingenio*, "but it did not fall in my way to examine it". The larger farms used variants of the lever press, including a hybrid which used a screw to raise and lower the lever, on which they could press astonishing quantities – as many as six hogsheads at a time – achieving very efficient extraction; but the process was slow, taking up to two days to press a single giant cheese of five feet square by five feet deep (in which straw was used, rather than hair cloths), and the equipment was vast, expensive, and unwieldy. Racking during fermentation was so haphazardly carried out that "it must be a matter of mere chance if a cask of palatable liquor be produced".

Most of the better west Devon cider was sold to local pubs, with very little going to dealers; the farmers themselves made do with cider made from windfalls and from the shavings taken from the sides of the cheeses during pressing, or with the "beverage" yielded by rehydrating and pressing the spent pomace. For the smaller farmers of the region, he said: "There can be no dispute about the superior profitableness of the orchard fruits to any other species of produce, and most especially to a small farmer who attends personally to the whole business and whose wife and children are his assistants." But for the larger, more commercial farms, he believed cidermaking to be more of a distraction than a moneymaking concern. "The business of making it interferes with the more important concerns of husbandry: even the business of harvest, and still more the cleaning of turneps, are too frequently neglected to give place to fruit picking; and the breaking and pressing are, afterwards, not less inimical to the saving of potatoes and the sowing of wheat." Finally, he was critical not only of the growers and makers of cider, but also of its consumers: "The drunkenness, dissoluteness of manners, and the dishonesty of the lower classes," he declared, "might well be referred, in whole or in part, to the baleful effects of cider."

It is well worth contrasting Marshall's work with that of the Board of Agriculture, set up in 1793 as the 18th-century equivalent of a quango under the presidency of the volatile Sir John Sinclair, with the agricultural writer Arthur Young as secretary. The board's most important work was to commission a number of reporters to compile a series of county surveys, the *General Views*. Young and Sinclair were soon at odds, with Young regarding many of Sinclair's appointments as incompetent; and when we compare their work with Marshall's we can only agree. Nathaniel Kent, for instance, commissioned to survey Norfolk in 1796, famously dismissed its entire top fruit industry in a single line: "Orchards very few, and much neglected, consequently no cider". And yet we know from other sources that the Gaymer family had already been making cider at Banham for two decades, and surely cannot have been alone; evidently, though, they escaped Kent's notice.

Arthur Young's own son was scarcely more cursory in his contribution to the series, *A General View of the Agriculture of the County of Sussex*, first published in 1801. He devoted not much more than a page to the subject of cider, noting that orchards were plentiful in the west of the county, around Petworth; that Lord Egremont made the finest in the county at Lodsworth and in surrounding parishes, having imported a new press from Herefordshire for the purpose; but that "it is only in a slip of land under the South Down Hills that cider culture is in any request"; and that apart from some local sales most of the cider made was consumed by farmers, their families, and their labourers.

Even some of cider's heartlands received no greater attention. In one of the first of the *General Views*, Somerset (1794), John Billingsley made just three mentions of cider (a quietness echoed, perhaps surprisingly, by Marshall a few years later, who in his report on the western counties had little to say about Somerset – not because there were not plenty of orchards, but because he did not linger there and preferred not to make judgements on less than first-hand information). In the west of the county Billingsley found the trees too closely planted and therefore not cropping as well as they might, and at Hutton he encountered a Mr Good who milled his apples twice before pressing, thus improving the extraction but at the expense (so Billingsley queried) of quality. In the Vale of Taunton he did encounter gentlemen farmers still making fine ciders in the old style: pruning the heads of the trees; allowing the apples to ripen fully; tumping them for up to five weeks; and preventing "excessive fermentation" by "early and frequent" rackings. These practices, he noted, made for "a rich and delicious flavour", increasing the value of the cider to £4 or even £5 a hogshead. On the other hand, he noted: "Cyder requires much greater nicety of management than malt liquor" – perhaps one of the reasons why fine cider was dying out. (Not completely, mind: in the 1820s the Rev Thomas Cornish planted orchards at Heathfield near Taunton and in the 1840s was supplying fine cider to aristocratic households including those of the Duke of Bedford, the Bishop of Bath & Wells, and even Queen Victoria herself).

To be fair, Thomas Rudge (Gloucestershire, 1807) and John Duncumb (Herefordshire, 1813) had far more to say on the subject of cider than had their colleagues, although without adding much to the catalogue of ills that Marshall had already compiled. But the low priority they accorded to orcharding and cidermaking in the agricultural hierarchy perhaps backs Marshall's principal finding: that the cider industry was, if not exactly moribund, certainly ossified, and lagging far behind the brewers of Eastern England in every respect. But Marshall was prescient enough to recognise its potential if only it could catch up in certain important respects, especially transport: "The late extension of canals, and other inland navigations, and most especially one which is now extending between the Severn and the Thames, together with the present facility of land carriage, have already extended, and will in all probability still farther extend, the market for fruit liquor," he wrote, "and there may be, henceforward, some encouragement for the manufacturing of sale liquor, the right management of which is a mystery few men are versed in." The challenge facing the more forward-looking growers, then, was to recognise and exploit the developments that had already transformed the whole nature of drinks manufacturing in the East.

7: New Foundations

For both William Marshall and the Board of Agriculture surveyors, the Napoleonic War was the elephant in the room. The agricultural economy had been dynamic enough even before 1793; the two decades of more or less uninterrupted and effectively global warfare that followed twisted and shaped it in entirely new ways – ways, perhaps, that the writers didn't understand well enough to factor into their reports. Therefore they glossed tactfully over the whole subject of war, mentioning it even less frequently than Jane Austen did in her novels.

Predating the problems created by the war was the progress of enclosure, now in its final phase and accompanied by a renewed wave of engrossment. As in the 15th and 16th centuries, many small strip farmers now found themselves possessed of discreet holdings, often on land that used to be common grazing and had never known the plough. And as in the earlier phase, most of the new small proprietors found they couldn't hold on to their land. Very few had the capital to drain, improve, fence and equip their farms, let alone build new farmhouses and yards: Board of Agriculture surveyors concurred that a farm of less than 400 acres would be too inefficient to survive, and an entire class of rural poor, landless, dependent on miserly wages, and without access to grazing or fuel, was created as village after village was enclosed.

Two additional elements that made holding on to a small farm even more difficult were both the direct results of the French wars. To pay and equip the hugely-enlarged army and navy, the Government taxed everything it could from income to clocks and windows, creating an overhead that small farms simply couldn't pay. Meanwhile rising demand from a growing urban population, coupled with chronic interruptions to the importation of grain from northern Europe, drove up the price of wheat, and hence the value of land. Larger landowners were therefore able to make the new generation of small proprietors offers they literally couldn't refuse: thousands made the obvious choice and sold up. "Of late, the practice of consolidating several estates in one has much reduced the number of small farms," wrote Duncumb in 1813. "Twenty years ago Holmer comprised of at least 10 farms; the number has reduced at this time to five." The arrival in the countryside of city-based land speculators during the 1820s merely added to the pressure on smaller farmers to sell up. The bigger, more efficient farms that were thus being created could afford to invest in the new methods of improvement, both in arable and stockrearing, that were continually being introduced, progressively increasing yields while driving down costs. Duncumb observed: "The demands of Government and the great manufacturing districts can best be supplied by great farmers."

While the war lasted, the big farmers profited from the inflated prices they could get for their grain. In the cider counties we have no evidence of orchards actually being grubbed up to create new arable; but what Marshall and the Board of Agriculture's *General Views* do tell us is that investment even in maintaining existing orchards simply dried up. As for investment in new orchards, the cost of anything up to £50 an acre for a crop that wouldn't show a return for a decade or more was already prohibitive: still more so when even marginal land was worth tilling. "It is a subject of controversy," wrote Rudge, "whether orchard planting be, on average of years, advantageous either to landlord or to tenant." His calculation of the cost of planting a 20-acre orchard, including interest on capital, was £320, which would show a profit to the tenant of at most £10 a year – and that after a wait of 20 years! All that could make new orchards worthwhile, it seemed, was that as Duncumb stressed, they could also be used as pasture.

It might have been hoped that the disappearance of French wines from the English market would open an opportunity, as in previous wars, for English fine cider. We have heard from the Board of Agriculture surveys that fine cider was still being made in West Sussex and the Vale of Taunton; Duncumb makes it clear that fine cider was also still being made for private consumption in Herefordshire. The premium it could command – 5-15 guineas a hogshead for Old Styre cider or Old Squash perry compared to 1-2 guineas for common cider (Sir John Sinclair, *The Code of Agriculture*, 1817)

– looks superficially like the foundation of a solid commercial proposition. But it never happened. Spain and Portugal supplied much of the deficiency caused by the end of (legal) trade with France; smugglers supplied much of the rest. Pitt, Fox, and the rest of their hard-drinking generation may have been deprived of their claret, but they still had access to all the port they could stomach. And anyway, given the time it took for new orchards to bear, the cidermakers were in no position to increase production in the short or even medium term. The disappearance through degradation of the noble old varieties such as Redstreak further weakened their position, and the labour costs involved in the hand-picking and frequent racking necessary to produce fine cider made the price premium more apparent than real.

Once the last salvo of musketry had been fired into the defiant bodies of the Old Guard at Waterloo and Napoleon had been safely immured in his Atlantic prison, the situation changed dramatically. With the English market once again open to foreign imports, wheat prices plunged. The Government responded almost immediately with a series of protectionist measures, the various Corn Laws, which until their repeal in 1846 guaranteed minimum prices and prevented British arable farmers from being undercut by cheap foreign imports. But grain prices never again reached their wartime levels; many farmers switched from arable to stockrearing; and all were closely concerned with maximising revenues from all the different aspects of their businesses. For cidermakers it was no great task to lop and prune existing trees and so revive their semi-derelict orchards; replacing and replanting, though, were not so easy. Decades of inattention to their orchards had been matched by inattention to their fruits: the grand old cider apples – Styre, Redstreak, and the rest – cloned for generation after generation (which is effectively what grafting is) had lost their resistance to canker and blight, and growers were actively seeking new varieties to succeed them. "Their renovation, or the introduction of others equally good, cannot be too strongly urged, and the public spirit of the present age has not been indifferent on the occasion," wrote Duncumb – perhaps a little optimistically, given the verdict of latter writers. "More endeavours have been perhaps directed towards this object in the last 20 years than during the century preceding."

With this observation, however exaggerated, Duncumb was acknowledging the enormous contribution made by Thomas Andrew Knight, whom we have already encountered measuring the specific gravities of the juices of different apple varieties. Born in 1759 of a landowning family of Downton Castle in the extreme north of Herefordshire, Knight was a gentleman scientist in the mould of the Royal Society's founding fathers and used the 10,000 acres at his disposal as a great breeding station or horticultural laboratory. Through exhaustive trial and error attended by minute observation he developed many new strains of cabbages, strawberries and peas as well as apples and pears. His assiduous work was recognised in his lifetime: a close friend of Sir Joseph Banks (the botanist who had accompanied Captain Cook on his expeditions), he was from 1811 until his death in 1838 founder president of the London (later the Royal) Horticultural Society.

Knight's principal work (although he is probably better-known to modern cider enthusiasts for the *Pomona Herefordiensis*) was the deceptively slim *Treatise on the Culture of the Apple and Pear and on the Manufacture of Cider and Perry*, first published in 1797 and running to five editions in 10 years. For much of its 182 pages it didn't do much more than repeat, albeit insistently, the familiar maxims of best practice in orchard husbandry and cidermaking. Where it was revolutionary was in its recognition that the old varieties were truly dead, and not to be rescued by any amount of haphazard experiments in grafting, planting, siting or "topical application". And more, the *Treatise* grasped that the cause of death was genetic – or hereditary, as Knight put it. He could not know the real cause, any more than 18th-century brewers and winemakers could know the true nature of fermentation. But like them, he scrutinised what he observed and came to an effective practical understanding of the problem, which was that these 200-year-old clones had simply been out-evolved by their pests.

If anything shows that Knight understood what was happening, his solution does. Every grower knew that apples grown from seed did not breed true; hence the tendency to graft and graft and graft from favoured trees. Knight, therefore, realising that these favoured varieties were exhausted, raised from seed on a huge scale, waiting patiently while his seedlings – 20,000 of them over nearly 20 years, according to his reckoning – came to maturity and then cross-pollinating them almost at random, selecting for further propagation only those adults that seemed hardiest and most productive. He experimented equally exhaustively on the stock on which the new varieties were to be grafted, recommending the Siberian crab as the strongest and most vigorous; and he discovered, again through experiment, that the soil in which the trees were planted was not nearly as important as the varieties themselves and the way they were managed. Consequently he believed that cider orchards could be planted with equal success in any part of the country – an observation supported by Arthur Young, who recorded cider varieties flourishing perfectly happily at Aspall Hall in Suffolk and, indeed, outproducing many West Country orchards.

As a gentleman scientist of substantial means, Knight had both the time and the money to experiment. Those who farmed for a living had neither – or at any rate, not enough to indulge in the long processes of trial and error involved in the artificial selection of satisfactory new varieties. Of course, new strains either grown from seed or discovered as wildings, just as Scudamore's Redstreak seems to have been, continued to come to light. Perhaps the best-known of these today are the Brown Snout, propagated by a Mr Dent from a wilding found on his farm at Yarkhill near Hereford in 1850, and the Yarlington Mill, found growing out of a wall beside the waterwheel at Yarlington Mill in Somerset a few years earlier. But making a commercial reality of Knight's recommendations called for specialised nurseries with the investment and expertise required to supply the growers with the varieties they needed via a continuous and systematic process of artificial selection: to all intents and purposes, a separate industry. But any thoughts in this direction were stymied – perversely, you might think – by an upturn in arable and livestock prices in the 1850s, '60s, and '70s. In the mixed agricultural economy of the western counties farmers had an incentive to shift their concentration from one area of production to another as prices dictated. Long-term strategic investment in artificial selection, modern orcharding techniques, and mechanised production were too expensive when times were lean, and must have seemed unnecessary and even foolhardy when wheat or cheese or beef prices were high. As Robert Hogg, whom we shall meet later on, summed it up in the 1880s: "The profits of agriculture from the growth of cereals and the production of cattle threw the orchards into a state of neglect from which they have yet to recover." So here, as in so many other areas of food technology and industrialisation, the more intensive and specialised east led the west by a long head.

The market gardeners and fruit growers of the counties immediately surrounding London had long done good business supplying the street markets and dining tables of the capital. From the 1840s on the spreading rail network opened the same opportunity to more distant rivals, and well-established nurseries such as Rivers of Sawbridgeworth, Hertfordshire, started in 1725, found themselves facing competition from newcomers such as Lindley's of Norwich, Laxton's of Stamford, founded in 1850 and removed to Bedford to be even closer to London in 1885, and Chivers of Histon, Cambridgeshire, best-known today for its jam but in the mid-19th century a possessor of extensive apple orchards. Another name from the era still familiar to modern ears and with a similar development curve to Chivers would be Wilkin's of Tiptree Heath, Essex, today a maker of jam but then a big grower of apples and pears. Falling grain prices were a further incentive for the planting of new orchards, especially on heavier soils that were expensive to plough: the fenlands around Wisbech began to regain their medieval status and reputation as a district of orchards, and the countryside to the south-east of Cambridge also became an important centre for top-fruit growing.

The specialised nurseries were actively involved in developing new culinary varieties based on a number of criteria, especially annual cropping, heavy yields, resistance to disease, and acceptability in the market place. They also tended to be late-cropping to reduce the risk of being "nipped in the bud" by April frosts. And it wasn't just the big commercial nurseries that were developing new apples: big farmers and landed estates were actively cross-breeding, too. The head gardener at Burghley House near Stamford, Richard Gilbert, was responsible for several crosses including one he modestly named after himself; and the Cox's Orange Pippin, today accounting for more than half of the UK's entire acreage of culinary apples, was the result of a cross between a Ribston Pippin and an unknown cultivar tried out in 1825 by a retired brewer, Richard Cox of Colnbrook in Buckinghamshire.

Farming in the mid-19th century followed a pattern that has become familiar again today, but on a much bigger scale. We are well-used to entrepreneurial farmers, often motivated as much by ethical concerns as by economic ones, starting to take control of the processing of their own produce. This is particularly true of stockbreeders who add value by slaughtering, butchering, and even retailing their own meat rather than accepting the slender margins allowed by supermarket chains. In the 19th century it was arable farmers rather than stockrearers who started to mill their own grain, often to malt it, and in some cases take the next step and start brewing with it too. Oxfordshire's Hook Norton Brewery came into being in precisely this way, as did Ridley's of Chelmsford. The Paine family of St Neots, Cambridgeshire, were farmers, millers, maltsters, and brewers from the 1860s to the 1980s; brewing historians could doubtless name dozens more. The country's first truly industrial cidermaker followed a similar route.

Belying Nathaniel Kent's curt dismissal of cidermaking in Norfolk, the Gaymer family appears to have been making cider at Banham in the 1780s (*Notes Towards a History of Norfolk Cider*, Owen Thompson, 1997, from which much of the following account is drawn). Gaymer's own literature makes an unsupported claim of an additional century's antiquity, but Robert Gaymer (1738-1821) appears to have settled at Banham as a farmer and cidermaker in 1784. His son Robert, known as Long John because of his height, married the daughter of an agricultural improver and cider merchant named Joseph Chapman, and was advertising his cider for sale in the local press in 1800. John's son William is listed in the 1846 Post Office Directory as licensee of the Crown at Banham, farmer, and cider manufacturer. In the 1856 and 1864 editions of White's Directory he is listed as cider manufacturer, farmer, and victualler, the changing order of words perhaps reflecting the shifting balance of his various enterprises. At this time, Gaymer was only one among many cider manufacturers and merchants listed in Banham and the surrounding villages; it was his son, William jnr (1842-1936), a much more progressive businessman, who took the decisive step when, in 1870, he bought a hydraulic press.

It was a defining moment: the moment when cidermaking stopped being a by-product of farming or estate management and became an industry in its own right. Of course William jnr's hydraulic press was not the first: he saw it at an agricultural show, so there must have been plenty in use. But he did more than merely venture into mechanisation: he turned Gaymer's into a specialised company with national ambitions, advertising extensively and even, after William snr's death in 1884, hiring a publicist named Henry Stopes to write a booklet, *Cider: the history, method of manufacture and properties of this national beverage* (1888), which was in reality, according to Owen Thompson, "not much more than a thinly-disguised promotion of Gaymer's product." A marketing ploy the book may have been; however it does demonstrate how rapidly mechanisation was being introduced at Gaymer's. Not only is the press hydraulic, but Stopes reveals that the traditional mill has been replaced by granite rollers, although sadly we are not told how they were powered.

In 1896 William jnr completed the transition from agriculturalist to industrialist by quitting the family farm and moving to a factory with its own railway siding in nearby Attleborough. The rail link was essential for distributing Gaymer's products, but it soon proved useful in another way: in 1903 the local apple crop failed, but Gaymer's was able to bring in supplies from Devon by rail to make up the deficiency. The separation between grower and manufacturer was – potentially if not yet actually – complete.

In this respect at least, the eastern counties were over a decade ahead of the more traditional cider country. From as early as 1856 Gaymer's had a competitor in Banham in the form of Rout's, which went through several changes of ownership before closing in 1957; but Percy Bulmer made not a drop of cider until 1887, and Henry Weston was only trading in his horse-driven mill and screw press for a roller mill, chain press, and steam engine at about the same time. Devon and Somerset had to wait still longer before their first modern cider companies – national in ambition, controlling their own supply chain and distribution, and deploying recognisable branding and marketing techniques – were to appear, although it seems that in Devon Gray's of Exeter, Henley's of Newton Abbott, and Hunt's of Paignton had already evolved from cider merchants into specialised manufacturers much earlier in the century (possibly as early as 1804 in the case of Hunt's). These, however, were companies of mainly local significance and certainly didn't have the ambitions or the reach of Gaymer's.

However, the western counties were not backward in all respects. If entrepreneurs and businessmen were slower to emerge than in the east, the west remained the centre of enquiry and research.

The Woolhope Naturalists' Field Club had been founded in 1851 to enquire into every aspect of Herefordshire's natural history. Based in Hereford City Library – still its headquarters today – its wide-ranging fields of study embraced geology, archaeology, and a range of other subjects including cider. A founder member was Charles Bulmer, the cidermaking vicar of Credenhill and father of Percy Bulmer. The founding chairman was a Hereford GP, Dr Henry Graves Bull. Club members scoured the county for different varieties of cider and perry fruit, holding annual exhibitions at which growers were invited to examine the comparative merits of different apples and pears, inspired by a manifesto that vowed "to restore Herefordshire to its true fruit-growing supremacy; to call the attention of the growers to the best varieties of fruit for the table and the press; to improve the methods followed in the manufacture of cider and perry, and the quality of these products; and thus to improve in every way the marketable value of its orchard products." In 1876 Bulmer invited the vice-chairman of the Royal Horticultural Society and chairman of its fruit committee, Dr Robert Hogg, to attend the Club's annual exhibition; and Hogg brought with him not only his compendious academic knowledge and his reputation as the author of *The Fruit Manual*, which went into five editions between 1860 and 1884, but also a close awareness of developments across the Channel in Normandy which might perhaps have been lacking in Hereford.

In 1864 the pomological committee of the *Société Centrale d'Horticulture de la Seine-Inférieure* had persuaded the French Government to finance a *Congrès pour l'Etude des Fruits à Cidre*. With phylloxera ravaging the country's vines, the Government was entirely receptive to the potential of – to quote Beale – "relieving the want of wine by a succedaneum of cider", although in the end it was disease-resistant American rootstock that provided the solution. Nonetheless, the money was forthcoming; and after nine years of research and deliberations the *Congrès* produced a scientific and economic report entitled simply *"Le Cidre"*, of which Hogg said: "It is thoroughly practical and has rendered very great service to the orchards of Normandy". It also prefigured an increase in the production of cider in France from 210,000,000 gallons in 1867 to 517,000,000 gallons in 1883 (Patrick Wilkinson: *Bulmers: A Century of Cidermaking*, David & Charles 1987), far exceeding the output of Great Britain. At the same time the *Société* itself was amassing at its headquarters in Rouen a collection of 400 drawings and wax models of native cider fruit varieties, accompanied by a catalogue describing each in minute detail and putting them into four classes according to their cidermaking quality. At Hereford in 1876, Hogg suggested that the Woolhope Club might try a similar venture.

Work stated on the *Herefordshire Pomona* that very year. Bull himself edited the work, whose chief glory is its 432 watercolour illustrations by his daughter Edith and a trained local artist, Alice Ellis. The *Pomona* was published in seven instalments between 1878 and 1884; so expensive was it to produce that only 600 copies were ever printed, Hogg remarking rather acidly: "It offers no pretensions to the complete and highly scientific character of *Le Cidre*, since the resources of the national government have not been available here for the long and expensive investigations required." Hogg and Bull quickly started work on a follow-up intended for much wider dissemination, *The Apple and Pear as Vintage Fruit,* published in 1886. Bull died, aged 67, soon after the book was started, and Hogg continued on his own,

Hogg's Norman connections continued to influence the work of the Woolhope Club and led directly to the importation of French varieties including the Médaille d'Or and the Michelin that became very widely planted, the latter being particularly important even today. "It was during a visit to Rouen on behalf of the Woolhope Club on the occasion of the Great Exhibition of Apples and Pears held there in 1884 under the auspices of *Société...* that the excellence of the orchards was remarked," he wrote in his introduction to *The Apple and Pear as Vintage Fruit.* "The care and attention evidently bestowed upon them, and the number of young trees planted, were the subject of special notice. It was felt that such results were largely due to the work of the *Société.* That similar results might be produced in the orchards of Herefordshire, this work was undertaken."

By contrast, he said: "The condition of the (English) orchards generally, at the present time, is most unsatisfactory, and close attention will be required for many years to restore their value. A century of neglect has caused the loss of many of the best varieties of fruit, for the number of vacancies from the prevalence of cold wet weather, the ravages of insects, the violence of storms, or the effect of age, that are constantly occurring in the orchards is very great. These vacancies must be filled up, by the conditions of the occupier's lease, and the young trees for this purpose seem to have been procured haphazard, that is, at the least possible expense and trouble, and thus a large number of chance seedlings, unproved and worthless varieties, have found their way into the orchards. They are without names, and for the most part do not deserve a name.

"The first step towards the improvement of the orchards will be to subject them to a gradual and thorough revision. Stock should be taken of every individual Apple and Pear tree on the farm, and its character and condition carefully considered. Such trees as are mere cumberers of the ground should be cleared off at once, root and branch; and such varieties as are proved to be unmistakeably inferior should have their places supplied by those which are known to be good."

In fact, Hogg's own figures show him as a little pessimistic in this regard. He reprints statistics from the Parliamentary Agricultural Returns showing that orchard acreage in the main cider-producing counties had actually increased in the six years 1877-1883 from 101,000 to 134,000. And there was considerable incentive for landowners to replant. After a run of good harvests in the 1850s and '60s, poor crops in the 1870s and the resumption of imports from the *postbellum* United States put arable farmers under great pressure: grain prices collapsed dramatically in 1884; there was drought in 1893; and during the years 1878-1907 there was widespread conversion of arable, especially on heavy clays, back to grassland. But the livestock industry was under pressure, too, thanks to the widespread use of refrigerated transport which saw big increases in meat imports and commensurate falls in the price of native-reared livestock. Although the various crises hit the eastern counties hardest, there must have been plenty of West Country farmers glad of the extra income they could get by planting up their grazing with cider apples.

It is clear, however, that the cidermakers Hogg described were still mixed farmers rather than the more specialised fruit growers of Norfolk: indeed, for many of them cidermaking was such a marginal activity that they did not even possess their own equipment and instead relied on travelling mills and presses such as that described by Thomas Hardy in *The Woodlanders* (1887), whose hero, Giles Winterborne, is a nurseryman who depends on various sidelines for his living including the operation of just such a press.

"In the yard (of the inn at Sherston Abbas), there progressed a scene natural to the locality at this time of the year. An apple-mill and press had been erected on the spot, to which some men were bringing fruit from divers points in mawn-baskets, while others were grinding them, and others wringing down the pomace, whose sweet juice gushed forth into tubs and pails.

"Down in the heart of the apple country nearly every farmer kept up a cidermaking apparatus and wring-house for his own use, building up the pomace in great straw 'cheeses', as they were called; but here, on the margin of Pomona's plain, was a debatable land neither orchard nor sylvan exclusively, where the apple produce was hardly sufficient to warrant each proprietor in keeping a mill of his own. This was the field of the travelling cider-maker. His press and mill were fixed to wheels instead of being set up in a cider-house; and with a couple of horses, buckets, tubs, strainers, and an assistant or two, he wandered from place to place, deriving very satisfactory returns for his trouble in such a prolific season as the present.

"The back parts of the town were just now abounding with apple-gatherings. They stood in the yards in carts, baskets, and loose heaps; and the blue, stagnant air of autumn which hung over everything was heavy with a sweet cidery smell. Cakes of pomace lay against the walls in the yellow sun, where they were drying to be used as fuel. Yet it was not the great make of the year as yet; before the standard crop came in there accumulated, in abundant times like this, a large superfluity of early apples, and windfalls from the trees of later harvest, which would not keep long. Thus, in the baskets, and quivering in the hopper of the mill, she (Grace, the heroine) saw specimens of mixed date, including the mellow countenances of streaked-jacks, codlins, costards, stubbards, ratheripes, and other well-known friends of her ravenous youth."

This was a state of affairs about which Hogg was decidedly ambivalent. On the one hand he praised small farmers as makers of generally better-quality ciders than their larger counterparts and was often disapproving of the effects of the introduction of technology; on the other, he was an advocate of much larger units of production to ensure uniformity.

"A traction steam engine in these days draws the mill and an attendant press into the orchard; grinds up the fruit heaps at a rapid rate; and presses the pulp forthwith," he wrote. "The math, or cake, is rejected on the spot, and the casks at once filled with the must. The whole process is completed with an economy of time and labour that can scarcely be exceeded. The economy is false when the result is taken into consideration, for the best cider is not to be made in this way. If the mill were taken from time to time to the orchard as the different varieties of fruit ripened, the economy would be lost. And thus it comes to pass that all the apples are ground up at once – early and late varieties, ripe and unripe – they are all submitted together to the mill and the press... No time is allowed for the pulp or pommage, as the old writers call it, to commence fermentation exposed to the air, or for the juice (to be) set free to extract the full flavour of the fruit from the rind, the pips, and the more solid parts, and thus the liquor loses flavour, and the so-called economy defeats itself."

And industrial technology was a threat in more ways than one, for steam ships with refrigerated holds were bringing more and more foreign fruit and other produce into Britain, undercutting the native producers. The only way forward for British farmers, said Hogg, was to go upmarket – a sentiment heard so often in our own times.

"The power of the steam engine, by land and by sea, enables space to be overcome by rapidity of movement, and lessens expenditure by gain on time and cheapness of conveyance; and thus wider markets are offered for all articles of trade," he wrote. "Nor have these changes by any means reached their limit. Every year sees some new economy effected, or some fresh article of commerce introduced ... to compete with those already in the field. Competition thus becomes world-wide, and according to the inevitable laws of trade the best and the cheapest must prevail in the end. The benefit to humanity at large is unquestionable, but to individuals and localities the result is often disastrous. Agriculture is now tried severely to contend with these great changes, and the struggle still goes on with increasing severity, in almost all the articles of its production. The result cannot be otherwise than to compel every district and every locality to produce those articles for which it is specially adapted in the best possible form.

"If free-trade in corn and the introduction of live and dead meat restrict the profit of the farmers, happy should they be who, living in the fruit districts of England, have their orchards to help them. Two hundred years ago it was the necessities of isolation that caused the orchards to be looked to as a good source of profit; in these times it is a world-wide competition that makes the same demand. Thus it has come to pass, by a curious revolution in the cycle of commerce, that the careful cultivation of English orchards has again become a necessity, and every effort must be made to improve their condition and to make them, as they can be made, one of the main sources of the profit of the farm.

"The products in which they are unrivalled, and for which therefore they need not fear competition, are cider and perry of superior quality. Here is the speciality that requires the immediate attention of our fruit growers; and it is one that will repay all the care they can bestow upon it ... It does not answer to produce a drink of inferior quality when it is possible to produce a better; and it may assuredly be said now, as truly as it ever could have been said, that so long as the quality is superior, however large the quantity may be, a ready market will be found for it at highly remunerative prices."

The establishment of large cider factories, he believed, would prod the growers into improving their orchards and the quality of their fruit and bring about the end of the still-common abuse of adulteration by middlemen. "There are private cider and perry makers now who will buy up the superior varieties of apples or pears they require, but who will not purchase at any price the enormous amount of poor fruit which at present pervades the orchards," he wrote. "The farmers, therefore, have to make the cider and perry themselves as best they can, and sell it in bulk at a very low price to the ordinary cider merchants. From their hands it passes on, if it will bear the saccharometer test, to other manipulators, eventually, it is believed, to reappear as Hock, Champagne, Sherry, or Port, as may be required in commerce at the time." (This allegation was borne out by Sabine Baring Gould who in the 1890s commented on London wine merchants buying up stocks of Devon cider to pad out their Champagne).

"The establishment of cider and perry factories would prove of the greatest advantage in the orchard districts. A ready home market for the best kinds of fruit would lead to the gradual extinction of the inferior varieties; and the manufacture of cider and perry of superior quality would soon cause these wholesome beverages to be properly appreciated, and the outer world to value their high character. Under present circumstances, when a great 'hit' of fruit occurs, the apples and pears are scarcely saleable at any price, and the waste is enormous. It sometimes happens at these times, that a barrel of cider is placed in the yard ready tapped, with a mug at hand, that all comers to the house may help themselves. Such prodigal hospitality is by no means desirable, and if the demand for good cider was as great as it might be made, its value would soon put a stop to such wasteful use.

"It is precisely in good seasons when fruit is so abundant and well ripened that the best liquor can be made. It would be the golden opportunity for a factory, supported by capital. Very large quantities of cider and perry could be made and laid by in cask and in bottle to meet the failure of succeeding years. With good management, a company formed for the manufacture of cider and perry could scarcely fail to give a very handsome return to the proprietors, and at the same time would greatly increase the value of the orchards."

Hogg's foresight may have fallen a little short of 20:20, but his instinctive understanding of the situation was vindicated the very next year when Percy Bulmer, son of Hogg's friend the Rev Charles Bulmer, started making cider in a dedicated works in Maylord Street, Hereford. And to compare the preceding paragraphs with Bulmer's early progress it seems he was very strongly influenced by Hogg's opinions, for he followed them in almost every particular.

8: Rebirth

If William Gaymer can be identified as the man who introduced cidermaking to the industrial revolution by installing a hydraulic press at his factory in Norfolk in 1870, it was Percy Bulmer and his brother Fred who carried the process of modernisation through.

Percy Bulmer was undoubtedly one of the greatest industrialists of his age, not just in the cider industry but in any industry. Determined, shrewd, equally strategist and tactician, and a magpie for new ideas, he must also have possessed considerable personal charm and had that quality the Romans called "*felix*" – not in the sense of happy, but fortunate: always being in the right place at the right time, able to learn from his accidents and misfortunes, and capable of turning any opportunity to advantage. The industry on his death in 1919 had undergone a complete transformation since he started making cider for sale in 1887, and it's fair to say that Bulmer was the driving force behind most of the changes.

He was not the first Herefordshire cidermaker to start embracing modern methods, though. That honour goes to Henry Weston, a tenant farmer in Much Marcle who in 1880 embarked on the same journey that so many arable farmers in other regions had done long ago. Where they had added value to their produce by evolving from grower into miller into maltster into brewer, Weston quickly progressed from fruit grower and stockbreeder to specialised cidermaker, replacing his old-fashioned trough mill and screw-press with a steam-powered roller mill and a mechanical press. His first market was the local licensed trade, which he supplied with draught Weston's Rough. His surpluses went to the cider merchants, who commonly bought farm-pressed juice as cheaply as they could and fermented it – and as often as not adulterated it – themselves. But after only five years a railway station was opened at nearby Dymock, and Weston was entrepreneur enough to see how it could be used to distribute direct to customers, cutting out the middlemen. This would allow him both to maintain the quality of his product and to increase his margin: in an interview with the Hereford Times in 1894 (quoted by Fiona Mac: *Ciderlore: Cider in the Three Counties*, Logaston Press 2003) he remarked: "A great many farmers just make cider in the rough and then send it to the merchants. If farmers would take the necessary precautions and make cider and perry themselves throughout, selling direct to the consumer, the latter would have more faith in it and a better trade would result." By keeping a close eye on the quality of his products, he soon found markets as far afield as Scotland and the House of Commons.

Weston, though, had started out as a farmer and at heart remained one. As a practical man he could see the advantages of investing in technology that would both increase production and reduce costs; but in other respects he was no revolutionary. Bulmer, by contrast, had never been a farmer and was a revolutionary (although he might not have described himself as such).

According to his younger brother Fred's short memoir, *Early Days of Cider Making*, privately published in 1937, Percy Bulmer was too severely asthmatic even to go to school. As an adult without qualifications he couldn't get a job and realised he would have to go into business on his own account. His father Charles, the vicar of Credenhill, was a Woolhope Club ciderist and a close friend of Hogg's and encouraged Percy to try his hand at making cider at the vicarage. In 1887 Percy made 40 hogsheads for sale, netting £157, and in 1888 he set himself up at a warehouse in Maylord Street, Hereford. In the following year he was joined by Fred, just down from Cambridge; and by borrowing against the security of a life insurance policy their father came up with £1,760 to fund a move to Ryelands Street, the company's home to this day.

Their father's gift, however, was not enough; and to start the business in earnest the brothers raised a mortgage of £1,700. How they raised a further £6,500 – an enormous sum in those days – makes for interesting reading and is a testament to the belief that people had in them. Their bank manager, who had known the family for 50 years, advanced them a second mortgage of £3,000 – unsecured! In addition, three of Fred's college friends demonstrated their confidence in the fledgling company by investing a total of £3,500, while a fourth became their unpaid legal adviser. You could say, perhaps, that this was the old boy network in action, and certainly private contacts played a larger part in financing new businesses then than they do today; but it is also perhaps evidence of their charm and credibility.

Their investors' confidence paid off. One of the first tasks at Ryelands Street was to excavate an enormous cider cellar. Fortunately the site stood on a mixture of sand and gravel which was relatively easy to extract and whose sale price repaid the entire cost of the work. The various loans they had raised enabled the brothers to equip the cellars with 200,000 gallons of tankage in the form of huge oak vats. This followed a catastrophically poor local crop in 1890 when they had had to buy apples from Somerset at huge expense, and meant that they could overproduce in "hit" years when apples were cheap and release the surplus to subsidise their wholesale prices in poor years when apples were expensive. Wildly fluctuating prices had bedevilled earlier generations of cidermakers: the ability to stabilise prices across good harvests and bad was a critical element in achieving consistent sales volumes in the wholesale trade and thus underpinned much of the company's growth.

At first the brothers relied on a horse-powered trough mill and a manual press, just as Henry Weston did; but not for long. In the days before there were specialised engineering firms servicing the cider industry, Percy was forced to become a great improviser. In 1891 he rented an ancient agricultural steam engine, and the year after that he installed hydraulic pumps and two more presses. The hydraulic pumps and one of the presses were made by a firm in Leeds, while the third press was a 17-ton monster bought from a candle factory which exerted a pressure of 300 tons per square inch and caused considerable operational difficulties. These improvised measures were far from satisfactory; fortunately, that same year the brothers made the acquaintance of Robert Worth, an engineer from Stockton-on-Tees for whom they secured a contract with the local water works and who, in return, helped with engineering advice and also made machinery for them.

Until 1895 Bulmers produced only bottled ciders, the reason being clear from 1885 prices reported by Bull and reproduced by Patrick Wilkinson. Best-quality cask cider fetched 1-2/- a gallon, said Bull, while second quality sold at 6d-10d a gallon, and "rough" at only 2½d a gallon. Draught cider's lowly social status, and commensurately low price, is neatly summed up by

Thomas Hardy's description in *The Woodlanders* of the refreshments at a timber auction: "Two women... conducted in the rear of the halting procession a pony-cart... with a barrel of strong ale for the select, and cider in milking-pails into which anybody dipped who chose." Bottled first-quality cider, by contrast, fetched up to 12/- a dozen and matured fine ciders could go even higher – 28/- a dozen for Taynton Squash perry and 30/- for Foxwhelp.

Bulmers' bottled ciders, like all others at the time, were made sparkling by secondary fermentation through the time-honoured method of adding a small piece of sugar. This, however, created a pressure of 70psi – easily enough to send an ordinary wine-cork soaring; so sparkling ciders were commonly packaged in Champagne-style wire-corked bottles. Bulmers used a corking machine bought from a firm in Epernay, and in 1894, on the basis of this slender acquaintance, Percy visited Epernay and was introduced to a Champagne house, Desmonet, where he learnt a great deal about making sparkling wines. He also studied for some months at the Municipal Wine Laboratory in Reims, where he learnt some of the finer points of the craft and acquired a selection of technical literature that was to prove useful when, in 1906, Bulmers started to produce a bottled cider by the *méthode champenoise*. This was marketed under the name of Cider De Luxe until 1916 when it was renamed Pomagne. Bulmers continued to produce and market Pomagne as "champagne cider" until 1974 when Bollinger took the company to court to prevent the use of the word champagne. Bulmers won, but had already stopped making Pomagne by the champagne process and in 1975 dropped the contentious word from the brand's descriptor.

Cider de Luxe was an early example of Percy Bulmer's inquisitive nature and his willingness to adapt technologies and innovations from other industries. Another instance was his visit in 1904 to the German mineral water firm Apollinaris to observe modern methods of artificial carbonation, which led to the launch of the carbonated Bull Brand in 1919. A tour of a German sugarbeet processing plant on the same trip persuaded him to buy a drier that would convert spent pomace (which had previously been dumped) at first into cattle cake and later into a source of saleable pectin. He also observed and promptly adopted the method of floating apples from the tumps to the mill which both washed them and separated out stones, rotten apples, and other orchard detritus.

But it wasn't only in the factory that Percy was an innovator and revolutionary. After the crop failure of 1890 he determined to safeguard his sources of supply and at the same time to encourage Herefordshire growers to plant the varieties he favoured. In 1898 Bulmers planted a 68-acre orchard at Broxwood which doubled as a nursery from which the company could supply recommended varieties to local farmers. This was the genesis of the now universal system of contract growing, which from the 1920s on led to the virtual demise of farm cidermaking in the West Midlands. From 1903 onwards Percy concerned himself more and more with the securing his supplies, planting experimental orchards on a scale Thomas Andrew Knight would have been jealous of and introducing a large number of new varieties. "If the cidermaking industry is to increase in Herefordshire," he said, "it will be necessary to have the raw materials; and in view of the demand for trees, I think a greater supply should be produced by the nurserymen. It will be necessary to grow trees on a larger scale than has hitherto been done in this country, and in a commercial spirit."

Fred, in his way, was no less innovative and no less ready to borrow and adapt. Put in charge of the sales and marketing side, he embarked in 1889 on a tour of every small town in Britain "between the Isle of Wight and Dundee", making good trade contacts but discovering a deep lack of awareness of cider beyond its traditional homelands. The late 18th-century days of Viscount Torrington's travels, when cider was universally stocked by inns far and wide, were evidently over: many publicans and grocers told Fred that they didn't even know what cider was, but would happily stock it if there were a demand. To create a demand, therefore, Fred virtually invented junk mail by sending sales letters to over 20,000 likely targets gathered from local trade directories – a massive task in the early days of the typewriter! Nevertheless, it paid off: Fred's initiative won Bulmers enough retail customers to enable the company to progress from selling directly to private customers to nationwide wholesaling. In 1892 Fred signed an exclusive contract with Browning's, suppliers to the Great Western Railway, paying 100 guineas a year for the privilege of being allowed to put the company's showcards in station refreshment rooms and dining-cars. Next, he signed an even bigger contract with Spiers & Pond, high society caterers and catering wholesalers. This time, the showcard rent was 500 guineas!

As innovators, the Bulmer brothers were matched by William Gaymer on the other side of the country. In the late 1880s and early '90s Gaymer was routinely exhibiting his products (still, like Bulmers and Weston's, all bottled) and utilising the many medals that he won for advertising purposes. He was also building a reputation for quality – and a large London customer base – by targeting prestige accounts such as gentlemen's clubs, military messes, the House of Commons, and even Buckingham Palace.

Railway refreshment rooms were, as with Bulmers, another prime target: winning sole concessionary rights with the Great Eastern, the Midland, the Great Northern, the Great Central and the North Eastern guaranteed distribution to hundreds of bars all over the country. The railway was useful in other ways, too: in 1896 Gaymer moved his entire operation from Banham to Attleborough, where he bought a much larger and more modern factory with railway sidings of its own. This enabled him to buy cider apples in bulk from Devon – until then he had mainly been using locally-grown culinary apples, especially the highly-esteemed Ribston Pippin – and even to import huge quantities of Canadian produce when the British crop failed in 1903. By 1900 the company also had a railway depot at Bishopsgate, enabling it to reach its London customers easily and cheaply. It was also exporting "Old Matured Cyder".

William Gaymer, Percy Bulmer, and Henry Weston pioneered the industrialisation of cider by mechanising their factories, by buying up the produce of other growers, by taking advantage of mass distribution by rail, and by marketing and wholesaling their own cider rather than relying on merchants. By these advances they all achieved huge growth in the last decade of the 19th century and the first of the 20th, a record of success that did not go unnoticed. Imitators proliferated. Rout's of Banham has already been noted as a local rival to Gaymer's, lasting through a number of changes of ownership until 1957. In Herefordshire two well-established merchants, William Evans (founded in Hereford in 1850 and moved to much larger premises in Widemarsh Common after being sold to the Chave family in 1884) and Ridlers of Clehonger mutated into full-blown cider manufacturers; while in 1898 an industrialist from a completely different sphere of operations, Henry Godwin, established his own steam-powered cider factory next to his tileworks in Holmer just to the north of Hereford.

In Devon, as well as Hunt's, Payne's, and Henley's, there was Symonds of Totnes, all well-known locally and mechanised to varying degrees. More successful and longlasting than any of them, though, was Whiteways. Henry Whiteway moved from Harbertonford, where his family had made cider for generations, to his wife's home village of Whimple in 1891. At Whimple he continued the family tradition, but the launchpad for his business was the death of his wealthy father-in-law – and hence a generous inheritance of orchards and other land – in 1894. Whiteway immediately moved the cidermaking from his farm to a large former tannery, and at the same time bought an acre of land next to Whimple Station for a new steam-powered factory. This opened in 1898, by which time Whiteways was already selling 100,000 gallons of "cyder" (the company's preferred spelling) a year largely by dint of an audacious advertising campaign embracing almost every periodical imaginable from the regionals including Exeter Express & Echo, the Western Morning News, the Manchester Guardian and the London Evening Standard to almost all the nationals of the day – the Daily Graphic, the Sketch, and the Bystander as well as the Mail, the Telegraph, the Mirror, the Times and the Express. Similarly Cydrax, a non-alcoholic cider introduced in 1904, was promoted and advertised in almost every newspaper or magazine with the word "Church" in its title.

But the process of industrialisation has other dimensions too. Specialised manufacturers require specialised technical support and specialised suppliers. And factories also require a very different kind of workforce. Chronologically, the last of these came first.

Truck was a longstanding abuse in British industry, requiring workers to accept part or even all of their wages either in the form of their employers' produce or of vouchers redeemable in their employers' shops, often against overpriced and substandard goods. As we have seen, farm labourers in the cider-producing counties were being paid partly in liquor as far back as 1597 when Gerard observed: "I have seen in the pastures and hedgerows about the grounds of a worshipful gentleman dwelling two miles from Hereford ... so many trees of all sorts that the servants drink for the most part no other drink but that which is made of apples." Their dole could be as much as two gallons a day; but it would be a mistake to assume that the workers thus remunerated spent their waking hours drunk. As we have seen, the liquor they were given was (except at harvest-time, said Knight) not cider but "ciderkin", the product of rehydrated spent pomace and probably no stronger than 3% ABV. Nor was the quantity as great as it would be today: before the standard 20fl oz imperial pint was introduced in 1825, a pint could be anything between 12 and 16 fl oz – the US pint today is still 16fl oz – and even the fluid ounce was subject to regional variations.

Modern writers tend to portray the abolition of the cider truck as the work of killjoy temperance campaigners. That temperance campaigners were involved is certainly true: that they were killjoy is anything but. Agricultural labourers doubtless appreciated a generous allowance of fluid to rehydrate them as they worked; but they were getting a bad bargain and they knew it. French, quoting figures from Worcestershire, says that in 1794 agricultural labourers were commonly paid a shilling a day and could commute their two-gallon cider dole for tuppence. By 1807, after 14 years of war, wages had risen to two shillings a day with the cider dole commutable for sixpence. It's hard to know how much their allowance was really worth in cash since ciderkin was not made for sale and therefore had no measurable market value. But a Poor Law Commission report on the employment of women and children in agriculture in the West Country in 1843 (quoted by James Crowden, *Cider: the Forgotten Miracle*, Cyder Press 1999) is adamant that "masters rated the value of the cider too high".

The first Truck Act made payment of wages in "current coin of the realm" compulsory as early as 1831 – but only for "artificers" or industrial workers. It took more than half a century of lobbying by workers' representatives including the National Agricultural Labourers' Union and largely Nonconformist ministers – and before these last are dubbed "killjoy", it should be remembered that the farm labourers of the West Country migrated entirely voluntarily from the Church of England to the various chapels, which they founded, owned, and ran themselves – before an amendment to the 1831 Act could be secured. The 1887 Truck Amendment Act did not specifically ban payment of wages in alcoholic beverages, as is sometimes said; all it had to do was add "husbandmen" to the list of workers classed as "artificers". The picturesque image of jolly farmworkers pouring their cider from little coopered costrels into cowhorn cups did not immediately disappear from the orchards, since it long remained common for farmers to allow their labourers a ration of cider on top of their wages. But the workers were vastly better off with their extra 1/6 or 2/- a week and cider as an entirely optional extra (a bottle of cold tea was an alternative preferred by many).

For the cider truck had undoubtedly been an abuse – one report from 1851 claimed that labourers in cider regions were obliged to accept up to 15% of their wages in cider – but, perhaps surprisingly, it wasn't necessarily popular even with its perpetrators. Various versions of the same anecdote exist from 1800 to the 1920s – in Marshall's version the farmer complains that his workers spend half their time making cider and half their time drinking it, while by the 1920s it has evolved thus: "I paid 'em to make it and I paid 'em to drink it and the buggers still weren't satisfied, so I stopped making it." The significant point here is that the curmudgeonly farmer of the 1920s version has actually stopped making cider altogether. To many farmers, once the great cider factories had started buying huge tonnages of apples at fixed rates, there seemed little purpose in making the cider themselves except to honour the tradition of paying part of their wage-bill in it. Cidermaking for many had become more trouble than it was worth; not overnight, but gradually, the tradition died out, and the farmers became contract growers, part of the supply industry that fed the vast appetites of the factories. Thus the abolition of the cider truck, if indirectly, assisted in the creation of the reliable specialised supply chain necessary to support large companies with national distribution.

In another area, though, the nascent cider industry was still groping in the dark. Breweries had been installing laboratories of ever-increasing sophistication since the late 18th century when the use of microscopes, hydrometers, and thermometers started to become widespread. Cidermakers, whether small farmers or large landowners, lagged far behind; and the microbiology of cider was scarcely understood except in the most general of terms until the very late 19th century. In the century since Thomas Andrew Knight's meticulous work on orcharding techniques and fruit varieties, both the practical and theoretical aspects of fruit growing had become much better and more widely understood. But a commensurately detailed understanding of the production process was almost entirely lacking: fermentation and maturation remained in many respects mysterious processes, governed by lore and tradition and controlled by rule of thumb. But industry demands a consistent product, one that can be reliably replicated from year to year. The groundwork of sound biochemical research required to guarantee it, and the facilities where such research could be undertaken, had to wait until the foundation in 1903 of the National Fruit & Cider Institute at Long Ashton near Bristol.

The choice of a home for the Institute is interesting. Until now, Herefordshire had made most of the running: Scudamore, Beale, Knight, Hogg, Weston, Bulmer – the great names in cider with one or two exceptions had been Herefordshire men. Now that other great cider-producing county came into its own with the appearance on stage of Robert Neville Grenville, squire of Butleigh near Glastonbury.

Although a commoner, Robert Neville Grenville came of an eminent family – his father Ralph had been a minister in the Peel administration that swept away the Corn Laws, and Robert himself by some strange chance was actually born in Windsor Castle. But his career path, by the standard of his class and times, must have seemed more than mildly eccentric, for he opted for a life in engineering. He was Cambridge University's very first engineering postgraduate (although his degree was an MA rather than an MSc, this being 1868), and while at Magdalene College he built himself a steam launch to go one up on his fellow undergraduates with their punts. From Cambridge he was apprenticed to an engineering company contracted to the Great Western Railway, in whose workshops at Swindon he built himself, in 1875, a steam car capable of 24mph. Later he built himself a more practical car powered by a petrol engine.

Neville Grenville succeeded to Butleigh in 1892 and in the following year set about a programme of research into cidermaking, much as Thomas Andrew Knight had done (and much as the Duke of Bedford was to do in 1894 at his family's stately pile, Woburn Abbey, with the establishment of a short-lived experimental fruit farm), but concentrating on the biochemical aspect rather than arboriculture. He hired a London-based analytical chemist, Frederick Lloyd, to direct the programme and – doubtless thanks to his county connections – was able to procure a grant of £100 a year from the Bath & West Society to fund it. The work was regularly reported in the Society's Journal and quickly came to the attention of the Board of Agriculture, which eventually took over the funding. By 1902 both the Society and the Board, as well as the county councils for the cidermaking regions, recognised that the work being carried on at Butleigh was of national importance and required a more permanent and publicly-owned base. In October of that year a conference was held at which the Society, the Board, and county council representatives from Herefordshire, Worcestershire, Gloucestershire, Somerset, Devon, and Monmouthshire agreed to set up and fund the Institute. Among them was a man who was even better-known on the public stage than Neville Grenville: Charles Radcliffe Cooke, representing Herefordshire.

Like Neville Grenville, Cooke was very much the patrician. His family estate was Hellens at Much Marcle, and he busied himself in county affairs as a justice of the peace, president of the Hereford Chamber of Agriculture and chairman of the Ledbury Highways Board. Like Hogg, he saw improved cider manufacture as a way out of the difficulties facing British fruit-growers owing to foreign competition and was instrumental in persuading Henry Weston, his near neighbour, to give up mixed farming and concentrate on cidermaking instead. From 1885 to 1892 he was, rather bizarrely, MP for Newington in South London but in 1893 fought the election for Hereford, won, and remained its MP until 1900. During his tenure he wrote *A Book About Cider & Perry* (1898) and became jocularly known as the MP for cider. But on this occasion, for once, Hereford deferred to Somerset, and it was a precondition demanded by the Bath & West Society that the Institute's home should be in Somerset, and that the annual meetings of its board of governors should be held at the Bath & West show.

A detailed account of the conference at which the Institute was established, written for the Society's Journal by AE Brooke-Hunt of the Board of Agriculture, set out the Institute's aims as, first, more research but, secondly, education.

"As the value of the work carried out at Butleigh became increasingly apparent," wrote Brooke-Hunt, "the question of the advisability of an extension of operations, especially in the direction of research into the action of the various yeasts and ferments which affect the manufacture of cider, came under consideration. It was felt too that, however true it may be that research must precede education, the educational side of the question required development, and that some provision was necessary for the instruction of those who might desire the same for some continuous period, with a view of eventually becoming practical and scientific experts in the art of cider-making.

"The work carried out at Butleigh had been of great value to cidermakers and had assisted to raise the standard of cider manufacture and place it on a scientific basis; but the time had now arrived when the work might, with advantage, be considerably extended. It appeared to the Board that this could best be brought about by the formation of a fixed Cider Institute, which should bear the same relation to cider-making as the fixed Dairy Schools did to cheese and butter-making. An Institute of this nature would, on the one hand, act as a centre to which farmers and cidermakers could come to obtain instruction of practical value to them in their business, and on the other hand, as a place where those who would act as peripatetic teachers on behalf of County Councils could get a thorough training and be placed in possession of the most recent information bearing upon so highly technical a subject as that of cidermaking."

A sub-committee was then formed to find a suitable site, and one was very soon forthcoming. Long Ashton was an existing cider farm, and was leased to the Institute by a relative of Neville Grenville's, Lady Emily Smyth, who also loaned the capital required to adapt the farm to its new purpose. The buildings, the sub-committee reported, were entirely suitable (although Brooke-Hunt described the cart-shed and poultry house as "not altogether pleasing"), and it was hoped that cidermaking and other commercial services would defray the estimated £1,100 annual running costs. Long Ashton already had a five-acre orchard, with eight more acres ready to be planted. An acre was to be used as a nursery with 11,000 stocks of cider apple and 2,000 of perry pear, to be "available as grafts for farmers and nurserymen throughout the district". In time it was hoped that "virtually every known variety" would be planted and properly noted and classified, "so that the Institute will really become a place where all information respecting varieties that it is possible to acquire will be available for the benefit of those who desire it".

The director for the first two years was to be Neville Grenville's chemist, Frederick Lloyd. He was to be succeeded by a Cambridge don already noted for his researches into yeast and fermentation, BTP Barker of Gonville & Caius College; and Brooke-Hunt concluded: "Thus the Institute is now fairly launched. It is beginning, as most things do which really last, in only a small way, but the potentialities are great; and it is hoped that its career may be one of increasing usefulness not only to this generation but to others which are to follow."

One token of its "usefulness" is the sheer volume of Barker's written output: between 1904 and 1954, he produced no fewer than 27 papers on topics as diverse as the use of spent pomace as animal feed and cidermaking experiments using culinary and dessert apples. Perhaps his most valuable contributions, though, were to analyse the chemistry of over 2,000 varieties and, in 1905, to systematise the traditional classification of apples as sweets (dessert apples), sharps (cookers), bittersweets and bittersharps (both cider apples). Sweets contain less that 0.45% acid and less than 0.2% tannin; sharps contain more than 0.45% acid and less than 0.2% tannin, bittersharps contain more than 0.45% acid and more than 0.2% tannin; bittersweets contain less than 0.45% acid and more that 0.2% tannin. This system of classification is still in use today.

The Institute did not long remain in its original format, though: in 1912 it was taken over by the University of Bristol and given a greater educational role. At the same time it adopted its more familiar name, the Long Ashton Research Station. The occasion was marked by the donation of more land by Lady Smyth, and the Station continued as a dynamic and vital resource for the industry until 1981, when the Agricultural Research Council closed its Pomology & Plant Breeding and Food & Beverage divisions. Thereafter its work focused more on arable crops, and it was finally closed altogether exactly a century after its foundation. It is now a housing estate, but in its heyday it not only provided practical research material for the industry but also trained many of its leading figures. It also worked closely with the East Malling Research Station in that other cradle of pomiculture, Kent. Founded in 1913 to serve the wider fruit-growing industry, East Malling's work on rootstocks under the directorship of Ronald Hatton led to the development of the "dwarf" or "bush" trees that began to replace standard trees from the 1950s on.

The proceedings of the conference that founded Long Ashton are notable for the absence of two names: those of William Gaymer and Percy Bulmer. Patrick Wilkinson notes that Bulmers supported the venture, but this is perhaps the last instance where the cidermaking gentry exerted their influence as landowners and patricians over the public affairs of their industry. Radcliffe Cooke and Neville Grenville were very different beasts from Percy Bulmer: perhaps they didn't recognise that the future lay with large, powerful manufacturers such as Bulmers and Gaymer's – who were not, it must be said, either very large or very powerful at that early stage. To be fair, there might be a far more prosaic reason for Bulmer's absence from the conference. Five years earlier, Cooke and Fred Bulmer had had a spectacularly public spat after Cooke – still then Hereford's MP – had proclaimed himself, following the publication of *A Book About Cider and Perry*, as "the leading authority on cider" and had announced his intention to set up as a cidermaker on his own account, provoking an explosive open letter to the Hereford Times drafted (according to Patrick Wilkinson) by Fred Bulmer and signed by six leading Herefordshire cidermakers including Bulmers.

"By virtue of your office as a Member of Parliament and your reiterated professions of disinterestedness you obtained the confidence of the cidermakers of the county," said the letter. "The same professions enabled you to secure in the columns of The Times and the press generally publicity which thousands of pounds spent in fair and legitimate advertising would have failed to procure.

"Armed with credentials of a public character, you frequently inspected the works and manufactories of cidermakers whom you systematically cross-examined in great detail as to the theory and practical methods of their businesses... What ground have you for the statement that you are "the leading authority on cider"? What apprenticeship have you served to justify this title? You have obtained the necessary superficial training which can be got by using the brains of others who have had to pay heavily in cash and labour for their experience; and this too while professing to act in the public interest."

By the time Long Ashton was founded, though, Bulmers was already deeply engaged in its own nursery and orcharding work and was about to appoint its own chemist, Herbert Durham. Another of Fred's university acquaintances, Dr Durham had given up surgery for medical research in 1895 and spent eight years working, mainly abroad, for the School of Tropical Medicine. His foreign assignments cost him his health; he joined Bulmers in 1905 and stayed for 30 years.

Percy Bulmer, always sickly, died in 1919 aged only 52 (he survived Henry Weston by two years; William Gaymer jnr, though, outlived him by 17 years, dying only in 1936 at the ripe old age of 94). In only 32 years Bulmer had seen cider in England transformed from an almost moribund by-product of mixed farming into a thoroughly modern industry, fully mechanised, with its own support and supply industries. He himself was responsible for much of the transformation. His factory employed 200 industrial workers in conditions far better than those of the farm labourers they had supplanted. His products were distributed nationally by rail from the company's own sidings. In 1894 he had launched Britain's first national cider brand, Woodpecker, which is still with us today (although, perhaps, only just). Taking a leaf out of Guinness's book, Bulmers had Woodpecker (in those days a still cider – artificial carbonation came later) shipped in bulk to breweries around the country for bottling and distribution to the brewers' tied pubs.

There were many things he hadn't achieved, though; achievements which had to be left to the stewardship of his brother Fred.

9: To Market

If modern cider-lovers could travel back in time to the early 1920s they might well think they had arrived in a golden age. With the economy enjoying its brief post-war boom, the nascent cider industry was flourishing. New manufacturers were appearing, among them names still familiar today, and many mixed farmers were taking their cidermaking more seriously. And the cider they were making for the national market was a high-quality product acceptable to drinkers beyond the confines of its home territory: not the rough draught cider beloved of Westcountrymen, but a sweeter, gentler, altogether more refined product, often made sparkling by the full-blown *méthode champenoise*.

World War I had not been kind to the cider industry. Supplies of raw materials were not restricted as they were with beer; but a general shortage of labour contributed to a great increase in apple prices from 30/- a ton in 1913 to 40/- in 1914 and an astronomical £20 in 1918 (worsened by an admittedly dreadful harvest). A fairly modest duty of 4d a gallon was introduced in 1916 – the first since Wellington repealed cider duty in 1830; worse was the "Excess Profits Tax", which according to Fred Bulmer was swallowing 85% of his company's profits by the end of the war. The duty raised only £144,000 in 1917, which implies a total national output of only 8.6 million gallons. Given an estimated national output of some 20,000,000 gallons or 560,000 brewer's barrels in 1920, it is clear that most cidermakers managed to avoid it. But even the higher figure represents a very considerable shrinkage in production before and during World War I. One estimate had put production at 55,000,000 gallons in 1890, and even if in an untaxed and unregulated industry any figure could only be an educated guess, the equivalent of 1,500,000 brewer's barrels for the whole industry doesn't appear too fanciful when beer production was just over 30,000,000 barrels and, moreover, is fairly consistent with a good estimate for 1830 when the cider tax yielded £260,000 from ten shillings per 100-gallon hogshead, equating to 52,000,000 gallons. The huge reduction in estimated cider output is also consistent with the better-documented figure for the brewing industry: output collapsed from 33,000,000 barrels in 1915 to a mere 13,000,000 barrels in 1919, so it is not unreasonable to suppose that cidermaking suffered similarly.

The end of the war, though, was followed by economic boom. True, the years 1918-21 saw a 25% fall in industrial production, largely accounted for by the winding down of the munitions industry. But the underlying trend – for the time being, at least – was upwards. Much of the visible unemployment was soaked up by returning servicemen ousting women from the workplace. Traditional ship-building areas flourished as the 40% of the merchant navy lost to German U-boats was replaced. New manufacturers of high-tech goods such as aeroplanes, cars, and radios sprang up in the South. Domestic and industrial demand for energy saw the process of electrification spreading rapidly across the country: the first coal-fired power station had been built near Newcastle-upon-Tyne in 1901, and the first regional grid was established in 1912 in the North-East. The national grid was created by the 1926 Electricity Supply Act; the process of linking the country's power stations was completed in 1938. The demand for electricity generated a new demand for coal: the number of mineworkers topped a million soon after the war and rose to 1,200,000 by 1921. It may be dangerous to use well-attested figures from the brewing industry to track developments in the all but undocumented cider industry, but beer production quickly recovered from its 1919 nadir to reach 26,000,000 barrels in 1921.

Despite enormous setbacks starting with the ill-advised return to the gold standard in 1925, which scuppered the export drive on which Britain's economic health depended, and followed by the Great Depression stemming from the Wall Street Crash of 1929, urbanisation and industrial development were proceeding apace. In October 1937 a senior Ministry of Agriculture official, Dr HV Taylor, told a gathering of growers and cidermakers at Burghill Hospital Farm's orchards in Herefordshire something that most of them already knew: that their world had changed forever. "Thirty or forty years ago, the bulk of the cider made in this country was drunk by people in the countryside, whereas today a very large proportion is drunk by the man in the town," he said. "Both growers and manufacturers have to realise that the cider of the townsman is a very different product from the cider the countryman used to drink." (quoted by Fiona Mac, *Ciderlore: Cider in the Three Counties*).

Dr Taylor's message was in fact already a quarter of a century out of date: the milestone year in which Britain's urban population outstripped its rural one had been 1910. During World War I rural depopulation accelerated as labour flocked to the munitions factories. Admittedly, many of these new factory workers were drawn from domestic service rather than agriculture; but the process accelerated after the war as farms became more and more mechanised and opportunities arose for better-paid work in industry to attract young countryfolk with no prospects in their ancestral villages. (Another aspect of mechanisation often cited by farmers as a reason for giving up cidermaking was that without horses, they couldn't turn their mills!) The cidermakers' traditional market was thus being steadily eroded, but a new, bigger, more prosperous urban market was growing around them. Unemployment and low wages in the older urban areas of the North were balanced by new industries in the South, and the middle classes continued by and large to flourish. For many if not most of the new inhabitants of the spreading London suburbs the "hungry '30s" were no more than a fearful rumour, a calamity that was engulfing someone else – foreigners, almost. These were the people at whom the burgeoning cider industry energetically set its cap.

The immediate post-war years were a period of extraordinary dynamism in the world of commercial cidermaking. At local level, the slow withdrawal of farmers from making cider for their own families and workers and neighbouring pubs created vacuums for commercial makers to fill, while the return of demobilised servicemen meant the regeneration both of custom and labour. An additional driver was the growth of mostly rail-borne tourism, especially to the Devon Riviera, which meant not only a seasonal sales boost but also increased awareness of cider among the urban middle classes in general and potentially, therefore, new markets in new territories.

One lesson the smaller regional makers quickly learnt from Bulmers, Gaymer's, and Weston's was an understanding of modern marketing, both the techniques available and the investment needed to exploit them. This was an era when shipping lines, railway companies and catering chains charged their suppliers hundreds of guineas for permission to display placards, posters, showcards and other point of sale material in their bars and restaurants, but the collections of ephemera enthusiasts show that even quite small makers – Sealey's, Magna, Clapp's, Cole's, Allen's, Ashford Vale, Lang's, some of them not much bigger than individual farms – were prepared to spend on both point of sale material and press advertising. Whiteways spent £250,000 in the press between 1926 and 1932, while Henley's of Newton Abbot had its advertisements emblazoned on the sides of Torquay trams. Much of this advertising trumpeted the West Country provenance of the makers, and the unadulterated natural goodness of the product. One Bulmers brand was touted as containing mineral salts that were good for the female complexion. That doctors could easily be found who were willing to write testimonials for cider's medical virtues, especially against gout and rheumatism, created another favourite and often-used theme for the copywriters.

The 1920s and '30s saw considerable growth for the old cider merchants and bigger cider farms that had mutated into full-time commercial concerns, and many long-forgotten names were well-known in their day. The period also saw a number of newcomers to the market, some large, some small. A number of them had been tenant farmers who were now able to take advantage of the gradual easing of the market for freehold agricultural property that followed substantial increases in death duties in the 1890s. As old estates slowly sold off parts of their landholdings to raise the necessary capital, more and more freeholds became available. Weston's bought itself out from the Homme House estate in 1924, buying a couple of neighbouring farms as well as Bounds; Perry Brothers was founded at Dowlish Wake in Somerset in 1921 by a blacksmith called William Churchill who bought Lot 9 when Major Sparkes was obliged to sell Dowlish Wake Manor. Still with us from this vintage is Wilkins of Wedmore; Coombes of Highbridge has only just closed; and Inch's of Winkleigh had its comeuppance in 1995 when it was bought by Bulmers only to be closed three years later. But of the many older cider firms that expanded and new ones that started up in the inter-war years, three grew to national significance, all of them from Somerset: Coate's, Taunton, and Showering's.

Of the three, only Coate's was strictly speaking new. In 1924 Redvers Coate had graduated with a degree in chemistry from Bristol University and was seeking a career. By then the commercialization of cidermaking was already well advanced in Devon, Gloucestershire, and Herefordshire, but not to the same extent in Somerset. With an eye to the opportunity, Coate put in a postgraduate year at Long Ashton and borrowed enough from family and friends, including £8,000 from his father, to open a cider works in a former timberyard at Nailsea with an experienced foreman, Charlie Higgins (headhunted from Williams Brothers of Backwell), a cooper, a cellarman, a clerk, and two labourers. From the start it was an ambitious venture. The works was fitted out with the most up-to-date equipment including three 10,000-gallon glass-lined concrete tanks – the precursor to stainless steel; and Coate's put a great deal of effort into sourcing the best-quality apples. Later, this extended to persuading farmers who had gone out of cidermaking to grub up inefficient old orchards and replant with modern varieties but in the early days Coate – who is said to have possessed considerable personal charm and probably needed it – toured his suppliers' farms in person to check up on the fruit he proposed to buy. The effort paid off early when, at the end of his first year's trading, Coate took three first prizes at the National Cider Competition.

Almost uniquely for the times, Coate planned from the outset to concentrate on supplying draught cider to the local pub trade rather than tackling the national market with bottled products. "I was out every night calling on the pubs that weren't tied," he later recalled. "I found this necessary pub-crawling hard work – I felt as if I was a commercial traveller in search of sales." (Quoted by Mark Foot, *Cider's Story Rough and Smooth*, self-published, 1999). Later, Coate was to revise his opinion; but in the 1930s his original strategy paid off when breweries started extending their beer tie to include cider as well. As a draught cider specialist, Coate's was well-placed to supply large tied estates and the company flourished. By the outbreak of World War II the workforce had expanded from five to 125.

Taunton Cider's origins are less well-documented, and surrounded by myths so oft-repeated they have become accepted as truth; but the company that came to be Britain's second largest maker always claimed a tenuous link with Somerset's 18th-century cider heritage.

The rector of Heathfield, Somerset, from 1786-1840, Thomas Cornish, was an enthusiastic cidermaker who had put 15 acres of his 70-acre glebe to orchards. His son, also Thomas, followed him as rector from 1840-56 and took his cidermaking even more seriously, supplying fine ciders to Queen

Victoria, Lord Melbourne, the Marquess of Bath, the Marquess of Worcester, and sundry other blue-blooded households. The Cornishes were succeeded by another father and son dynasty of cidermaking rectors, Edward Bryan Combe Spurway (1856-96) and Edward Popham Spurway (1896-1914). According to the *Heathfield History* website (www.oake.org.uk): "It was said that EBCS made the best cider and had the best hands in Somerset. He had 70 acres of glebe so rich that if you stuck your walking stick into it, next year it would have grown into a tree... It was said that a Mr Cattle did the actual work of making the cider.

"The year revolved round the orchards. First in the early winter pruning the trees which had grown for 100 years in the rich red loam of Taunton Deane. The trees were 7' in the bole, and one was 40' high. The applewood was burnt on the rectory fires, and in the winter came the wassailers with blackened faces for the pagan ceremony of singing to chase the evil spirits off the trees. They would sing in the rectory drawing room too: and then (with a more vulgar song because they thought the rector could not hear) they would dance in the backyard with the serving maids. In the spring the bees would work, and in the autumn the old horse worked the mill. The apples were gathered from the trees and placed in racks shaped like a V and then covered with thatch so that all water would drain off before they went into the press.

"Morgan Sweets were mixed with the standard Kingston Blacks sometimes. The apple juice was three days in the vat. In long cellars across the yard were all the barrels, and there at Heathfield Rectory 5,000 gallons of cider a year were made."

Edward Popham Spurway continued to make cider and in 1901 won a gold medal at the Bath & West Show, and it was his cidermaker Arthur Moore – who was not, as is often (and impossibly!) repeated, Thomas Cornish's gardener – who became Taunton Cider's first master cidermaker. There is some confusion about the date, too. It is always said that Moore left Heathfield in 1911 to join a company founded in Norton Fitzwarren by George Pallett and John Vickery, called Pallett's Cider until 1921 when it was incorporated as the Taunton Cider Company. However EPS's son Michael (born 1909), also quoted in *Heathfield History*, clearly recalls Moore being excused morning prayers in the rectory – a remarkable feat of memory for a two-year-old! It is more likely that Moore left to join Pallett's Cider when EPS died in 1914 since the next rector, Guy Hockley, had no interest in cidermaking; the rectory's equipment was sold during World War I.

The third of the Somerset trio, Showering's, was by no means a newcomer, the family having been brewers and cidermakers at Shepton Mallet since at least 1843, owning three tied houses. It was incorporated as a company in 1932. The cidermaking side of the business, though, only started gaining prominence in the late 1930s when one of the three Showering brothers, Francis, started researching the fermentation of fruit juice – research that led to the launch of Babycham in the early 1950s and the company's rapid rise to the national stage.

Throughout the 1920s and '30s the new generation of industrial cidermakers expanded at the expense of the traditional mixed farmer. Patrick Wilkinson in *Bulmers: A Century of Cidermaking* estimates that at the end of World War I 76% of production was in the hands of farmed-based cidermakers, while commercial manufacturers were still developing new markets beyond cider's old heartlands. By 1937 more and more farmers who had previously made their own cider had instead become raw materials suppliers to the cider companies, whose share of the country's total production had risen from 24% to 68% – 13,000,000 gallons out of the 19,000,000 produced nationally, according to Wilkinson. Small scale rural cidermaking proved a slow beast to kill: indeed, it was officially encouraged as a way of helping farmers increase their income during the agricultural depression. Devon County Council's agricultural committee, for instance, produced several editions of a free booklet, *Cidermaking on the Farm*, which guided small cidermakers on best practice and would still be a perfectly viable manual for the aspiring cidermaker today. And, of course, Laurie Lee's *Cider with Rosie*, from which this book derives its title, emphasises the importance of farm-made cider in village life in 1920s and '30s Gloucestershire.

But all the time, the commercial cider industry was becoming more a coherent and powerful institution, continuing the processes of building its supply and distribution chains and developing its technology, and finding a voice of its own at national level. The foundation of the National Association of Cidermakers in 1920 was actually a refoundation – a first attempt in 1894 had flopped, perhaps because the industry lacked a sense of identity or was indifferent to the need for representation, perhaps because of the spectacular falling out of its two moving spirits, the old patrician Radcliffe Cooke and the young radical Fred Bulmer.

By 1920, though, and with Cooke long dead, Bulmer was in charge and free to revive the project. The Association was launched that year with 46 members and in 1923 was successful in its first major lobby, persuading Stanley Baldwin, then briefly Prime Minister in the first of his three administrations, to repeal the wartime cider duty. It might have helped that the Chancellor's nephews were among Fred Bulmer's oldest friends and that one of them, Harold, had been appointed manager of the company's orchards at Broxwood having had difficulty finding work because of his epilepsy. But it was nonetheless a solid start for a fledgling lobby, as well as an effective demonstration to the world of how well-connected Fred Bulmer was. The Association showed its effectiveness even more formidably in 1931 when it overrode the brewer's protests and persuaded the new National Government's Chancellor, Philip Snowden, to continue to exempt cider when he increased beer duty in his supplementary Budget. As a result beer rose to 6d a pint while cider, actually the more alcoholic of the two, remained at 4d. That same year the Association gave its wholehearted support to the Board of Trade's extension of the National Mark scheme – a way of promoting domestic produce against foreign competition by guaranteeing and certifying its purity and quality – to cider. The Board was headed by none other than Stanley Baldwin and in 1932, in the continuing round of political *quid pro quo*, Fred Bulmer, acting in the Association's name, prevailed on Baldwin to exempt the French cider apples on which large manufacturers depended in poor years from a £4 10s a ton duty on non-Commonwealth imports. In return the Association promised to pay growers a minimum of £4 a ton for five years, demonstrating the industry's cohesion only two years later when every single member abided by the pledge even though 1934 was a glut year when apples could have been had for the asking.

Ensuring a steady supply of the right sort of fruit had always been an issue of critical importance for commercial cidermakers whose brands had to be consistent from year to year, and as their share of the market increased the headache only intensified. Chronic underinvestment in orchards over many decades meant irregular and unpredictable cropping of a multitude of varieties, many of which the cidermakers considered unsuitable. Work in this direction had been an early priority: Bulmers had followed the purchase of the 68-acre nursery and experimental orchard at Broxwood by buying two neighbouring farms comprising another 180 acres and was selling seedlings of approved varieties to its growers, who were now being offered long-term contracts at fixed prices provided they supplied the varieties that Bulmers wanted (and many of which Bulmers had either developed itself or imported from France). In 1932 the company bought another 120 acres with 10,000 trees when the King's Acre Nurseries near Hereford came on the market. But that same year Professor Barker of Long Ashton was warning that another 30,000 acres needed to be planted to supply future needs, while by 1936 it was estimated that the acreage of cider and perry orchards in the western counties had actually fallen from 116,000 in 1894 to just 67,000. Early experiments with bush trees, which could be planted at 2-300 to the acre rather than the 40 per acre possible with standard trees, and which started cropping after five years rather than 10, offered a long-term solution to the supply chain. In the shorter term, intensive education and incentivisation of growers both by individual companies and by NACM, as well as practical financial support in the form of subsidies for seedlings and grants for spraying equipment, went some way towards alleviating the supply problem. Companies also invested more and more heavily in tankage, especially in the Swiss-made glass-lined concrete vats that were the forerunner of stainless steel, so that they could overproduce in hit years.

But the immediate reality was that even though overall production seemed stuck at 19-20,000,000 gallons a year for much of the interwar period (but dipping sharply towards the end of the 1930s) the bigger manufacturers' demand for the right varieties of apples was outstripping the growers' ability to satisfy it. Maintaining a constant supply of suitable fruit, therefore, inevitably meant importing – some from Canada, some from Spain, but mainly from the enormous orchards of Brittany and Normandy. The amounts imported fluctuated depending on the growing season at home, and in some years it was as little as 2,500 tons. But in bad years it could be many times more – 12,350 tons in 1931, and 19,100 tons in 1932. And it wasn't just apples that were being imported, either: imports of finished cider from France, nearly all of it for blending, topped 2,000,000 gallons in 1925 and 1932 when British crops failed. But carriage by sea was both expensive and chancy, and there was an import tax of 4/6 a gallon; so in the early 1930s significant amounts of apple concentrate were also imported, mainly from Canada. The total for 1932, a very bad year in British orchards, was 300,000 gallons. Thereafter, though, the total sank until 1939, when 100,000 gallons were imported as a precaution following the outbreak of war.

Much of the imported concentrate was only used for experimental purposes. It derived from cooking and eating varieties – "pot fruit" – which were rarely if ever used for cidermaking in the western counties: indeed, Bulmers had specifically warned growers against bring pot fruit to the mill, and even Gaymer's in Norfolk was by this time using West Country cider apples brought into its sidings at Attleborough by the trainload to supplement the culinary and dessert apples grown closer to home. And if the cidermakers were extremely cautious about what went into their cider, it was because they still saw themselves, even at this stage, as being primarily the inheritors of the old "fine cider" tradition that had so nearly died out in the preceding century, rather than suppliers of draught "rough cider" to the alehouse-frequenting working class. Bulmers didn't put a drop of its cider into cask until 1895, and at the end of World War I still only had a single cooper; and even Redvers Coate, who started out mainly by supplying local pubs, recanted. "I came to the conclusion that bottled cider was the thing of the future, and so it proved," he said. "To me, cider was something to be sold in the off-licences and shops rather than the pubs." (Quoted by Mark Foot, *Cider's Story Rough and Smooth*).

And here the old dichotomy between the fine bottled cider nosed and sipped by the gentry and the rough draught cider swilled by the peasantry, outlined in 1753 by Hugh Stafford, rears its head once more.

For many of the new wave of cidermakers in the last decade of the 19th century, private customers from large farms to stately homes had been their most important source of revenue. Much of this trade was draught – Stanley Baldwin, that great friend of the Bulmer family, had his private stock delivered in 20-gallon casks – but it had to be of the finest quality to satisfy the discerning palates of the gentry. To exploit the wider trade – the grocers, the wine merchants, the hotels, the railway refreshment rooms – these fine ciders had to be bottled, for they were competing not against beer but against wine. And in the early years of the 20th century, this trade seemed to offer the most promising direction. Close to home there was a lively pub trade to be serviced; but as Fred Bulmer had discovered, many in the licensed trade outside the cider-producing regions hadn't even heard of cider. And bottled ciders offered the same advantages that they had in the 18th century – greater portability and profit margins for the producer and distributor, less risk for the retailer, and a veneer of gentility for the bourgeois suburban customer.

In tackling the bourgeois market, *cachet* was all. The branding played sedulously to the petit bourgeois would-be wine snob: Bulmers' Pomagne had a host of imitators including some that might sound ridiculous to our ears, such as Avalagne from Clapp's of Baltonborough. Whiteways had an Apple Sauterne on its list. Gaymer's Sparkling Pommette was touted as having "somewhat of the character and flavour of a hock". And the celebrity endorsements were as blue-blooded as the cidermakers could get. Bulmers had its Royal Warrant as early as 1911. Gaymer's trumped it with two: one to the Royal Household in 1928 and one to the Prince of Wales in 1933. There were excited stories in the gossip columns (placed there by whom, one wonders?) of cider's new found favour in the most fashionable circles: in 1923 cider cup – a long cocktail of cider, brandy, orange curaçao, and maraschino, served cold and, like Pimm's, under an improbable top-hamper of sliced fruit – was said to be the *dernier cri* in West End cocktail and hotel bars; in June 1924 there was even greater excitement when the Daily Mirror reported that cider cup had been served at three royal occasions: two evening courts and a state ball.

This appeal to snobbery was certainly successful as far as it went, with cider sales increasing outside the producing regions as fast as they declined at home. But it was a limited appeal, and the truth is that while the larger cidermakers were growing, overall production was stagnant and much of the growth for Bulmers, Coate's and Whiteways came from cannibalisation in their home markets. What they needed if they were to continue their expansion outside the western counties was a more democratic product. At first this took the form of artificially carbonated brands for a brighter, longer-lasting, and cheaper bottled product. Once Bulmers had launched Bull Brand in 1919 the others soon followed suit, with Whiteways installing a German-made sterile filter at its new London depot and bottling hall in Vauxhall in 1924. Two years later Bulmers launched Woodpecker in two-pint bottles closed with an internally-threaded black vulcanised rubber screwcap sealed with a soft rubber washer: hardly chic, but an innovation that remained the industry's standard packaging format for over 40 years. The potential of carbonated bottled cider even attracted the attention of Schweppes, which bought three small cider farms – at Hele in Devon, Wear in Somerset, and Bledisloe in Gloucestershire – in 1923 and won a gold medal at the 1928 Brewers exhibition for its efforts.

But successful though these strategies were, the cider industry could not ignore the pub trade and its demand for draught "rough" cider altogether. Regional this demand may have been, low-margin it may have been, but it was on their doorsteps and it offered the opportunity, especially to the larger makers, to build substantial volumes very quickly and for a marketing spend much, much lower than the bottled trade demanded. And much of it was there for the taking: as farmers gradually went out of cidermaking, the local pubs (including hundreds of cider houses that sold no beer at all) they had previously serviced had to look elsewhere for their supplies.

These were lean times for country brewers, though. The mid-1920s saw the beginning of an agricultural depression that lasted until the outbreak of World War II, and many of them were in deep financial trouble. In response, they started adding cider to their lists of tied products in order to profit from the wholesale margin – which could be quite significant when in some West Country pubs cider outsold beer by a margin of 10:1. That action in itself squeezed out the smallest producers, who might have been able to supply one or two local pubs but couldn't meet the requirements of six or seven, and caused a great deal of anger among cidermakers. In 1928 the Daily Mail (quoted by Mark Foot, *Cider's Story Rough and Smooth*) reported: "Many are of the opinion that the tied house system will crush the farmer-cidermaker out of business." It quoted Henry Coles of Coles of Chardstock as saying: "We created the public demand for cider, and the public resents being deprived of that source." One victim was Broughton's of Littledean, frozen out when West Country Brewers tied its pubs to Bulmers. One WCB tenant was evicted for persisting in buying his cider out of tie, and the rest fell into line. Given the importance of the pub trade to local cidermakers, it is legitimate to ask why they never considered buying pubs of their own. One answer is that the pub trade itself was in a parlous condition at the time, with village populations decreasing, most rural workers existing in a state of extreme poverty, and local justices extinguishing licences they considered superfluous. Another is that the capital that would have been required simply wasn't available to those who needed it most – the smaller makers.

In fact only Weston's dipped its toe into pub ownership, and not in Herefordshire but in London, where it bought a pub in the Harrow Road and supplied a second in Wandsworth in the early 1930s. Forty years later, both suffered the same fate: compulsory purchase and demolition for road-widening. As for the more commercially-minded producers, they simply didn't need to, for the widespread imposition of the cider tie worked to their advantage. Vallance's Brewery of Sidmouth, for example, tied its pubs to Horrell's of Stoke Canon. This stood Horrell's in good stead when Vallance's was bought by Devenish of Weymouth: the trading arrangement continued until 1974 when Horrell's sold out to Devenish, which closed the factory 18 months later. Clapp's was supplying West Country breweries including Frome, George's of Bristol, Eldridge Pope of Blandford, and even Showering's as well as breweries in Birmingham and Cardiff as early as 1916, while Burnett Champney of Theale supplied Holt's Brewery of Burnham until the 1950s. Other producers successful in the pub trade included Wickwar Cider, set up in 1924 by a consortium of growers in the old Arnold & Perrett Brewery in Wickwar – which had just been bought by Cheltenham Brewery – with a contract to supply Cheltenham's pubs; Brake's of Nailsea, which supplied 64 pubs in and around Bristol; and, surprisingly, Schweppes. Schweppes had decided to close its cider operation in the early 1930s citing the squeeze on outlets caused by the imposition of the tie. Yet when it sold its Hele plant to Whiteways for £16,000 in 1934, a contract to supply Starkey Knight & Ford of Bridgewater's tied estate in Devon and Somerset was part of the deal.

That same year Whiteways took a pioneering step when it decided to access investment capital with a £350,000 stock market float. Buying out Schweppes' cider interests was the first fruit of the flotation; later that year Whiteways bought Hunt's of Paignton from its owner, Simond's Brewery of Reading, for £34,000. The acquisition came with a contract to supply the Simonds estate, which covered the south of England from Devonport to London, for seven years; and Hunt's had also supplied Hall & Woodhouse, Strong's, Usher's, Ind Coope, and Whitbread, as well as prestigious London outlets including the Savoy, Claridge's, and the Berkeley hotels and Simpson's Restaurant in the Strand. Glamorous these hotel accounts may have been; but in the boardroom at Whimple there was no doubt as to which were more important. For Simond's was expanding fast, buying Rogers of Bristol in 1935, Cirencester Brewery in 1937, Lakeman's of Brixham and Style's of Bridgend in 1938, and Marsh & Sons of Blandford Forum in 1939; and whither Simond's went, there too went Whiteways. It must have seemed like a magic carpet ride.

Securing supply deals with large brewery tied estates offered the big cidermakers a springboard out of their traditional heartlands and towards the truly national distribution that had always been their aim; and it seemed by the late 1930s that draught "rough" cider and not bottled "fine" cider was, after all, the way ahead. But as war loomed there was still a long way to go. Overall national output was still stagnant at around 20,000,000 gallons, and cider's profile beyond its traditional markets was still low. In 1938 Mass Observation conducted a comprehensive and exhaustively detailed survey of the pubs of Bolton – their locations, styles of trading, customer bases, and product ranges – that was published in 1941 under the title *The Pub and the People*, with Bolton disguised as "Worktown".

It doesn't contain a single mention of cider.

10: The Brewers' Coat-Tails

With memories of World War I still fresh in their minds, the cidermakers were not taken by surprise by the restrictions imposed on production following the outbreak of World War II. There were, of course, some unwelcome novelties. Petrol rationing was one: in the 1930s Bulmers, Gaymer's, Whiteways and the rest had become gradually more dependent on road haulage, and their sales representatives travelled the country by car. These activities had to be sharply curtailed, especially as many lorries were requisitioned for military use. Bulmers sold its orchards at Broxwood and planted more trees at King's Acre, which was closer to Hereford; it also bought a local haulage firm purely for its petrol allocation.

Another was the total disappearance of imported fruit. Supplies of cider fruit from Normandy and Brittany, available during World War I, were cut off after the 1939 harvest. Apples were still grown in huge quantities in Canada, but there was not the shipping to carry them. The 63,000 acres of cider orchards in England and Wales were unable to supply enough fruit, especially in poor years such as 1945, and cidermakers had to stoop to using windfalls and pot fruit. Sugar, increasingly used to equalise the fermentable content of the juice from harvest to harvest and thus maintain the consistency of national brands, was also in short supply, especially as so much was required for jam-making, and cidermakers were rationed to a shrinking percentage of average prewar consumption. (Jam was regarded as a wartime essential, much to Bulmers' advantage. The company had started making pectin out of its spent pomace before the war, and production rose from 970 tons in 1940 to 3,400 tons in 1945). The availability of glass, too, was limited, especially damaging to an industry that still depended heavily on sales in bottle: refundable deposits were introduced to ensure the return of as many flagons and bottles as possible. More problematic was the supply of stoppers and washers, which did not always come back with the bottles. Bulmers was reduced to placing press advertisements almost pleading for their return, using the slogan: "You Can Replace The Stopper, We Can't".

Other exigencies were more familiar, especially the shortage of labour. Typically some 20-25% of the workforces of the larger factories were called up, and although farmers and farm labourers were exempt from conscription, the seasonal labourers they depended on to pick and press the crop were not. Office staff, refugees, and later on prisoners of war were drafted in to help with the picking, and Whiteways urged its growers to repair their old mills and presses and deliver juice to its factories rather than fruit. These shifts, though, were never enough and inevitably fruit prices rose until in 1941 the Government had to fix a maximum of £18 a ton. It fell to £14 in 1943, which was a great relief but still a sharp contrast to the average £4 a ton paid in the 1930s. At least there was no attempt this time round to charge duty on cider – much to the disgust of the brewers, who saw beer duty rise from £4 to £14 per standard barrel in 1943.

Under the circumstances, cider production held up remarkably well. In 1940 Whiteways produced 3,300,000 gallons. This fell to 1,800,000 gallons in 1941 but rallied to 2,300,000 gallons in 1945. The same figures for Bulmers were 5,200,000 gallons, 3,700,000 gallons, and 5,100,000 gallons. A zoning system introduced in 1944 to reduce wasteful competition undoubtedly helped the national cider companies regain lost ground and expand their footholds outside their home territories: Gaymer's got Scotland and Eastern England; Bulmers got the Midlands, Wales, and the North-West; and Whiteways got the south and south-west. Customer swaps were organised by the National Association of Cider Makers. The system only lasted until 1946, but it had the effect of squeezing smaller players including Weston's, Coate's, and, for the time being at least, Taunton out of the wider national market.

If, in 1945, the cidermakers had expected business to return to normal as quickly as it had done after World War I, they were in for a cruel surprise. The labour shortage might have eased, but rationing and shortages persisted for years as Britain struggled to pay off its war debts and build new homes for hundreds of thousands of bombed-out families. Sugar and glass remained in short supply, and petrol was rationed until 1953. In the factories, worn-out parts were hard to replace and building materials – even for repairs, let alone for expansion – could only be obtained by negotiating with the relevant ministry. Only a run of poor harvests persuaded the Government to allow apples to be imported free of tax again from 1948 – a critical year, as it turned out, for relations between the manufacturers and their contract growers.

The price per ton had been set by the Government at £14 for 1943-46 and with the end of emergency controls in sight the growers, represented by the National Farmers' Union, were not unnaturally anxious to maintain the wartime price. NACM, however, sought to reduce it to £10. The NFU threatened to boycott the cider industry and grub up members' orchards, for which Government subsidies were available. In 1948 NACM agreed to maintain the wartime price, but for one year only. But the growers' bargaining position was fatally undermined that same year by the lifting of price controls and the ending of tax on imports. Bulmers promptly bought 3,500 tons of French apples, 400,000 gallons of concentrate, and 1.1 million gallons of French cider "for blending"; enough, in fact, for the company to do without English apples entirely at a pinch. The fact that Bulmers was prepared to pay £19 a ton for its French apples and that it imported no more fruit until 1953 and no more concentrate until 1956 indicates that it didn't actually need these supplies (as Patrick Wilkinson suggests in his company history), especially as the 1949 harvest turned out to be a better one, but that they were brought in to defeat the growers. The growers capitulated, and in 1952 the price was duly set at £10 – or £12 delivered, which saved the cidermakers precious petrol. This price remained stable throughout the 1950s and well into the 1960s.

As a result of all these various difficulties, investment in plant and orchards was slow to pick up again and production remained flat for the remainder of the 1940s. The only immediate opportunity for growth lay in an aggressive policy of takeovers such as Whiteways had pursued in the 1930s, but capital was limited and only Bulmers was positioned to make significant acquisitions in the late 1940s. In 1946 it completed the purchase of Magner's of Clonmel in the Republic of Ireland, in which it had bought a 50% stake nine years previously. To satisfy Irish law Magner's had to be run by a citizen of the Republic, so Bulmers took on a local businessman called Thomas Jackson. In the mid-1950s Jackson bought the company from

Bulmers for a mere £27,000 but kept the Irish rights to the Bulmer name, which has been the cause of much confusion since – especially as Jackson later sold out to C&C, a consortium that included Allied Breweries. Allied by that time owned Showering's, so the Irish rights to the Bulmer name belonged to one of its deadliest competitors, a state of affairs that raised few smiles in Hereford.

Then in 1948 Bulmers bought Godwin's of Holmer – not, as is often said, in the hope that Golden Godwin perry might compete with Showering's Babycham, which wasn't even launched until 1953, but simply for its goodwill, its contract growers, its petrol and sugar rations, and its production capacity. This last was important at a time when accessing building materials was a bureaucratic nightmare. The almost continuous process of expansion and modernisation at Bulmers' Hereford site had stalled, and the Godwin's factory remained in production until 1960 when it was downgraded to storage depot.

As postwar restrictions on domestic consumption gradually eased, production returned to growth – a process heralded by bumper crops in 1950, 1951, and 1953. But developing a national market was still a problem for the cidermakers. All of them except Whiteways were still private companies, with limited access to investment capital unless they were prepared to borrow heavily. Nor were any of them particularly big: Bulmers' 1945 output of 5,100,000 gallons equated to about 140,000 brewer's barrels, which in comparison to the larger breweries did not put the company in the first rank. The route to expansion that had been embarked upon in the 1930s was buying market share through the acquisition of mid-ranking producers, and thereby piggy-backing on the growing tied estates of the bigger breweries. Bulmers was first to restart this process with the acquisitions of Magner's and Godwin's, but once the economic recovery of the 1950s had got under way it was Showering's that set the pace.

Before the war, Showering's had been a small family-owned brewer and cidermaker based in Shepton Mallet, Somerset, owning a handful of pubs. In the lean years after the war dozens of such small country brewers sold up: two world wars and the Great Depression meant that for over 30 years they had been unable to invest in their brewing plant and tied estates, which in many cases were near-derelict. Showering's was made of sterner stuff, partly because one of the four brothers who then ran the company, Francis Showering, had a plan. In the 1930s he had formulated a "champagne perry", as indeed had many other cidermakers. "Champagne de la Pomme", as it was rather misleadingly called, won several medals and built up a strong regional following in the years immediately after the war; but it wasn't until 1953 that the company decided to exit brewing altogether and launch its champagne perry nationally with a new name – the racier, more modern "Babycham" – and a revolutionary single-serve bottle. Aimed fair and square at women as something more up-to-date and glamorous than the bottled Guinness or port and lemon which, according to *The Pub and the People*, had been the staples of female pubgoers in the 1930s, it was perfect for the zeitgeist and was an instant hit. In 1954 supplies actually ran out, and Showering's had to lay in two years' worth of juice and plant 3,000 acres of perry pear orchards to ensure it could meet future demand – demand that was stoked by intensive advertising on Radio Luxembourg, in cinemas, and, from 1957, ITV (it was the first alcoholic drink to be advertised on British television). All these media were consumed mainly by the younger half of the demographic; and given that Babycham was a "solus" or standalone brand like Guinness, there was no problem getting distribution through brewery tied houses. And by being first into the market, Babycham was able to beat off not one but four challenges from its much bigger competitor. Bulmers' first attempt was the subject of a legal action by Showering's in which the Hereford company claimed that the name "Chamlet" did not infringe Showering's chamois trademark but was an obsolete word meaning coarse silk. The court didn't buy it (especially as the obsolete word in question was actually "camlet"), so Bulmers instead attempted to launch Godwin's existing sparkling perry as an alternative under the name Golden Godwin. In the words of Patrick Wilkinson, Golden Godwin "proved short-lived", as did the third bid to enter the single-serve market, Limelight, a lime-flavoured version launched in 1960 and withdrawn soon after. Baby Pom, Pomagne packaged in single-serve bottles, fared little better. Showering's in its later manifestations went on to dominate the single-serve market with brands including Pony, a pale cream British sherry originally a Whiteways product, and Snowball, an advocaat-based cocktail originally made by another company in the group, Goldwell of East Malling, Kent.

With only a single, albeit stellar, brand in its portfolio at this stage, Showering's needed both to diversify and to find more production capacity, and by 1956 was ready to make an acquisition. Coate's was an obvious target. A comparative latecomer, it boasted a well-equipped and modern factory on a 13-acre site at Nailsea just outside Bristol and strong local distribution, but had never grown to join the first rank of cider producers. Its agreed acquisition in March 1956 was followed within a few months by the purchase of Magna Cider of Marston Magna near Yeovil, a much older-established firm with its own orchards. Redvers Coate became managing director of the new group, and production was swiftly rationalised. The Shepton Mallet site was given over entirely to Babycham; Nailsea made the cider; and Magna was converted into a winery and the home of Cherry B – another brand, like Babycham, packaged in single-serve bottles and aimed at women. Showering's was now able to propel Coate's cider towards national brand status using its distribution channels and marketing muscle, but once again finance was a constraint and in 1959, only six years after the launch of its star product, the little Somerset brewery went public with a £1.5 million share issue.

The late 1950s and early '60s saw a frenzy of mergers and acquisition that was to shape the brewing industry for the next 30 years. Larger brewers had been swallowing up smaller competitors since the Depression, but the process of creating genuinely national combines started in earnest with the merger of Courage and Barclay Perkins in 1955. This was followed by the merger of Watney Combe Reid and Mann Crossman & Paulin in 1959 (helped along by the 1958 Budget's reduction in beer duty, a historic first), while 1960 turned out to be a truly momentous year. Courage Barclay Perkins bought Simond's of Reading; Scottish Brewers and Newcastle Breweries merged to form Scottish & Newcastle; and in two great coups United Breweries was formed first by the merger of Hope & Anchor, John Jeffreys, and Hammond United in February, and then by the acquisition of five more breweries in Scotland, one in Northern Ireland, and one in Wales in October. United merged with Charrington's in 1962 to form Charrington United and with Bass Mitchells and Butler's in 1967 to form Bass Charrington, which remained Britain's biggest brewer until the 1990s. Meanwhile Allied Breweries had been created in 1961 by the merger of Ind Coope, Tetley Walker, and Ansells, while Whitbread merged with Flowers in 1962.

None of this activity escaped the notice of the cider industry, for which 1961 was almost as big a year as 1960 had been for the brewers. The big cidermakers had just the same ambitions as the big brewers, and also saw consolidation as the quickest way to establish corporations with the production, distribution, and marketing clout to step up to the national plate. In June, the merger was announced of Showering's, the comparative newcomer, and Gaymer's, the pioneer of the modern cider industry. The new combine almost rivalled Bulmers, with a share capital of nearly £10 million; national brands in the form of Babycham and Gaymer's Olde English (originally intended in 1939 for the American market, a plan stalled by the outbreak of war, and launched in the home market immediately after hostilities ended); a secondary national brand in Coate's Triple Vintage; and a growing presence in the British-made wine market, which was recovering from the impact of must shortages and stratospheric duty increases during and after the war. Immediately after the merger, a series of talks began at the Great Western Hotel, Paddington, between Francis Showering, Ronald Henley of Whiteways, and ADW Hunter of Surrey-based Vine Products, the biggest producer of British wines. The talks progressed with astonishing rapidity and on 12 September the formation of the awkwardly-named new combine, Showering's Vine Products & Whiteways, worth £20 million, was announced to the press.

Bulmers, meanwhile, had not been letting the grass grow, although its expansion plan was less ambitious than those of Showering's or Whiteways since it was still a private company and had a prudent aversion to borrowing. Acquisitions therefore had to be financed from revenue, and only then once the competing demands of expanding and modernising the Hereford factory and acquiring more orchards had been satisfied. Nevertheless, in 1959 it seized an opportunity to buy the goodwill (along with the locally very popular GL brand) of the Gloucestershire Cider Company, based in the old Arnold & Perrett works at Wickwar and put up for sale by its owner, the Cheltenham Brewery. This was part of a complicated deal that saw the merger of Cheltenham with the Stroud Brewery to form West Country Breweries, in which Whitbread also took a stake. Cheltenham had previously bought breweries in Hereford and Tredegar, so the new combine had an estate of over 1,200 pubs stretching from South Wales to the West Midlands; and thanks to its takeover of Gloucestershire Cider, Bulmers was now listed in all of them. The Hereford company also gained a toehold in Somerset and Devon, since Gloucestershire Cider had earlier acquired Creed Valley Cider. It was a devastating blow to Weston's, though, whose listing with the 600-strong Stroud tied estate represented a third of all sales which disappeared literally overnight. Fortunately for lovers of traditional cider

Weston's was able to recover by changing tack completely, more or less abandoning the race for mass distribution through brewery tied estates and concentrating on making high-quality natural ciders mainly for the grocery trade. Later, after the big cidermakers had gone over to mass-produced keg brands made with high proportions of concentrate, Weston's became virtually the only standard-bearer for the traditional product with any sort of national presence. For Bulmers, however, the deal led on to greater things – in 1963 WCB was bought by Whitbread, which started listing Bulmers brands in its 6,000-strong national tied estate.

In 1960 Bulmers was able to buy the goodwill of William Evans of Hereford from Webb's of Aberbeeg. Webb's was the Welsh brewery bought by Northern United in its second phase of acquisitions that year, and as a result Bulmers gained distribution, for the time being at least, in a further 88 South Welsh pubs. Another advantage of the purchase was that William Evans was Bulmers' only serious rival in the pectin business, which was rapidly expanding beyond the ability of the cider industry to supply it. Bulmers now had to look further afield for sources of pectin and ended up buying supplies of discarded citrus peel first from Rose's, of lime cordial fame, and then from Schweppes. Evans's pectin and cider plants were immediately closed, and production was transferred to the ever-swelling Bulmers site.

Taken one by one, Bulmers' acquisitions in the 1960s were modest – certainly nothing like as headline-grabbing as the creation of Showering's Vine Products & Whiteways. From 1962 it cautiously built up a small tied estate, starting with the historic Red Lion in the picturesque Herefordshire village of Weobley and followed by the Maesllwch Arms at Glasbury, the Cider House at Wootton, Shropshire, the Blue Bell at Hockley, Warwickshire (where Bulmers closed one of the country's last pub breweries), the Stag's Head at Watford Gap, the Hempstall Cider House at Stourport, the Ram at Godalming, the Swan at Abergavenny, and the Lord Nelson at Pontlottyn. This, however, turned out to be a dead end and eventually all the pubs were sold. More important was the purchase of Tewkesbury Cider in 1965, which brought with it a supply deal with Ansell's (by now part of Allied).

But climbing on the backs of the fledgling brewing behemoths implied acceptance of a certain loss of control, as Weston's had found when it lost the Stroud Brewery business and as Bulmers was also to discover more than once. For it was one thing for ambitious breweries to seek scale by acquisition and merger, and quite another to fit all the pieces together in a way that worked; and in the processes that followed the creation of the national giants their suppliers, including cidermakers, were among those who found they had no voice. Two momentous developments in the 1960s forcibly reminded the cidermakers that they were only passengers on the big brewers' voyage of discovery, and if decisions take in the brewery boardrooms worked against them there wasn't much they could do about it.

The brewers – by now the Big Six, which were to dominate the pub trade so completely that it was to take a Monopolies & Mergers Commission investigation to break their stranglehold – not unnaturally wanted as much control over their suppliers as possible, and also wanted to add the margin that their suppliers made to their own bottom lines. Even before the war brewers had been taking over cidermakers, and in the early 1960s Courage, whose tied estate had just been massively swollen in the south and south-west by the acquisition of Simonds of Reading, pursued the same logic by buying a stake in Taunton Cider. In a rare example of competing brewers working together, Courage, Guinness, Scottish & Newcastle and Bass M&B had joined forces in 1961 to create what came to be known as the Harp Consortium, building a brewery at Alton in Hampshire to produce Harp lager and launching the brand through their own estates and those of regional brewers including Greenall Whitley and Greene King in 1964. Much the same cast – excluding Guinness but including Watney Mann, although Watney's left the consortium and Guinness briefly joined it only a few years later – then came together to buy Taunton Cider outright. Taunton had been quietly growing since the war, acquiring a number of smaller local competitors including Brutton's, Horrell's, Ashford Vale and Quantock Vale and building distribution in its West Country heartland, but like Coate's had never broken into the first rank of national cidermakers. However it had the production capacity and the efficiency to satisfy the requirements of the consortium – and that meant that Bulmers was frozen out of the small tied estate of Webb's (now part of Bass Charrington), while Showering's suffered the same fate in the much larger estate of Simond's (now part of Courage). It also meant that Taunton Dry Blackthorn started to eclipse Gaymer's Olde English as a national brand, with production at the Norton Fitzwarren factory climbing to 4,700,000 gallons, or more than 130,000 brewer's barrels, by 1970.

Bulmers' main avenue of on-trade distribution was now with Whitbread, which gave it access to some 6,000 tied houses and an even larger tranche of free trade accounts, including a huge number of working men's clubs and miners' welfares in South Wales, and, thanks to the Tewkesbury Cider acquisition, with Ansells. But on 20 May 1968, Allied Breweries (Ansells' parent company) and Showering's Vine Products & Whiteways "merged". Effectively it was an agreed takeover; but as Keith, Francis, Herbert and Ralph Showering all joined the board of Allied, it could be made to look like a cosy arrangement between equals. For Bulmers it meant a significant loss of distribution. But only three years later the mad merry-go-round of brewery mergers and acquisitions turned full circle once again when Grand Metropolitan, a giant hotel group which already had a supply arrangement with Bulmers, took over Watney Mann. Watney's, as we have seen, promptly sold out of the Taunton Consortium and turned to Bulmers instead, giving Bulmers access to over 12,000 pubs and, almost overnight, a national market share of 60%.

If the journey to national distribution on the coat-tails of the Big Six brewers could be an uncomfortable one at times, it worked. Annual output, having been stagnant at the prewar level of around 20,000,000 gallons throughout the 1950s, climbed steadily in the '60s as pub customers all over the country got used to the presence of cider in their locals and as the number of supermarkets soared, spurred by the relaxation of off-licensing in the 1964 Licensing Act. In 1970 production passed 30,000,000 million gallons (or over 800,000 brewer's barrels), of which Bulmers alone produced 20,000,000. Remarkably, the company had funded this growth entirely through retained profits, neither borrowing nor issuing shares outside the family. But retained profits also had to fund the continual processes of expanding and modernising its now huge factory, marketing new brands – its 1967 advertising spend was almost £500,000, a titanic sum in those days – acquiring new businesses, and buying more farms and orchards. Clearly its resources were spread far too thin, and the crisis which prompted the company finally to go public was a big tax bill following the deaths, both in 1968, of the two family matriarchs, Percy's widow Mildred and Fred's widow Sophie (Fred himself had died in 1941). It was floated in December 1970 with a share issue valued at over £3 million, but with 65% of the shares remaining in family hands.

At this stage, most cider sold outside the traditional producing counties was still bottled, in a wide range of formats ranging from single-serve to gallon flagons including, since 1959, cans. Draught cider was mainly still rather than sparkling – although Bulmers' Traditional was dosed with a little yeast and sugar to create a light fret – and was still filled into coopered oak barrels. Spin-off products alongside Babycham and its various siblings and imitators included Whiteways' non-alcoholic Cydrax and Peardrax and, between 1955 and 1961 a competitor from Bulmers, Cidona. The big firms sought to diversify not only their ranges of products, though, but also their spheres of operation. Whiteways had ventured beyond cider production as early as the 1920s, when it started making ginger wine to keep its plant busy year-round. It had then expanded into producing British port and British sherry from imported grape concentrate, and in 1939 had also started producing Sanatogen, a "tonic wine" made by mixing a patent "nerve tonic" (basically sodium glycerophosphate, a form of sugar that can be metabolised very quickly to produce a sudden burst of energy, and iron) with sweet British wine. The 1960 merger with Vine Products made it by far the country's biggest maker of these cheap and cheerful products.

Bulmers took a very different course, buying three reputable wine shippers – H Parrott, Dent & Reuss, and Findlater Mackie Todd – between 1964 and 1968. These acquisitions gave it a portfolio of agencies that included Fonseca port, PF Heering liqueurs, Pol Roger champagne, Hine cognac, Findlater's sherries, and Dry Fly South African sherry. This side of the business continued to expand into the 1980s, when Bulmers also became UK distributor of Red Stripe lager from Jamaica, Perrier sparkling mineral water, and a French soft drink, Orangina, among other brands. It also took a fateful step in 1968 when David Bulmer was despatched to Australia to found a subsidiary there: a factory capable of producing 250,000 gallons a year from English concentrate was opened in late 1969 and the product was launched during a fortuitous heatwave in January 1970 in a country where, according to Patrick Wilkinson, "most people did not even know cider was an alcoholic drink".

The most important newcomer to the Bulmers family, though, was Strongbow, launched in 1960 in response to the public perception revealed by consumer surveys that sweet ciders such as Woodpecker were drinks for women and children. Strongbow was drier and was aimed with great success at males aged 18-26, early fans (says Wilkinson) including "branches of what were later to call themselves Hell's Angels". Another consumer survey conducted 10 years later led to a very major step indeed: lager was identified as cider's chief rival, and shortly after that Strongbow joined the keg revolution.

This, a traditional cider purist would say, was where the rot set in – where "real" farmhouse cider was displaced by a mass-produced "industrial" version. Arguments over quality are, of course, subjective. Nevertheless the introduction of the pasteurised, filtered, and carbonated keg product does mark a key moment in the evolution of cider: it was the moment when the big cidermakers abandoned their position as inheritors of a tradition of "fine cider" – cider as wine, which technically it is – and adopted instead a modern interpretation of "rough cider" – cider as beer, which it isn't. But in truth there had already been milestones along the way. Pomagne had ceased to be made by the *méthode champenoise* in the 1950s and was now artificially carbonated: the court case in which champagne houses successfully contested the use or indeed suggestion of the word "champagne" on any product but theirs merely wrote the epitaph for a fine cider tradition that was already dead. Most manufacturers were now only producing a single standard fermentation, boosted up to 10% ABV or more by the use of corn sugar and then diluted, sweetened, and coloured as required to produce different brands (although at this stage even the bigger makers still produced smaller special fermentations for particular minority brands such as Pomagne and Bulmers No 7). And since that first experimental dalliance with concentrate in the 1930s its use had become commonplace: in 1962 Bulmers had built an evaporator capable of concentrating a million gallons of fresh juice during the pressing season. This was a commonsense step rather than a cynical one: any large manufacturer that depends on vintage raw materials needs to find a way of storing them so that they can be processed throughout the year rather than in one great autumnal burst. Bulmers had invested a fortune in the 1950s and '60s in a forest of 550,000-gallon fresh juice storage tanks: if it had not found a way, as output grew, of condensing its main ingredient it would have had to turn the whole of Hereford into one vast tank farm.

Whatever consequences for the nature of the product might have arisen from these changes, the identification of cider as a draught long drink competing for the same market as lager had a transforming effect on sales. The 1970s was a peak period for British brewing, with annual production rising from 36,000,000 barrels in 1970 to 44,000,000 million barrels in 1979; and now that the cider industry was almost completely integrated into the brewing industry it shared in the latter's success. Access to genuinely national distribution chains meant that keg fonts marked Woodpecker, Strongbow, Olde English or Dry Blackthorn were installed in pretty well every pub in the land, while packaged versions appeared in every supermarket. And cider had two advantages over lager that helped boost its sales to an average annual growth rate of 13% – it was much more alcoholic, and it was not liable to excise duty. In the first half of the 1970s annual cider production rose quite spectacularly from 30,000,000 gallons to 44,000,000 gallons – or, as we must now say, 2,000,000 hectolitres (or 1,250,000 barrels).

Then came financial emergency, with the IMF riding to Britain's rescue; and in September 1976 Chancellor Dennis Healey imposed excise duty on cider for the first time in over 50 years. The growth which cider had enjoyed for more than 10 years went into reverse.

But although this was the first time excise duty had been charged since the 1920s, it was not the first time cider had been taxed in the postwar period. In 1956, at the instigation of the Brewers Society, cider of 8.5% ABV and above was defined for excise purposes as wine. In 1962, cider and soft drinks were made liable for purchase tax at 15%, increased to 20% a couple of years later. The replacement of purchase tax by VAT at 10% in 1973 actually gave the cidermakers a brief respite – although when duty was reintroduced VAT was charged on top of it. On the other hand, Mr Healey's cider duty was a mere £8 a barrel for a drink of anything up to 8.4% ABV, whereas session-strength beer was dutiable at £20 a barrel and strong beer was charged far more. The duty was followed by a dip in sales that lasted until 1978; but the new-found popularity of keg cider as a rival to lager, coupled with some heroic advertising spends, ensured that in 1979, a record year for beer production, cider sales picked up as well, to 2,500,000 hectolitres, 48,000,000 gallons, or 1,500,000 barrels. A second sales dip followed in 1980, but growth resumed in 1981 and continued until 1984, when it a cash-strapped Nigel Lawson imposed a stunning 47% duty increase.

The effects were dramatic and immediate. Cider went from cheap to expensive overnight, and national sales went into a 2% annual decline that lasted for five years. Bulmers, without the cushion of brewery ownership enjoyed by Taunton and Showering's, was forced to lay off 400 staff as profits fell. Fortunately for the company's independence its main agency brands, Perrier and Red Stripe, had both entered their respective markets at exactly the right time and were performing strongly. But it wasn't until marketing director John Rudgard – the man responsible for the successful positioning of Strongbow as a male drink and for the strategic decision that the lager market was now cider's market too – was appointed chief executive in 1989 that firm action was taken. Rudgard, with the support of chairman Esmond Bulmer, doubled the company's marketing spend to £16,000,000 at a stroke. As in the late '70s, TV advertising turned the situation round: the industry returned to growth, and Bulmers' profits and share price recovered.

It's very noticeable, from the production graph produced by NACM, that two of the steepest growth spurts since 1976 have occurred during the recessions of the early 1980s and '90s, and that the post-2008 recession has had no impact on robustly positive growth. This may well be a result of the way duty was reintroduced in 1976. The temporary impact on national production notwithstanding, three concessions from 1976 stood out for their longer-term implications. The first was that production and sale of up to 1,500 gallons or 7,000 litres a year was (and remains) duty-exempt, principally to placate the remaining cidermaking farmers in the West Country to whom "farm gate" sales to tourists were still a considerable source of income. The second was that duty was charged at a very much lower rate than the duty on beer, reflecting the overhead involved in planting and maintaining orchards – an overhead not shared by the brewing industry. The third was that the duty was assessed – unlike that on beer – without regard to alcoholic content, so that a cider of 7.5% ABV was charged exactly the same duty as a cider of more modest strength.

The cidermakers were rather slow to catch on to opportunity presented by the last of these three concessions. But in 1986, inspired by the success of premium bottled beers whose market was being ignited by fashionable imported lagers such as Red Stripe, Tiger, and Singha and by the cloudy Belgian wheat beer, Hoegaarden, then just beginning its phenomenal and counterintuitive period of vogue, Taunton launched a new kind of strong cider. Diamond White was carbon-filtered to remove all trace of colour and, although it was bottled at 7.5% ABV, occupied the same price point as the fancy small-pack lagers. Heavily promoted and aimed principally at the pub trade, it soon became the brand-leading small pack cider and was widely imitated by other makers both large and small. Gaymer's K was even stronger at the maximum permitted alcohol content of 8.4%; and while these brands were originally aimed at the premium end of the market and were never intended to attract under-aged and problem drinkers, their successors eventually did – of which more in the following chapter.

By the end of the 1980s, then, the cider industry was firmly embedded within and consciously modelled itself on the brewing industry. Taunton and Showering's were actually owned by brewers, and Bulmers, although on paper still independent, was in reality dependent on Whitbread and Grand Met for almost its entire on-trade distribution. So when, after many false starts, the Monopolies & Mergers Commission finally decided to look into the "complex monopoly" exerted by the Big Six national brewers on the supply of beer, its enquiries inevitably embraced the cider industry as well.

11: Boom and Bust

In 1988, just as it was completing what was to be almost its last major acquisition in the UK – that of Symonds of Stoke Lacey, Herefordshire, from Warrington brewer Greenall Whitley – Bulmers was compiling its evidence to the Monopolies & Mergers Commission's inquiry into the supply of beer.

The two events were closely related. In its evidence to the inquiry Bulmers explained that it wanted to buy Symonds partly to gain distribution throughout the Greenall's estate of more than 1,200 pubs, many of them in Bulmers' West Midlands home territory. Before Greenall's had acquired Symonds in 1984, Bulmers had supplied its pubs. Now Greenall's had decided to rein back its diversification strategy – it also owned De Vere hotels – and focus on its core business of brewing, distilling, and retail. Bulmers seized the opportunity not only to acquire a newly rebuilt and re-equipped factory, a strong heritage, and some potentially useful brands (especially Scrumpy Jack, which had been launched in 1973, was on sale in 800 pubs in 1988, and grew to 13,000 accounts by 1993), but also "to re-establish access for its ciders... and... soft drink brands to the large Greenall Whitley tied estate".

Bulmers' evidence to the inquiry and the ripostes of the brewers and brewery-owned cidermakers provide an extremely rare glimpse behind the scenes which is worth recording at some length: after all, large companies are not often called upon to state publicly what they really think of each other, and the tensions revealed by the inquiry clearly ran very deep. In its summary of evidence, the MMC reported:

7.2. Bulmers stated that in its view the present ownership and control of on-licenced and off-licensed premises was detrimental to its business. The detrimental effects stemmed from:

(a) the progressive concentration of ownership of licensed retail outlets, both on- and off-trade, in the hands of a limited number of brewers;

(b) the vertical integration of those outlets with manufacturing and wholesale interests in beer and other drinks;

(d) exclusive purchasing policies pursued by the brewers through the managed and tenanted on-trade and through loans to the nominally free on-trade; and

(e) price discrimination against cider in the on-trade and against Bulmers' products in that part of the off-trade owned by some major brewers.

7.5. Bulmers considered that the difficulties created by the lack of any effective regulatory action had been compounded by the continuing concentration of power in the hands of the big six brewing companies as a result of takeovers and mergers. In Bulmers' view the takeover of smaller brewers by the four of the big six brewers with their own cider interests ... had resulted in Bulmers' ciders being systematically and in many instances rapidly excluded from large numbers of public houses in which they were formerly stocked.

7.6. Bulmers considered that the fall in its market share was principally due to the longer-term effects of the brewery mergers and, in particular, to the constraint which the tied-house system placed on Bulmers' ability to increase its representation in the extremely important keg cider market, which represented 75% of all cider sold in the on-trade and which provided much of the cider industry's growth in the early 1980s.

7.7. Bulmers considered that it was particularly affected by the regional concentration of public house ownership and contractual power through the tie. For example, mainly as a result of their ownership of Ansells and Mitchells & Butlers respectively, Allied and Bass now controlled 53% of the managed and tenanted public houses in the Midlands (Central Television area). Yet Bulmers' ciders were largely excluded from the Allied and Bass estates.

7.9. Bulmers considered that the concentration in ownership had also meant that it was faced with a concentration of buying power in the hands of a limited number of companies which to a significant extent controlled Bulmers' access to the on-licensed consumer. Bulmers had little or no access to the Allied or Greenall Whitley estates or to the estates of most of the shareholders in Taunton. According to Bulmers, this meant that over half the brewer-owned public houses in Great Britain – and an even greater proportion by value of sales – were effectively closed to it.

7.10. Bulmers believed that tied loans to the free trade severely restricted its ability to achieve higher levels of distribution for its existing products, and were an additional barrier to the launch of new products. Thus, they were detrimental to competition.

7.16. Bulmers gave us the following (non-exhaustive) list *(22 in all)* showing those brewers which were acquired by or merged with Allied, Bass, Courage or Greenall Whitley between 1960 and the present day. It said that in each case Bulmers' ciders were strongly represented in the public houses of the acquired company prior to the acquisition but the position now was that Bulmers had no effective presence in any of those public houses.

The overall impression given by Bulmers' evidence is of an extremely ambitious company that felt itself held back by the very system that had given it privileged access, through its links with Whitbread, Grand Met, Greenall Whitley and a number of smaller brewers, to a third of Britain's pubs and clubs, and a national market share of around 60%. It claimed that unlike the tied supply deals of Allied and the breweries comprising the Taunton consortium, its arrangements with Whitbread and the rest were not formally exclusive (although how true this was in reality is a moot point); and it produced figures to show that wherever its brands were able to compete freely with those of its rivals it always outperformed them. It seems to have struck a chord, because in its final report the MMC recommended that the cider tie should be abolished in the national breweries' leased estates; and this was one of the recommendations that actually survived the two-year political process that led to the 1990 Beer Orders. At the time this provision was not much commented on, so attention-grabbing were the other clauses in the Beer Orders; but it led to the radical and almost immediate restructuring of the entire cider industry.

One of the drawbacks of the tied house system was that it acted as a drag on ambition, which is perhaps one reason why British brewers have traditionally neglected the export markets. An estate of 6-7,000 pubs is a very comfortable cushion, and while Allied and the Taunton consortium were very active at marketing their beer brands, they had rather taken cider for granted, perhaps seeing it more as a commodity market than a branded one. It was part of the genius of Bulmers, and John Rudgard in particular, that it identified the supermarket trade as the key battleground early on and poured resources into dominating it; but marketing on this scale was no part of the plan for Allied or the Taunton consortium. Bulmers' evidence to the MMC suggests that the brewers artificially boosted the wholesale price of cider to their tied tenants (the only operators in the pub trade, after all, who have to pay full list price for their stock) and that to them, cider was in effect a cash cow. Now that the tie was dissolved, their cider assets became liabilities. It was not that their tied lessees suddenly switched brands en masse: it was that they could now buy on the open wholesale market at free trade prices, so that to maintain share the brewers would now have to market their ciders more aggressively and more expensively. Faced with the same problem in maintaining supplies to their now rapidly-disintegrating tied estates, which were in the process of being snapped up by pub companies, the brewers suddenly lost interest in cider.

Having only just closed the original Whiteways factory in Whimple, Devon, Allied was the first to bail out altogether. For Showering's the glory years were past: neither Babycham nor British sherry had fitted well with the shoulder-padded aspirations of the 1980s, and the Coate's and Gaymer's cider brands would need huge investment to compete with Strongbow and Dry Blackthorn. No sooner had the ink dried on the Beer Orders than Showering's – or the Gaymer Group, as it was now called – was put up for sale: after a short-lived management buyout it was knocked down to an old-established West Country wine merchant-turned-wholesaler, Matthew Clark, for just £45,000,000, a price that would have seemed laughable not long before.

The Taunton consortium, with wider distribution and more credible brands, lasted a little longer: it too was sold to its management; but in 1995 – the same year that the Gaymer's factory at Attleborough in Norfolk, was closed down – it too was soon sold on to the ambitious Matthew Clark, but for rather more money: £271,000,000. The purchase gave Matthew Clark almost 40% of the market and, in Diamond White, the brand-leading small-pack cider; but it seemed a high price and in later years even the company's chairman Peter Aikens admitted it was too much.

Bulmers, by contrast, was looking for opportunities to expand; and if the home market was saturated it would fulfill long-held ambitions and go global. Having just paid £7,000,000 for Symonds, in 1992 it bought the Belgian family firm Stassen for an undisclosed sum and in the following year started building its war-chest by selling its pectin division, Citrus Colloids. Progress, though, was interrupted by a new crisis in the home market: in the hot summer of 1995 Merrydown launched its Australian alcoholic lemonade, Two Dogs, while Bass came up with a concoction of its own, Hooper's Hooch. The alcopops took the youth market by storm, with more than 50 rival brands appearing within a year: the 9% annual growth of the first half of the decade turned into a downward lurch. The key to the success of the alcopops was not their alcoholic strength, which tended to be in the standard 4.5-5% ABV range, but their sweetness and their fruit flavours. This was something the cidermakers could not tackle head on: flavoured ciders attracted the same rate of duty as made wine, which at that time would have made them hopelessly uncompetitive with the alcopops. These were taxed as beer until 2002, when – far too late to have any effect – the Government levelled the playing field. (Hooper's Hooch was delisted in 2003, by which time its bolt had long been shot).

Matthew Clark responded by announcing an £8,000,000 advertising campaign to turn the tide. Bulmers, however, took a different approach and spent £23,000,000 on buying Inch's, the Devon independent best-known for its White Lightning strong white cider and at that time the largest of the independents with a 7% market share and strong distribution in its home territory.

Denied access to the heavily-tied pub trade, firms like Inch's had been forced to rely on the grocery trade with its cut-throat pricing. White Lightning was inspired by the success of Taunton's Diamond White, but rather than targeting the premium bottled lager market was sold as cheaply as possible in two and three-litre plastic bottles. Its combination of low price (helped by cider's preferential duty regime) and high alcoholic strength naturally attracted the custom of under-aged and problem drinkers, and it became even cheaper to produce when the makers stopped using cider apples as a base and turned instead to imported dessert apple concentrate – although the suggestion that the glut of ultra-cheap 7.5% ABV white cider brands that followed White Lightning, notably Frosty Jack from Aston Manor, were made by soaking spent pomace in alcohol derived from maize syrup were always stoutly denied.

White ciders, it has to be said, never made up a great percentage of overall cider sales – 6% at most – and were never consciously intended for the constituency among which they found most favour. But in the 25 years between the introduction of Diamond White and the separate decisions by the Coalition Government to increase duty on cider of more than 7.5% ABV and to redefine cider as consisting of at least 35% juice (the juice content of Diamond White had been a mere 24%), they inflicted enormous damage on the image of cider as a whole and cider drinkers as a class. Even the industry, or part of it, admitted as much: in 2009 Bulmers delisted White Lightning on the grounds that responsible manufacturers should not be marketing such a product; in 2010, the very day after a visit to a London homeless shelter by senior management, the company withdrew Strongbow Black as well.

At the very same time that alcopops and white ciders were flooding the youth market, though, the national cidermakers were also looking in completely the opposite direction. Showering's had launched Addlestone's, unfiltered and therefore described as a "cask-conditioned cider" and served on a handpump, as early as 1986. The brand succeeded draught Coate's Farmhouse in the handful of pubs where it was stocked but never really caught fire, and the genuine handpumps were soon replaced with dummies that actuated a carbonated keg dispense system – much to the fury of the Campaign for Real Ale, which threatened any pub caught using "fake handpumps" with exclusion from its *Good Beer Guide*. By 1996, though, "real" cider was perceived to be making a comeback, partly because Weston's and Thatcher's were making inroads in the pub trade (Thatcher's, cannily, had signed a distribution agreement with the Ringwood Brewery of Hampshire, one of the better-established micros, which although it owned no pubs had built up a delivery route of 700 free trade accounts); partly because CAMRA at that time was putting a greater emphasis on its traditional cider campaigning. Bulmers already had a draught still cider in Traditional; at the time of surveying for CAMRA's 1996 *Good Cider Guide*, the brand had over 750 accounts, many of them in South Wales. But it was felt that Traditional's appeal was too regional and too old-fashioned, so Bulmers launched a new "traditional" draught brand, Old Hazy, to capture a more diffuse, more up-to-date, more urban market. By the time the 1996 guide was published Old Hazy already had more than 400 accounts and was being sold in many of them alongside the Inch's traditional brands, Stonehouse and Harvest. In response – and having already squandered the authenticity of Taunton Traditional by carbonating it – Matthew Clark returned Addlestone's to genuine handpump dispense. The real cider revolution proved to be a flash in the pan, though: the mass-market simply wasn't ready for it. Old Hazy was quietly withdrawn before 2000; the Inch's factory was closed in 1998 and Stonehouse became a keg and PET brand; and in 2003 production of Bulmers' five traditional brands – Bulmers Traditional Medium and Dry, West Country Dry, Inch's Harvest Dry, and Woodmancote (specially branded for the Cider House at Woodmancote, Worcestershire) – was contracted out to Weston's. By 2012 the list had been reduced to just two, Bulmers Traditional Medium and Woodmancote, both at significantly lower volumes. Addlestone's, meanwhile, soon went back to keg dispense, and the "real" cider field was left to its best exponents – the independents.

The attempt to position national cider brands against real ale, worthy though it may have been, did nothing to offset the harm done by the popularity of alcopops. Cider sales slipped appreciably in 1997-98 which, combined with continued supermarket price-cutting, forced Bulmers to issue a profit warning as its share price halved to 332p; Matthew Clark shares, meanwhile, collapsed from 801p in 1996 to 193p in 1998. Bulmers responded by closing Inch's, much to CAMRA's fury (again), while Matthew Clark took even more drastic action and actually closed Taunton in July 1998, concentrating production at a single site in Shepton Mallet. It wasn't enough. The low share price attracted takeover attention, and in November of that year the giant US wine conglomerate, Constellation Brands, snapped it up for £215,000,000 – £101,000,000 less than Matthew Clark had paid for Gaymer's and Taunton combined. Dry Blackthorn and Gaymer's Olde English were now stablemates of world-famous brand names such as Paul Masson, Mondavi, Hardy's, and Banrock Station wines and Corona and Tsingtao beers.

The following year saw cider sales rally briefly, but from 2000 they started a three-year downward drift. Bulmers – which in 1998 saw the veteran John Rudgard hand over the helm of Bulmers to Mike Hughes – had by this time already resumed its global expansion drive, buying Harvest Wines of New Zealand in July 1977 for £1,000,000 and Green Mountain Cider of Vermont for £8,700,000 in August 1998. In 1999 it struck twice more, buying Diageo's South African cider brands and factory for £2,300,000 in February, and American Hard Cider for £21,000,000 in November. In July that year it had announced its intention to expand its overseas interests still further by setting up joint ventures with foreign companies: in December it agreed to set up a cider factory in China, in partnership with the San Kong brewery of Qufu, and in February 2000 it announced a deal with Synebrychoff of Finland to make and package Woodpecker there.

But the situation in the home market was too threatening to be left alone, and a decision was taken to seek new opportunities for the company's beer and soft drinks portfolio. In April 2000 it bought the Dawes Group, parent company of Somerset-based free trade wholesaler The Beer Seller, for £32,000,000. It was all too much. In the past five years – in a difficult market, with shares and profits slipping – Bulmers had spent £88,000,000 to shore up its position at home and to try to establish itself worldwide. At the same time it had continued the never-ending process of expanding and modernising its Hereford base, had invested heavily in marketing to fight off the alcopop menace, and had committed funds to new operations in China and Finland. Worse – and unknown outside the company at the time – a "black hole" was opening up in its pension fund, which had overinvested in equities. It was time to retrench. In July 2001 it unveiled plans to shed 10% of its 2,300 workforce as part of a two-year £10,000,000 restructuring plan; 12 months later it had to issue a £7,000,000 profits warning, shed another 100 jobs, and withdraw from South Africa; in December 2002 a further 200 jobs went, and the Australian operation was sold to Foster's for £22,000,000. It also announced that it was temporarily suspending all growers' contracts, despite a continuing decline in the price of apples from £133 a ton in the early 1980s to £85 a ton.

By that time the end had already been signalled when, in September, Mike Hughes issued yet another profit warning but also revealed a £3,300,000 hole in Bulmers' accounts arising from the costs of promoting Strongbow in the supermarket and cash-and-carry trades. By this time the pension fund shortfall had widened to £29,000,000 and was getting bigger as the equity market continued to slide. The City was not impressed with Bulmers' diversification into the UK beer and soft drinks markets, nor with its foreign ventures, nor with its gearing of 172%; and by now Bulmers' own share price had collapsed to 231.5p. Some analysts were suggesting that the company was really only worth 153p a share, or £110,000,000. The situation was hopeless. In January 2003 Bulmers tried one last throw, announcing that it would make a rights issue or, if that failed, put the company up for sale. The £6,000,000 raised from the sale of surplus land in March was no more than a sticking-plaster. The rights issue failed. Mike Hughes departed to be succeeded by former Whitbread boss Miles Templeman, who had but one mission: to find a buyer and get a good price. That buyer turned out to be Scottish & Newcastle, a former member of the Taunton consortium, and the price Templeman secured was not the gloomily-forecast £110,000,000 but a more realistic £278,000,000. The sale was announced in April, to take effect in July; in the interim, Bulmers managed both to recover a little more of its missing cash and complete the process of abandoning its international ambitions by selling its US operations to a management buyout for an undisclosed sum.

After 114 years, the voyage of Bulmers as the family-owned and proudly independent leader of the British cider industry was over. The timing, for the many members of the Bulmer family who were forced to sell their inheritance for a fraction of what it had recently been worth, could not have been worse. In Scotland, just as Esmond Bulmer was handing over the keys of Plough Lane to Sir Brian Stewart, his opposite number at S&N, the Irish cidermaker Magner's was test-marketing its Original brand; and the cider market in Britain was about to be transformed beyond recognition.

Magner's of Clonmel had been sold to Irish owners C&C half a century before, along with the rights to the Bulmers name in the Republic, and had subsequently been sold to a consortium headed by Allied Breweries. Allied in turn sold C&C in 1999 to a venture capital house which was planning to build it up and float it on the stock exchange. The man chosen to oversee the operation was the former Tesco Ireland chief executive Maurice Pratt, who was already well-known for his marketing expertise. The flotation plans had to be put on hold in 2001 when Ireland hugely increased its cider duty; instead, Pratt turned his attention to re-energising the Bulmers brand. His first step was to reduce its strength to 4.5% ABV, make it considerably sweeter, abandon the downmarket cans and PET in which it had previously been sold in favour of a brown glass pint bottle, and recommend that it be served over ice. The new formula was a huge hit in the Republic, where the brand quickly made the transition from a discounted take-home brand into a premium on-trade one; the next step was to launch it in the UK. For this, C&C had to use the Magner's name. Original, as the brand was dubbed, was as successful in Northern Ireland as it had been south of the border and was test-marketed in Scotland from 2003. Here the company was soon claiming brand leadership in the on-trade; and in 2006 Magner's Original had its UK national roll-out. Fortunately it was a hot summer, and the trick of serving it in a pint-glass half-full of ice proved timely. (It also meant that customers took a half-full bottle back from the bar to their table with them, where the label served as an advertisement – "badge drinking", as it was called in the bottled lager boom of the 1980s).

For a year, Magner's swept all before it, not only converting existing cider drinkers but bringing in a whole new audience as well. Magner's drinkers crossed all demographic boundaries; one admiring but perhaps somewhat jealous competitor credited the brand with "refeminising" cider. Less than a year after the launch, C&C's cider sales had soared by 85%, profits more than doubled to £70,000,000, and the share price shot up. Its success threatened C&C's ability to produce enough of it, and Pratt committed C&C to a £200,000,000 expansion of the Clonmel factory. Then in 2008 Bulmers hit back, reviving and reformulating its own Original brand as a frank imitation of Magner's, but selling it to the trade at £5 a case less. Magner's sales slid, its share price fell, and in November Pratt resigned, to be replaced by ex-S&N chief executive John Dunsmore.

Magner's star had risen like a rocket and, despite its difficulties, it had not fallen completely to earth. There was to be another chapter to the saga. But before dealing with that, the "Magner's effect" is worth studying. In effect, it undid the damage to cider's reputation that white ciders had done 10 years earlier.

Interviewed for the 2009 *On Trade Review*, Richard Luscombe – sales manager for the rival St Helier brand – recalled coming off the golf-course one hot day with "a bunch of middle-aged guys" whose natural tipple, one suspects, would be beer. They all settled for an over-ice cider instead. And Weston's commercial director Roger Jackson commented in the same publication: "When Magner's was launched people were saying that we ought to be concerned. But we were delighted because we saw them revitalising a cider market that had been growing only very slowly.

"The amount they were investing kicked off the whole category. They reintroduced whole sectors of the population to cider, which is now in the repertoire of thousands of people who wouldn't have drunk it before. Young adults who found alcopops didn't deliver what they wanted suddenly discovered that cider could deliver both refreshment and flavour."

What they are saying is that, thanks to Magner's, the "ciderhead" image of high-strength budget rocket fuel has been smashed forever and that cider is now an acceptable option for almost all drinkers.

Magner's success also opened the door to a Swedish import, Kopparberg Pear Cider, launched in the same hot summer of 2006 and, like Magner's, primarily an on-trade brand but aimed mainly at younger drinkers. The significance of Kopparberg was that it more or less created the pear cider category (even if an independent, Brothers Drinks, had come up with the name first, on the grounds that consumers didn't understand what perry was). Kopparberg, along with the Bulmers/Stassen brand Jacques, then defied the higher duty imposed on flavoured ciders, reasoning quite correctly that consumers would pay a premium price for a premium product and that the addition of exotic fruit flavours would add a value that, in the opinion of the consumer, constituted a premium. More recently other imports in a broadly similar style have arrived on supermarket shelves: Rekorderlig, also from Sweden; Savanna Dry from South Africa; even Cidre Artois, a rather unlikely brand extension of the Stella Artois range.

The "Magner's effect", and the success of the new brands that followed it into the market, has been electric. In 2003-04, according to HMRC, cider clearances (all dutiable consumption, both home-produced and imported) totalled 5,966,000hl, slightly up on 2002-03 but still below the previous peak year of 1999-2000, when clearances reached 6,200,000hl or 3,800,000 brewer's barrels. In 2004-05 clearances topped 6,000,000hl again. They then rose steeply every year until in 2010-11 they reached 9,421,000hl or 5,750,000 barrels. At the same time, annual beer consumption fell sharply from 34,000,000 barrels to 28,272,000 barrels. In other words, during the first decade of the 21st century cider's share of the long drinks market rose from about 11% to a touch under 20%. An astonishing achievement – perhaps the cider industry should erect a statue to Maurice Pratt!

And yet... Quite apart from any sentiment about the fact that 90% of the British cider industry is now foreign-owned (Bulmers' parent, Scottish & Newcastle, having been bought out by Heineken in 2008), there is an undeniable fly in the ointment. Cider may have become respectable, but it has lost the premium pricing and premium margins that Magner's UK marketing manager Scott Fairbairn said (*On Trade Review* 2009) were key aims when it was launched. Two factors are to blame: competitive price-cutting as exemplified by Bulmers' response to Magner's initial success, and the crisis in Britain's pubs that has seen the weight of sales switch from the on-trade to the much lower-margin supermarket trade. The on-off split is now 35% to 65% – almost the reverse of what it was a decade ago. The loss of value in the industry was starkly outlined in 2009 when Constellation Brands decided to sell the Gaymer's Group because it no longer fitted with CB's portfolio of high-value international brands. By that time the group's output of 1,500,000hl represented perhaps 15% of the UK market, well below the 44% share it enjoyed at its peak; and 80% of its sales were in the low-margin take-home trade. The buyer was Magner's parent company, C&C. And the price – for the whole group, Taunton as well as Gaymer's – was exactly what Matthew Clark had paid for Gaymer's on its own nearly 20 years earlier – £45,000,000.

12: Piggies in the Middle

The postwar period has seen the national cidermakers becoming ever more deeply embedded in the distribution structures created by the much bigger national breweries, and benefiting as a result from spectacular increases in sales. The progress of the independent makers has also, in some ways, mirrored that of their counterparts in the brewing industry, especially in the perceived cycle of decline and revival. There are, however, as many contrasts as there are similarities, determined by the different histories, scales, and structures of the two industries.

At the end of World War II there were fewer than 600 breweries in the UK, ranging from home-brew pubs or "brewing victuallers" which retailed their own beer on the premises, through very local breweries with a handful of pubs within a stone's throw of the mashtun, up to regional superpowers with tied estates of 1,000 or more. The cider industry, although very much smaller, was of a superficially similar shape, with half-a-dozen regional superpowers, three of them with near-national distribution; a second tier of independents with local followings, some of them quite large and based in modern mechanised factories, others still essentially mixed farms but producing cider in serious commercial quantities; and a "tail" of small makers selling their own produce at the farm gate and perhaps supplying a handful of local retailers. And there the similarity ends.

The first and most obvious difference is that with exception of farm gate sales, very few of the independent cidermakers had retail outlets of their own. They were almost completely dependent on a mixture of private customers, direct-supplied local independent grocers and publicans, brewers' tied estates, and local or national wholesalers and caterers. A particularly critical limiting factor was the barrier that the brewery tie posed to open competition.

The second was one of size. Bulmers, as we have seen, produced 5,100,000 gallons or about 140,000 barrels in 1945, making it the equivalent, in terms of output, of a respectable middle-ranking regional brewer. Whiteways, one of its leading competitors in the national arena, produced less than half that. At the bottom end of the table were farmers still producing a few hundred gallons. Many of these latter – hundreds, perhaps – didn't even match the handful of surviving brewing victuallers in output: 500 gallons is quite a lot of cider to mill, press, and store, but still only adds up to 14 barrels or three months' sales for quite a small pub. For this scale of producer cidermaking was increasingly a hobby, and an expensive one at that: many farmers dipped in and out of production as circumstances dictated, and one by one the mills and presses came to a stop as the farmers turned an outgoing into an income by selling their apples to the factories.

Between these extremes, the middle-ranking concerns were struggling in an ever-narrowing market. Even before the war, as we have seen, the imposition of the brewer's tie had cost them dear. The zoning system of 1944-46 excluded them from the national market, a handicap from which they took 40 years to recover; and the increasing concentration of pub ownership as breweries merged froze more and more of them out of both tied houses and loan-tied free houses (owner-operated pubs whose landlords had accepted cheap finance from brewers in return for stocking only their products). A number of the medium-ranking independents didn't survive: in the 20 years after the war Bulmers and Taunton each bought four of them, while Rout's of Banham, Gaymer's only competitor in Norfolk, struggled on through changes of ownership – and an attempt to compete with Sanatogen with the launch of "Slimvin" – only to close in 1957. Mark Foot's *Cider's Story: Rough and Smooth* includes a roll-call of well-established and often quite sizeable Somerset cidermakers that failed to make it into the 1970s: Allen's of West Bradley, founded in 1900, went out of cider production in the late 1950s; Clapp's of Baltonsborough, founded 1916, making 260,000 gallons or over 7,000 barrels a year at its peak, sold and closed in 1946; Lang's of Hambridge, also a brewer with 56 pubs of its own, stopped brewing in 1953 in order to buy its beer in from Ind Coope, finally sold up to Ind Coope and closed in 1958; Magna Cider of Marston Magna, bought by Showering's in the late '40s and turned into a winery; Williams Brothers of Backwell, whose head cidermaker had been poached by Redvers Coate, closed in 1989 when the second generation retired; Coles of Chardstock, whose founder had been so forthright in 1928 on the imposition of the brewery tie, once employed 18 men, closed in 1961; Sunshine Cider Mills of Chard, expanded into soft drinks in 1936, took over an old factory with seven acres in 1941, closed in 1967 when the sales director retired. Retirement was often the reason for the closure of these and similar firms: their distribution depended on personal relationships with local retailers built up over many years, and personal relationships are a wasting asset. By the time the principals called it a day, all too often there wasn't the trade to persuade their heirs to carry on; and in many cases where the heirs did try to carry on, they found they hadn't the social networks or the personal status and motivation to maintain the business and soon had to close. These companies were, in a sense, unstable: they never developed as corporations separate and distinct from their individual proprietors, and in all too many cases when the proprietors bowed out their enterprises went with them.

Having said that, a sizeable core of independents did soldier on through the lean years and down the generations: Thatchers, Sheppy's, Inch's, Wilkins, Countryman (originally Lancaster's), Symond's, Perry Brothers, and Hancock's were among the biggest of the 20-odd makers with prewar origins identified in the Campaign For Real Ale's first *Good Cider Guide*, published in 1987; the two subsequent editions (1990 and 1996) identified the same number again including Aspall, Heck's, Coombe's, and Richards. The stock of local free houses where their products were appreciated never dried up completely (and contemporary estimates, as well as the author's personal experience, reveal many of them to have been by modern standards very high-volume accounts); and there were still local independent grocers and off-licences that saw a commercial value in stocking distinctively local products not just for local loyalists but also for the seasonal influx of tourists for whom farm-made (or apparently farm-made) cider was all part of the experience.

On the national scene, though, Weston's was almost alone in carrying the flag for the independent sector thanks to a well-developed grocery trade and a number of supply deals with smaller regional breweries such as Davenport's and its 100-strong tied estate in Birmingham. These connections with regional breweries, although small beer to the national cidermakers, proved their value when Cameron's of Hartlepool approached Weston's to produce an own-label keg brand, dubbed Stowford Press after two picturesque Cotswold towns – Stow-on-the-Wold and Burford – that caught the brewery's eye. Cameron's and its sister brewery, Tolly Cobbold of Ipswich, owned more than 500 pubs between them, so the contract was a substantial one for what was then quite a small cidermaker; it became even more so when in 1988 Cameron's and Tolly were sold by their owners, the Barclay Brothers, to the 1,200-strong Brent Walker pub chain, which grew to over 2,000 pubs before eventually being sold on to Punch Taverns. Even though Brent Walker delisted Stowford Press shortly after the takeover, by then it had become established almost by accident as a national brand and is Weston's biggest seller to this day.

Adventures in PET, own-label and white ciders were not, however, the core strategies chosen by the more established independents, however narrow the retail market was becoming. Not that they were above such work when the opportunity arose – Weston's, for instance, made Sainsbury's own-label Vintage and in the mid-1990s launched a range of flavoured ciders – but they sensibly decided to occupy, in the main, a position at the premium end of the mass market. To companies like Weston's, Sheppy's and Thatcher's fell the task of trying to interpret traditional cider for a market unaccustomed to the tannic, astringent, and sometimes even acetic character of the genuine article; a mission in which they risked pleasing neither the mass market nor the traditionalists. But even if carbonated brands such as Sheppy's Bullfinch and Goldfinch were not what diehard traditionalists would have regarded as "real" cider, in terms of juice content and authentic flavour they were immeasurably closer to tradition than market-leading national brands such as Bulmers Strongbow, Gaymer's Olde English, or Taunton Dry Blackthorn ever set out to be.

Following a period of dipping below 3,500,000 hectolitres (66,000,000 gallons or 1,800,000 brewer's barrels) after the 1984 Budget duty increase, cider sales began to take off again from 1990 on. The more commercially-minded independents benefited particularly from increased sales in supermarkets, taking advantage of the growth in premium bottled ales by launching premium bottled ciders. One innovation that stood out came from Thatcher's, which went against the tradition of blending ciders from a large number of apple varieties by launching single varietals. In 1994 Thatcher's went one further by including two culinary varieties – Katy and Cox – in the range, although other makers who followed suit preferred to use traditional cider apples of vintage quality such as Dabinett. As a result of its delicate balance between tradition and innovation, by dodging the alcopop trap, and by maintaining its premium positioning in the market, Thatcher's reported a 55% sales increase in 1997. Sheppy's, which had never enjoyed much of a presence in the pub trade, saw its output almost double from around 70,000 gallons or less than 2,000 brewer's barrels to 130,000 gallons or 3,600 barrels between 1999 and 2009 – again, as a result of focusing on high-quality bottled ciders mainly for the supermarket trade. And between the publication of the fourth and fifth editions of CAMRA's *Good Cider Guide* (2000-2005) Weston's, which stuck more closely to tradition by producing strong blended ciders including the cloudy Old Rosie, also doubled its output from 1,000,000 gallons (more than 27,000 brewer's barrels or 45,000 hectolitres) to 2,000,000. Today its output is closer to 6,000,000 gallons (more than 160,000 barrels or 270,000 hectolitres). Another venerable name that came to prominence thanks to supermarkets was the long-established Suffolk family firm, Aspall. The 1996 *Good Cider Guide* listed it as producing little "cyder" (its preferred spelling), and that for a narrowly local trade; but its premium cyder vinegar was becoming a supermarket staple and on the back of that it was able to gain national distribution for its premium ciders in their distinctive flask-shaped bottles.

The supermarket trade from the mid-1980s onwards provided a good growth platform for producers efficient enough to live with low margins and frequent "promotions". But at the same time the pub trade was becoming gradually less restricted too. The boutique pub chains founded in the 1970s, such as David Bruce's Firkin brewpubs (eventually taken over by Allied) and Tim Martin's JD Wetherspoon Organisation sought premium and (for the times) slightly quirky draught ciders to match their real ale offerings. Weston's fitted the bill nicely, matching an authentic brand (the strong, cloudy Old Rosie) with efficient production and therefore competitive pricing; and as these chains grew, so did Weston's sales and visibility. Then in 1990 came the Beer Orders following the Monopolies & Mergers Commission's investigation into the beer tie. Among its clauses was the abolition of the cider tie in national brewery tenanted pubs, and although most affected tenants regarded this new freedom more as an opportunity to shop around for better prices on the national brands they already stocked rather than as a chance to try out craft-made guest ciders, nevertheless the opportunity was occasionally fruitful for the independents to exploit. Weston's, as we have seen, was able to build national distribution for Stowford Press on the back of its relationship with Cameron's of Hartlepool, a relationship that stood it in good stead when independent pub companies were able to flourish in the post-Monopolies Commission environment. Thatcher's also benefited in the mid-1990s when Taunton decided to carbonate its Traditional draught brand. At the time, according to the 1996 *Good Cider Guide*, Taunton Traditional had around 300 outlets, mainly in and around Bristol: many of their landlords, indignant at the change, took advantage of the loosening of the cider tie to switch to Thatcher's. Aspall, too, was tempted back into the draught market – again, at the premium end – thanks to encouragement from the Suffolk family brewer Adnams, with which it enjoyed a very warm relationship.

To balance the steady post-war erosion of the cidermaking base there were also newcomers, and not all of them were minnows. Merrydown, Knight's, and Broad Oak (now the Original Cider Company) all grew quite rapidly once they had evolved marketing strategies that lifted them out of their local trading areas, even if their strategies did not necessarily meet the approval of traditionalists and purists.

Merrydown was founded in November 1946 by wine buffs Jack Ward, Ian Howie, and John Kellond-Knight, all from Eastbourne and friends since childhood, and found a home in the outbuildings of the derelict Horam Manor in East Sussex. The plan was to go upmarket, making pure fruit wines (the fruit wines then made by Whiteways being based on imported grape concentrate) as well as an Eastern-style cider from cooking and eating apples, using an ancient stone press loaned by a neighbouring farmer. The high rate of duty made the fruit wines uncompetitive, but cider of any strength was then untaxed, and amid the shortages of postwar Britain the partners soon found a ready market for a fine still cider of 11% ABV (sold out of necessity in recycled hock bottles but emphasising that this was, in reality, not merely cider but an apple wine more fit for the dining table than the pub). The imposition in 1956 of wine duty on ciders of more than 8.5% ABV pushed the price of Merrydown up by a third, and the company diversified into cider vinegar. At the same time, though, it persisted with its distinctive cider (the only Eastern-style brand on the national market) advertising heavily and investing in new equipment. Its efforts, and its faith in its product, were rewarded with handsome sales growth, and by the early

1960s it was producing 250,000 gallons a year. The rapid increase in the number of supermarkets that followed the 1964 Licensing Act provided the ideal platform for a product that was still traded as being more refined than other ciders; Vintage, Merrydown's first carbonated mass-market brand and rather less alcoholic than the original, was launched in 1975 and quickly gained nationwide distribution.

By the early 1990s, however, Merrydown was in trouble, affected like all other cidermakers by price-cutting in the supermarket trade on which it depended so heavily. After two years of losses, company chairman Richard Purdey took a giant step that at first looked like Merrydown's salvation but in the end brought the whole company down. In June 1995 he took on the UK agency for Two Dogs, the Australian brand that launched the era of alcopops. Two Dogs was originally a genuine lemon wine, made in a glut year by a citrus-grower with a huge surplus to dispose of. At the same time, though, Bass was preparing to launch an alcopop of its own. The infamous Hooper's Hooch was a concoction of lemon pulp soaked in corn-derived alcohol and then diluted and carbonated. Putting its huge marketing and distribution muscle behind a much cheaper and more profitable product Bass easily outgunned Merrydown, leaving the Sussex company with all the overhead of a national product launch and none of the returns. Briefly it seemed that Purdey's gamble had paid off: Merrydown's share price recovered from 67p in early 1995 to 140p by the end of it. An annual loss of £2,700,000 was turned into a profit of £2,100,000. But it didn't last: competition from Bass was compounded by the launch of more than 50 imitators such as Lemonhead, while a media witch-hunt against alcopops generally led some retailers to ban them altogether. Sales collapsed, and the profits dried up. Richard Purdey departed after 32 years, and in 1997 the Two Dogs agency was sold to Scottish Courage. Ironically, at the time of its disastrous excursion sales of Merrydown's core product – cider – were growing 13% year-on-year. Nevertheless, in 1998 the company was put up for sale as a going concern – only to fail to find a buyer. Instead, a new board raised £7,000,000 to refinance the company and axed 50 jobs. It struggled on, supported by success of its UK agency for Schloer grape juice; but in 2004 the factory at Horam was closed after nearly 60 years and production was outsourced to Belgium. The following year Merrydown was sold for £37,000,000 to SHS of Northern Ireland where ironically, given that alcopops were the original source of its problems, among its stablemates is the WKD range.

Less well-known to the public but enjoying greater long-term success were Broad Oak in Somerset and Knight's in Herefordshire. Broad Oak was started in his garage by factory fitter and cider enthusiast Brian Brunt in 1974. Eventually cidermaking grew beyond a hobby and the operation was moved to a unit on a former feed mill and pig farm that had been turned into an industrial estate. Here Broad Oak continued to make traditional ciders, winning several awards, but also diversified into low-cost industrial ciders, packaged in two and three-litre PETs, for the grocery trade. This might be seen as a brave strategy, given that bigger producers with lower cost bases could and did occupy the same territory. But it paid off, and by the mid-1990s Broad Oak's output was 1,000,000 gallons or more than 27,000 brewer's barrels a year. Many old-established regional brewers would have been delighted to produce so much!

Demonstrating the diversity of the people attracted to cidermaking, Knight's had a very different and perhaps more conventional genesis than either Merrydown or Broad Oak. Keith Knight bought the 140-acre Crumpton Oaks Farm at Storridge in the Malverns in 1969 from a mining company which had been refused planning permission to quarry it. It was, according to Fiona Mac's *Cider in the Three Counties*, near-derelict and growing only a few acres of soft fruit, so Knight took advantage of the assistance Bulmers offered to contract growers and planted 25 acres of cider orchards. These took several years to get established, and Knight's finances were stretched, so in 1979 he started making cider on his own account as well as growing apples for Bulmers. In his first year he made 18,000 gallons, and soon afterwards started supplying Aston Manor Brewery in Birmingham, which had evolved from a microbrewer into a major contract-brewer and wholesaler. The link proved to be a short-cut to expansion as Aston Manor became one of the country's biggest contract brewers and cidermakers, enabling Knights to complete the planting of Crumpton Oaks and buy two more farms totalling 200 acres. The company produced brands across the spectrum from award-winning traditional ciders under its own name to own-label products for supermarkets: the range included Frosty Jack high-strength white cider, which became notorious for its appeal to under-age and problem drinkers. In 2006 the relationship between the two companies was consummated when Aston Manor bought Knights outright. It now claims to produce an astonishing 1,400,000 hectolitres (30,000,000 gallons or more than 800,000 brewer's barrels) a year.

More recently there have been other newcomers to the middle ranks of the independent sector. Mike Henney was actually a trade marketing executive at Bulmers when he started making his own cider at his home in Bishop's Frome, Herefordshire, using apples including the now quite rare Foxwhelp from a neighbour's semi-derelict orchard. Winning a trophy in the 1995 Hereford Cider Museum's annual competition persuaded him to become a registered duty-exempt producer for sale, and in 1996 he made and sold 300 gallons. Unlike many such enthusiasts, though, he took matters a stage further and, with his wealth of contacts and experience, was able to build up a healthy business. By 2010 he was selling 200,000 gallons (more than 9,000 hectolitres) of premium bottled ciders to all the national supermarket chains.

More headline-grabbing has been the explosive growth of Brothers Cider of Shepton Mallet, Somerset – in large part because the surname of Francis, Jonathan, Matthew, and Daniel is Showering, and they are the sons of Keith Showering and the nephews of Francis Showering. They set up their own business in 1992 making and bottling alcopops including WKD under contract, and also launched a perry of their own called Straight 8. The brand proved to be no Babycham, but in 1995 the brothers set up a bar at Glastonbury Festival selling their strong perry. It was a big hit, and the bar became a regular feature at the event.

The company's main business remained – and still is – contract production of other brands, a business in which Brothers is now a major player. Its branded range of Festival Strength Pear Cider at 7.4% ABV and a family of mid-strength flavoured variants (strawberry is their biggest seller) was not launched to the retail trade until 2005. The marketing trades heavily on the Glastonbury connection, and the company claims to have originated the term "pear cider" because staff on the bar grew tired of explaining to festivalgoers what "perry" was. The pear juice that goes into the Brothers range is derived entirely from imported concentrate – and of culinary pears at that – but the fact that Brothers can co-exist with long-established Somerset arch-traditionalists such as Wilkins, Heck's, and Perry Brothers (which actually makes no perry) shows if nothing else what a broad church the cider industry's independent sector has become.

13: The Craft Revival

The number of commercially-minded independents in a position to exploit the new opportunities in the pub and grocery trades in the 1980s and '90s was small. But beneath them existed a vast substrate of craft cidermakers producing anything from a few hundred to a few thousand gallons for themselves, for local customers, for holidaymakers. This is the territory of folklore and stereotype: the bewhiskered old farmer beside a tourist route in Mummerset, whose family has been making scrumpy in the same old way for generations. (Scrumpy, as a footnote, is one of those cider words with as many meanings as there are wiseacres. It's sometimes defined as inferior cider made of the windfalls that labourers were allowed to gather for themselves; but as I have not come across any record of labourers being allowed to gather windfalls I tend to discount it. The verb "to scrump" in its most recent currency means to steal apples; and since many 18th-century writers did actually bemoan the widespread theft of apples by cottagers it seems to me likeliest, on balance, to have originally meant cider made from stolen or, at least, "gathered" apples. But we shall never know for sure). But who were – and are – all these small-scale rustic cidermakers? How well do they represent cider's past as an aspect of mixed farming in the South-West? How many have survived the modernisation of agriculture? Is there really a revival going on? And how many of them are there?

The last of these is the hardest to answer, and bedevils the question of whether there's really a craft cidermaking revival along the lines of the microbrewing revolution going on at all. CAMRA's five cider guides never managed to identify more than 150 cidermakers, including the national giants; www.ukcider.co.uk lists about 450; and although even duty-exempt makers producing less than 7,000 litres a year for sale have since 1976 been required to register with their local HMRC officer, no central record has ever been kept. NACM's estimate is 4-500, in line with ukcider.co.uk's. Rumours keep surfacing of old farmers in this backwater or that still discreetly making a couple of hundred gallons for themselves (and in some cases distilling it on makeshift stills, which would account for the discretion), but they are uncounted and uncountable. Perhaps NACM's estimate is the closest we shall come to a workable figure. But what we can't know, either, is how many small cidermakers there were 50 years ago, how steeply their numbers fell in the 1940s, '50s, '60s and '70s, and how far, if at all, they have recovered since; and without being able to quantify the decline, can we really assess the revival?

Fortunately, it's not just a numbers game. We may not be able to know whether craft cidermaking is growing in scale as microbrewing has done; what we can say is that it is changing its nature, becoming more dynamic and interactive, and attracting a greater diversity of entrants.

There are no formal local studies that I am aware of that attempt to characterise the small-scale cidermakers of the immediate pre- and post-war years. But the mass of anecdotal evidence compiled in interviews by Dave Matthews of the Welsh Perry & Cider Society (www.welshcider.co.uk), by Fiona Mac in *Cider in the Three Counties*, and by Alan Stone in his *Somerset Cider Handbook* (self-published, 2009) demonstrates vividly the nature of farm cidermaking half a century ago; how its existence was, even then, still a given for many country people in the West Country and West Midlands; and how much of the tradition had disappeared by the time the various interviews were conducted.

The lack of formal data is also an obstacle in defining the increasing diversity of craft cidermakers since the 1970s. I have therefore attempted to fill the gap by making a (necessarily vague) comparison between the 139 small-scale producers listed in the 1996 *Good Cider Guide* and the 135 listed in the cidermaking counties of Cornwall, Devon, Gloucestershire, Herefordshire, Somerset and Worcestershire on the ukcider.co.uk website as at January 2012. Neither source gives more than sketchy background details, but I have attempted to divide them into three rough categories. "Traditional" includes old-established makers (such as Wilkins, Heck's, Rich's etc which have been producing for more than a generation); fruit growers who have diversified into cidermaking (I have included the many vineyards that also make cider, the best-known of them being Biddenden in Kent, founded in 1969); and mixed farmers who have started or re-started cider production recently. "Newcomers" I class as makers who have come to cidermaking from other regions and professions, some of them in search of the good life, others being more earnestly commercial. "Miscellaneous" embraces pubs and tourist businesses making cider as an added attraction (and including Prinknash Abbey!) and producers for whom insufficient background is given to make a judgement. In the 1996 guide the "traditional" category numbered 99 compared to 26 "newcomers" and 14 "miscellaneous". On ukcider.co.uk the respective totals were 80, 37, and 18.

These figures by themselves do not reflect the kind of diversity of origin we see among the microbrewing sector. Most of the early microbrewers were refugees from the mainstream brewing industry then in the throes of concentration of ownership and rationalisation of production, which created a pool of highly skilled workers with redundancy cheques in their pockets. Today, though, new brewers come from all walks of life and few have had more than home-brewing experience (although the vast majority have undergone formal training before starting up). On the sole basis of the comparison between the 1996 *Good Cider Guide* and ukcider.co.uk, craft cidermaking seems not to have attracted such a diversity of entrants as microbrewing. However one crucial difference between the two sources is that the cidermakers of 1996 were almost all concentrated in the traditional cidermaking regions, with only a handful in other southern counties as Berkshire or even further afield. Ukcider.co.uk, on the other hand, shows that craft cidermaking has expanding far beyond its traditional boundaries: it lists four producers in Cheshire, four in Cumbria, three in Derbyshire, one in Northumberland, four in Leicestershire, seven in Lincolnshire, four in Northamptonshire, six in Yorkshire (including Ampleforth Abbey), and even two in Northern Ireland and three in Scotland. Clearly none of these fit into the "traditional" category, not even the handful of fruit growers among them who have decided to make a little cider out of the produce rejected by the supermarkets.

Anecdotal evidence also supports the idea that craft cidermaking is attracting entrants from a wide variety of backgrounds: Roy Bailey of Lambourn Valley Cider, a former TV cameraman; Ivor and Suzie Dunkerton of Dunkerton's, respectively a former TV producer and theatre producer; Ron Barter of Brimblecombe's, a former engineer in the oil industry; Martin and Janet Harris of Butford Organics, respectively an RAF officer and an RAF doctor. For some of these new entrants, cidermaking is a thoroughgoing commercial business; for others, it's a second career after retirement; for others again, it's part of a mixed lifestyle that also embraces small-scale farming and other crafts.

The resurgence of cidermaking in Wales is worthy of special mention. Historically, Gwent was an apple-growing and cidermaking (and, as a neighbour of Gloucestershire, pear-growing and perrymaking) county, while references to cider are fairly liberally sprinkled through the pages of *Kilvert's Diary*, recording the life and times of the curate of Clyro in Radnorshire in the 1870s, Francis Kilvert. By the 1980s, though, the tradition appears to have died out, other than the rumour reported by Dave Matthews of a small group of farmers in the Usk Valley still producing a few hundred gallons for themselves. The 1987 *Good Cider Guide* found no producers in Wales at all, and the 1996 edition listed just one – Ralph Owen of Kinnerton, Powys, who is cited as having been making cider there since 1986, and who for 10 years previously had made cider on Anglesey as farm manager on Bertram Bulmer's private estate. Undetected by CAMRA's researchers were Troggi Cider at Earlswood in Gwent, founded by hospital pathologist Michael Penney in the same year, and Radnor House four years later. The Welsh cider revival really got under way in 2000-2001, though, when three of today's leading producers – Seidr Dai, Gwynt y Ddraig, and the Clytha Arms – all started up. Since then the tally of producers has grown to 34, mostly clustered in South-East Wales but including one in the hills near Wrexham. The Welsh Perry & Cider Society not only represents their interests but is also closely involved in identifying and rescuing old varieties of native perry pears and cider apples threatened with extinction by the gradual disappearance of the old orchards. These are planted at Llanblethian Orchards near Cowbridge, where owner Alex Simmens not only supplies cuttings for other growers to graft but also makes award-winning cider and perry on his own account.

In 2009 the Society received Supply Chain Efficiencies Scheme funding from the Welsh government and the EU for a three-year project to help support and develop traditional cider and perry orchards, which typifies the readiness of the new wave of craft cidermakers to get involved in initiatives beyond their own purely commercial activities. Many craft cidermakers work both with local authorities and DEFRA and with voluntary conservation groups such as Common Ground to rediscover and restock the traditional apple and pear varieties that the big producers haven't used for generations and that often survive only as a handful of aged specimens in some half-derelict orchard. This is perhaps best embodied by Kevin Minchew of Tewkesbury, who has made rescuing near-extinct varieties – especially of perry pear – a personal crusade, and the Orchard Centre at Hartpury, Gloucestershire, now home to the National Collection of Perry Pears.

The drive to locate and revive historic varieties is partly pragmatic: in contrast to mass-producers, who for the sake of consistency require a continuous supply of a fixed range of ingredients, identical as far as possible from year to year, craft makers need a large and changing palette in order to create their individual identity. So where the mass producers have over the years deliberately narrowed the number of varieties their contract growers may plant, the craft producers struggle to re-establish sources of varieties they can experiment with. This is particularly the case with perry: perry pear trees are larger and longer-lived than cider apple trees, but they're also very slow-growing – hence the saying "he who plants pears/plants for his heirs". Large cidermakers have, over the years – as they will confess themselves – underinvested in planting new perry orchards, and there is a chronic shortage of native fruit. Bulmers gave up making perry altogether many years ago, and the industrial perries and "pear ciders" you will see on the market today are made mostly or entirely from imported fruit or imported fruit concentrate. Showering's invested heavily in planting 3,000 acres of perry pear trees in several orchards across Somerset when Babycham was at its peak: I believe, although I have been unable to confirm it, that most of these have now been grubbed up. So not only the WPCS, Kevin Minchew, and the Orchard Centre but also Dunkerton's at Pembridge in Herefordshire and many others have had to invest in plantings of their own, facing not only business risk implicit in such long-term investments but also a natural risk: most perry pear varieties are early croppers, whose buds are therefore frequently exposed to destruction by late frosts.

A close involvement in securing sources of raw materials is one of the many points of difference between the superficially similar microbrewing and craft cidermaking sectors. There are, true, microbrewers who concern themselves closely with sourcing their malt and hops, but not out of actual need. An already well-established supply industry of maltsters and hop merchants adapted itself to the needs of microbrewers in the early days of the

1970s and '80s so that all the microbrewer has to do to secure adequate supplies of, say, Maris Otter pale malt or organic New Zealand Green Bullet hop cones is pick up the phone. The craft cidermaker who wants to experiment with varieties less obvious than Yarlington Mill or Brown Snout has to go out into the lanes and fields and find them.

But there's more to it than mere pragmatism. There's a strong romantic element as well. The connection between the cidermaker and his or her apples is a much deeper, more visceral, one than that between a brewer and his or her malt. Most craft cidermakers – and many of the larger producers, for that matter – are very conscious of their place in the farming cycle and the farming community. Where they can, they grow what they use; and where they can't, they get their ingredients from as close by as possible, from familiar orchards and from growers who are personal friends rather than anonymous wholesalers. Perhaps that's because they see themselves not just as businesses but also as custodians of features of rural life that have become virtually extinct and have to be safeguarded or even reinvented. In a surprising number of cases the attraction of reinventing a lost heritage even extends to the resurrection of a family tradition of cidermaking – Brothers Drinks is the most obvious example; Dennis Gwatkin of Abbeydore in Herefordshire is another; a third is Robinson's Cider of Tenbury Wells in Worcestershire. The Robinson family had been substantial cidermakers and pub owners in "the town in the orchard" for two centuries until 1959, when they stopped cidermaking to concentrate on their highly successful soft drinks business, Wells Drinks. But after Wells Drinks was sold in 1998 the urge to make cider – using the original press, which was still *in situ* and fully operational at the family home – resurfaced, and Robinson's Cider went on sale again in 2006 after a gap of almost half a century.

The influx of newcomers and resurrectionists implies a discontinuity in the tradition of craft cidermaking, especially as regards the new wave of producers in counties outside the old heartlands. Unlike, say, the current generations of the Sheppy and Heck family, the newcomers do not have the first-hand experience of their fathers to guide and instruct them. They have to relearn – in effect, to reinvent – the entire business from orchard to retail. They cannot simply contemplate and imitate (and perhaps improve upon) the methods of the past; they have to make a considered and detailed examination, taking nothing for granted. But a fresh eye, or an enquiring mind that has been conditioned in other industries and disciplines, often lights upon aspects of the tradition that the traditionalists themselves have completely forgotten or, at least, pushed to the back of their minds as no more than an interesting but impractical footnote. Nowhere has this been more clearly manifested than in the reintroduction of two aspects of cidermaking that everyone thought defunct: bottling by the *méthode champenoise,* and distilling cider brandy.

Of the two, bottling by *méthode champenoise* is the most recently extinct. It was widespread before the war, and Bulmers' Pomagne was fully crafted with *pupîtres, dégorgement* and the rest of the paraphernalia until the 1960s. The art was revived in the 1980s and '90s by a number of craft makers including Burrow Hill and Bridge Farm in Somerset, Gospel Green in Sussex, and Bollhayes (the cidermaking arm of Vigo Vineyard Supplies) in Devon. The volumes were not great – both Gospel Green and Bollhayes were below the 7,000-litre tax-exempt ceiling – but these ciders were commercially important to their makers and were positioned very firmly at the premium, high-margin, end of the market. They also represented an opportunity for other craft cidermakers to seek to reacquire the skills of the past. But in 1998 the *méthode champenoise* makers found themselves caught up in a passing-off war between the Italian sparkling wine industry and the manufacturers of Lambrini, a sparkling industrial perry positioned against the likes of Asti Spumante and, especially, Lambrusco, but very much cheaper. The Treasury, whose Chief Secretary at the time was Dawn Primarolo, immediately gave way, charging sparkling ciders closed with a mushroom cork, of three bars of pressure or more, and of 7.4% ABV or less, an extra £90 per hectolitre, and commensurately reducing the duty on lower-alcohol sparkling wine. It could perfectly legally have excluded *méthode champenoise* cider from the duty increase by using the same wording that had been employed to distinguish cask ale from keg beer in the 1990 Beer Orders, but it chose not to. The producer of Lambrini easily sidestepped the new rate of duty simply by altering its packaging; the only producers caught by the trap were Burrow Hill and Bridge Farm. Bridge Farm gave up using the *méthode champenoise* but Burrow Hill persisted, producing high quality Kingston Black and Stoke Red varieties to this day – but at £8 a bottle. It could be argued – and was at the time – that the interest at stake was too small to be worth defending; but what was lost was not merely one small part of two small companies' businesses, but a very promising potential development opportunity for the industry as a whole.

Interference from across the Channel had scarcely been more helpful just over a decade earlier, when the art of (legal) distillation was reintroduced by the newly-retired chairman of Bulmers, Bertram Bulmer. A major retirement project of his was the foundation of the Hereford Cider Museum in the building in Ryelands Street where (perhaps ironically, in view of the above) Pomagne had once been made by the *méthode champenoise*. To help fund the Museum, which opened in 1981, it was decided to use an old pot still acquired from Normandy to make cider and perry brandy under the King Offa label. A licence to distill was granted by Customs & Excise in 1984 and in 1987 the first fruits went on sale. (The first bottle, actually, was given to the Queen while the second went to Prince Charles, both of whom had donated oak from their estates to be turned into barrels). At this point the French objected to the use of the name "cider brandy" on the grounds that the word brandy could only be used to denote a distillate of wine – which came as news to companies that had been calling their fruit macerations "cherry brandy" and "apricot brandy" for generations. Bulmer simply ignored an instruction to rename his product "cider spirit"; and unlike Customs & Excise 11 years later, British officialdom went in to bat for King Offa and the French objection was headed off. This did not stop distillers from Spain, Scotland, and Italy raising the same objection against Julian Temperley of Burrow Hill Cider, who in 1987 had started making cider brandy on another ancient French still in partnership with Charles Clive-Ponsonby-Fane of Brympton D'Evercy Hall near Yeovil. It took four years of legal wrangling to overcome the objections this time, perhaps because Temperley wasn't quite as well-connected as Bertram Bulmer. In 1989 Temperley moved out of Brympton D'Evercy and set up the Somerset Cider Brandy at Thorney nearby, using two French continuous stills dubbed Josephine and Fifi. Somerset Royal Cider Brandy and its various extensions – different ages and bottlings, eaux de vie, aperitifs and liqueurs – provoked intense interest in the food and drink media and have more recently inspired a great many other cidermakers too. Temperley now distils cider for Bridge Farm and Yarde Farm of Stoke Gabriel, Devon, and for the monks of Ampleforth Abbey in North Yorkshire. Healey's Cornish Cyder at Penhallow uses a small Scottish pot still to make its cider brandy; while Herefordshire potato grower William Chase (best-known for Tyrells Crisps, which he sold for £40,000,000) turns distilled cider not into brandy but into William's Gin and Naked Vodka. (His potatoes no longer go to make crisps but are transformed into Chase Vodka). It might also be reasonably claimed that Bertram Bulmer and Julian Temperley are the inspiration behind a whole new wave of microdistilling: whisky is now made in Wales, Cornwall, and even Norfolk; and artisan gin distillers such as Sipsmith's are breathing new life into a sector that many commentators had thought moribund.

Despite these innovations, the craft cidermaking sector faces many difficulties, mainly as a consequence of its diminutive size – and not just of the size of the sector as a whole, but of many of the producers within it. The 1,500-gallon duty exemption ceiling permitted in 1976 was intended to protect the remaining cidermaking farmers whose principal business was generally either rearing livestock or growing cider fruit under contract. In the 35 years since then it has acted as an encouragement to many people – possibly thousands of people – to start making cider for sale, offering them a buffer between semi-professional status and full-time commercial production. But for many the buffer is also a barrier: take a single step over it and the whole nature of your business changes from a casual and unregulated lifestyle option into an intimidating bureaucratic tangle. So, rather like the shallow end of a swimming pool, it's as much an encouragement to timidity as a base from which to splash out. This has its advantages for the individual producer, who can dip below the 1,500-gallon ceiling when circumstances dictate, but there are also disadvantages. Larger craft cidermakers sometimes dimiss the exempt producers as glorified hobbyists who hold back the whole sector by creating an unrealistically low consumer price expectation. If the hobbyists were eliminated by the abolition of the exemption, they argue, a more commercially-minded independent sector could start addressing some of its serious weaknesses: lack of access to training and research, lack of public awareness, and lack of access to retail.

In any industry, training and research are critical to maintaining product quality. In other areas of food and drink production there is adequate publicly-provided training to degree level and beyond. You can even study oenology in the minutest biochemical detail (at Plumpton College, Lewes). But you can't study cidermaking. Long Ashton Research Centre was closed in 1985 on the grounds that it was too "near market", meaning that the bigger cidermakers should foot the training and research bill themselves. From 1994 there were publicly-funded BTEC courses (the vocational equivalent of an A level) in cidermaking at Hindlip Agricultural College in Worcester which were transferred to Pershore Horticultural College after the two merged in 1997. In 2000 a brand new special facility was built at Pershore to be a National Centre of Excellence for cidermaking; it closed after only three years, and Pershore now offers only part-time and short courses that earn no qualification more prestigious than a certificate of attendance. Other than that, as far as vocational training is concerned, the NVQ in Brewing Skills has two units directly relating to cidermaking – maturation and blending and storage and fermentation – and units in areas such as materials handling, bottling, hygiene and so forth that are equally applicable to both industries. There is also provision in the new Qualification & Credit Framework for training in cidermaking, but no colleges that actually teach it.

Training for small cidermakers is, therefore, only really accessible in the private sector. Peter Mitchell, who headed the training at Hindlip and Pershore, set up the Orchard Centre at Hartpury in 2008 where he runs the Cider & Perry Academy offering one-day, five-day and advanced courses as well as training in processing and packaging. The academy attracts about 250 students a year but has no Government or industry funding. Andrew Lea, formerly of LARS, runs a training and consultancy operation from his base in Oxfordshire. Many smaller cidermakers also run courses, but generally only of one or two days' length and more as weekend breaks for enthusiastic amateurs than as repositories and disseminators of microbiological and pomological expertise. It is perhaps not the role of a history to make predictions, but the shortage of academic training in cidermaking is bound to have a long-term impact on quality. We know from William Marshall, and from the conditions that caused Long Ashton to be founded in the first place, that the informal father-to-son transmission of the basic mechanics of cidermaking causes a gradual erosion of knowledge and skills, and that properly-funded and continuous research and training are necessary foundations for the maintenance of quality and consistency and to create the possibility of informed innovation. The small independent sector, however, is simply too small to sustain any such research and training without help either from the public purse or from the larger players, perhaps under the umbrella of the industry's own association.

Lack of public awareness is another disadvantage of the small scale of independent cidermaking; and lack of public awareness of traditional cider is the chief cause of low public demand. People who have been on holiday in the west and south-west will be aware of farm cider as part of the tourist experience, but it's not necessarily an experience they want to take home with them. They might expect to find farm cider on sale at the campsite shop in Devon; they don't expect to find it on sale at the pub or supermarket back home. The whole subject of traditional cider is surrounded with quaint myth – rats in the vat and so forth – which some small cidermakers gleefully promote as a marketing tool unaware that while it may help sales in their home areas it actually holds back demand in non-cidermaking regions. Cider myth labels the product as a quaint curiosity, acceptable while on holiday but not a mainstream choice.

In the absence of a nationwide association of independent cidermakers (although there are two regional associations), the Campaign for Real Ale has been almost alone in preserving and promoting traditional cider across the country. It has been doing this almost since its inception, and has a national committee, APPLE (it's not an acronym!), dedicated to the task. It produced five editions of the *Good Cider Guide* between 1987 and 2005 and between 1996 and 2000 published a periodical supplement, *The Cider Press*. However APPLE has no resources of its own and its work is, understandably, not the highest of priorities at CAMRA's St Albans head office, although its national awards are prominently publicised in the campaign's newspaper, *What's Brewing*. Many cidermakers are sceptical about the value of CAMRA's support at national level, although at local level enthusiasts among the Campaign's members have played an active part in introducing consumers to the unfamiliar delights of traditional farmhouse ciders and perries. At most local CAMRA beer festivals you'll find a dedicated cider bar, and most local CAMRA branches have members who are enthusiasts and who work tirelessly to persuade pubs to stock "real" cider.

But pubs, even though the Big Six brewers have entirely disappeared, are still for the most part tied and access is denied to the local craft cidermaker just as firmly today as when Ivor and Suzie Dunkerton set up in business at Pembridge in 1982 and found that there wasn't a single pub nearby to which they could sell their products. The rapid decline of the pub trade since the beginning of the century has, in addition, seen the loss of many rural free houses which could once be relied on to stock locally-produced farmhouse ciders. With lack of demand fuelled by lack of public awareness, there is very little motivation for pubs outside the cider-producing regions to stock traditional ciders on a regular basis; those that do so tend to be the minority that specialise in craft-brewed real ale and also provide focal points for local cider enthusiasts; there is very little sign of demand increasing to the point where traditional cider tips over into the mainstream. A handful of cidermakers such as Ralph Owen have opened on-licensed "cider barns" of their own, but with a few exceptions (such as the Cider Shed in Banham, Norfolk) these outlets are within the cider-producing regions where local demand is boosted by the tourist trade.

The situation in the off-trade is, if anything, even worse than that in the pub trade, with independently-owned local shops disappearing in droves to be replaced by national chains of supermarket and convenience stores whose stocking policies exclude all but the bigger independents – Weston's, Thatcher's, Sheppy's, Henney's – or (within the cider-producing regions) a token representation of local producers. Even the traditional standby of farm gate sales has been bureaucratised almost to extinction by the Licensing Act 2003: wholesalers can operate without a licence; but whereas before the 2003 Act the term "wholesale" denoted the sale of a minimum quantity both to retailers and consumers, it has now been redefined to denote sales from manufacturers/distributors to retailers only. A cider farm that wants to sell to private customers or passing tourists these days has to possess a regular off-licence – which the 2003 Act also made much more onerous and expensive to get. But this is precisely what many of them are doing and it's here that the craft cidermakers' identification with farming is a strength: the farm shop selling locally-reared meat and dairy and locally-grown fruit and vegetables is a natural arena for the local cidermaker. The same association makes cider stalls a natural fit at farmers' markets, although here there are sometimes licensing issues. Some independent cidermakers have developed museums and visitors' centres complete with sales counters, Weston's, Sheppy's, and Perry Brothers among them; Whin Hill Cider at Wells-next-the-Sea in Norfolk has a shop dedicated entirely to its own products. And of course, many cidermakers sell over the internet. But even here, the size of most of the producers in the sector is another handicap: without the funds to afford proper packaging and design, they tend to offer their ciders in clunky, unattractive screwtop bottles – or, worse, oversize plastic flagons – with unappealing home-made labels that undermine the premium status their often excellent ciders ought to be flaunting.

Taking all the above into account, can we really claim that there is a craft cidermaking revival going on? Certainly the larger and more efficient independents have been able to access national distribution vectors and have seen sales rise dramatically as a result; but whether the changing nature and attitudes of the participants at the lower end of the scale has sparked off anything that could be defined as a revival is more doubtful. The craft cidermaking sector, for all its strengths, has shown little of the vigour of the microbrewing sector, and craft ciders have enjoyed nothing like the acceptance of microbrewery beers. Without national institutions – a trade organisation as effective as the Society of Independent Brewers; a college to act as a focal point for research and training (perhaps, given the extra income that vineyards could generate from cidermaking, Plumpton might be persuaded to expand its curriculum?); a genuinely national wholesaler with the reach of independent beer wholesalers such as the Flying Firkin – it is frankly hard to see the craft sector ever living up to its potential, or its products ever achieving the cachet of "wines of the west". The energy and imagination are certainly there; what is lacking is the sort of organised infrastructure that Percy Bulmer had to create for himself. If we had that, we would have our revival.

Postscript: A Plea for a Vintage

Roger French concluded *The history and Virtues of Cyder* 30 years ago with a plea for a vintage, by which he meant ciders made as the Pomona ciderists made them – perfect fruits; judiciously selected varieties; tumped to concentrate the sugars; gently pressed; keeved; racked over and over again. Smooth ciders, Hugh Stafford would have called them.

In repeating French's plea, I am not merely being wistful or romantic (although I would dearly love to be able to grace my dining table with the sort of cider that John Beale or Hugh Stafford appreciated so much). But while the demotic ciders that have captured the public imagination so strikingly are all very well, they are the heirs of what Stafford would have called rough cider, and this is the age of the super-premium. Look at the spirits market: artisan-distilled gins, rums and vodkas – even craft-made mixers – are all the rage. The cider industry offers many fine products, but has nothing to compete with the New World white wines that sell so well, let alone the best white wines of Alsace, Burgundy, and Bordeaux. Not because cider inherently can't be as good as wine, but because the cider industry has chased the false god of volume at the expense of value.

There have, it is true, been many attempts at producing a table cider of wine quality: Gaymer's County and Single Orchard ranges have won praise; the various makers of *méthode champenoise* ciders were heading in the right direction until the category was fatally undermined by a neglectful Government; Dunkerton's has pursued this aim since it was founded 30 years ago; Whin Hill ciders from Norfolk definitely deserve to be categorised as "fine", despite their clunky packaging; and more recently Once Upon A Tree from Herefordshire has started making elegant ciders and perries that definitely belong in the wine-merchant's window rather than on the supermarket shelf. But in the past 40 years the public perception of cider has taken a battering: fine cider as a concept has slipped almost entirely from view, and even the enthusiasts rhapsodise over the inheritors of the rough cider tradition while forgetting that there is another tradition that is just as honourable and has, perhaps, an even greater potential.

It would take either a heroic effort by the larger players in the industry, or the continual drip-drip of insistent small makers, to re-establish fine cider. But in the long term it would be worth it.

Bibliography and Further Reading

Barr, Andrew: *Drink, A Social History*, Pimlico Books 1995.

Bulmer, Fred: *Early Days of Cidermaking*, Hereford Cider Museum 1996.

Bolton, Mark and others: *Cider*, CAMRA Books 2009.

CAMRA Books: *The Good Cider Guide*, ed David Kitton 1987.

CAMRA Books: *The Good Cider Guide*, ed David Kitton 1990.

CAMRA Books: *Guide to Real Cider*, ed Ted Bruning 1996.

CAMRA Books: *The Good Cider Guide*, ed unattributed, 2000.

CAMRA Books: *The Good Cider Guide*, ed Dave Matthews 2005.

Clark, Peter: *The English Alehouse*, Longman 1983.

Crowden, James: *Cider, The Forgotten Miracle*, Cyder Press 1999.

Crowden, James: *Ciderland*, Birlinn, 2008.

Ellis, William: *Complete Planter & Cyderist*, ECCO Print Editions 2010.

French, Roger: *The History & Virtues of Cyder*, Robert Hale 1983.

Foot, Mark: *Cider's Story Rough & Smooth*, self-published 1999.

Hagen, Ann: *Anglo-Saxon Food & Drink*, Anglo-Saxon Books 2006.

Hornsey, Dr Ian: *A History of Beer & Brewing*, Royal Society of Chemistry 2003.

Mac, Fiona: *Ciderlore, Cider in the Three Counties*, Logaston Press 2003.

Marshall, William: *Rural Economy of the West of England* (2 vols), David & Charles 1970.

Russell, James: *The Naked Guide to Cider*, Tangent Books 2010.

Stone, Alan: *Somerset Cider Handbook*, self-published 2009.

Whiteway, Eric: *Whiteway's Cider, A Company History*, David & Charles 1990.

Wilkinson, Patrick: *Bulmers, a Century of Cidermaking*, David & Charles 1987.

Texts Available Online

Amherst, Alicia, *A History of Gardening in England*, 1895.

Digby, Sir Kenelm: *The Closet of Sir Kenelm Digby, Knight, Opened*, 1669.

Evelyn, John and others: *Pomona*, 1664.

Hale, Thomas: *Compleat Body of Husbandry*, 1758.

Hitt, Thomas: *A Treatise of Fruit Trees*, 1757.

Hogg, Dr Thomas: *Apples & Pears as Vintage Fruits*, 1886.

Knight, Thomas Andrew: *Treatise on the Culture of the Apple & Pear and on the Manufacture of Cider & Perry*, 1797.

Markham, Gervase: *The English Husbandman*, 1614.

Marshall, William: *Of the Management of Orchards & Fruit Liquor in Herefordshire*, 1785.

Parkinson, John: *Paradisi in Sole Paradisus Terrestris*, 1629.

Phillips, John: *Cider, a Poem in Two Books*, 1708.

Risdon, Tristram, *Survey of the County of Devon*, 1811.

Salzmann, LF: *English Industries of the Middle Ages*, 1913.

Stafford, Hugh: *A Treatise on Cyder Making*, 1753.

Westcote, Thomas: *View of Devonshire*, 1630.

Index

—1—

1964 Licensing Act, 149, 173

—2—

2003 Licensing Act, 187

—A—

Adam out of Eden, 58

Addlestone's, 160

Adnams, 172

adulteration, 85, 87, 110

advertising, 104, 117, 118, 125, 129, 144, 149, 152, 153, 159, 172

Agricultural Research Council, 124

Alcock, Thomas, 89

alcohol, 11, 12, 14, 28, 29, 36, 52, 63, 67, 153, 159, 173, 182

alcopops, 159, 160, 161, 164, 173, 175

ale, 11, 27, 29, 30, 33, 35, 36, 47, 52, 53, 55, 56, 65, 70, 72, 83, 115, 161, 171, 182, 186

Allen's, 129, 168

Allied Breweries, 143, 145, 149, 163

America, 74

American Hard Cider, 161

Amherst, Alicia, 34

Ampleforth Abbey, 178, 183

Anglo-Saxons, 25

Ansells, 145, 149, 156

Aphorisms, 59, 62, 71, 72, 73

APPLE, 186

apple varieties, 19, 30, 41, 81, 92, 101, 170

applejack, 28

Aqua Vitae, 70

Aspall, 66, 91, 102, 169, 171, 172

Aston Manor, 159, 174

attenuation, 67

Attleborough, 105, 117, 135, 158

auge et pil, 50, 95

Austen, Ralph, 58, 59, 64, 65

Australia, 150

Axe-Tees line, 48, 65, 73

—B—

Babycham, 132, 143, 144, 145, 146, 150, 158, 175, 180

Bacon, Francis, 53

Bailey, Roy, 178

Baker, George, 88, 89

Baldwin, Stanley, 133, 135

Banham, 34, 96, 104, 105, 117, 168, 187

baptism, 34

Barclay Perkins, 145

Barker, BTP, 123, 134

barley, 27, 48, 60, 91, 92

Bass, 145, 148, 156, 157, 159, 173

Bass Charrington, 145, 148

Bath & West Society, 10, 121, 122

Beale, John, 45, 58, 59, 60, 61, 62, 63, 65, 67, 81, 106, 120, 189

Bede, the Ven, 26

beer, 9, 11, 13, 15, 19, 20, 21, 27, 29, 48, 53, 55, 56, 60, 63, 65, 71, 72, 73, 76, 79, 83, 90, 91, 92, 126, 127, 130, 133, 135, 137, 141, 145, 151, 152, 153, 154, 155, 156, 157, 159, 162, 164, 165, 167, 168, 169, 171, 182, 186, 188

Beer Orders, 157, 158, 171, 182

beetle and tub, 50

beor, 27, 28, 29, 30

Berkshire, 62, 178

Biddenden, 29, 178

Big Six, 148, 149, 154, 186

Billingsley, John, 96

Black Death, 37, 38, 39, 40

Board of Agriculture, 96, 98, 99, 121, 122

Bollhayes, 182

Bordeaux, 11, 32, 60, 78, 189

bottling, 62, 75, 76, 77, 79, 85, 87, 88, 115, 125, 136, 141, 144, 145, 159, 171, 172, 175, 182, 185, 187

Brake's, 138

brandy, 11, 71, 72, 74, 75, 82, 92, 136, 183

Brent Walker, 170

Breton Ballads, 20

brewer's barrels, 90, 126, 143, 148, 149, 165, 170, 174

brewers, 28, 29, 56, 73, 85, 90, 91, 92, 97, 101, 104, 125, 131, 137, 141, 143, 145, 148, 149, 154, 155, 156, 157, 167, 168, 174, 178, 186

brewing, 9, 15, 33, 35, 47, 60, 73, 86, 90, 91, 92, 103, 127, 143, 145, 147, 151, 153, 154, 155, 156, 167, 168, 178

Bridge Farm, 182, 183

Brimblecombe, 178

Bristol, 31, 41, 52, 56, 74, 83, 85, 87, 89, 92, 93, 120, 124, 129, 138, 145, 172

British sherry, 144, 150, 158

Brittany, 22, 73, 134, 140

Broad Oak, 172, 174

Brogdale, 43

Brothers Drinks, 165, 175, 181

Brown Snout, 102, 181

Broxwood, 116, 133, 140

Brunt, Brian, 174

Bull Brand, 115, 136

Bull, Dr Henry Graves, 105

Bulmer, 105, 111, 112, 113, 115, 116, 117, 120, 124, 125, 126, 132, 135, 143, 150, 153, 163, 179, 183, 191

Bulmer, Fred, 112, 113, 116, 124, 125, 126, 132, 133, 135, 149, 191

Bulmer, Percy, 105, 111, 112, 113, 114, 115, 117, 124, 125, 149, 188

Bulmers, 106, 114, 115, 116, 117, 124, 125, 128, 129, 132, 133, 135, 136, 137, 140, 141, 142, 143, 144, 146, 147, 148, 149, 150, 151, 152, 154, 155, 156, 157, 158, 159, 160, 161, 162, 163, 164, 165, 168, 170, 174, 175, 180, 182, 183, 192

Burrow Hill, 182, 183

bush trees, 134

Bute,Lord, 79, 89

Butford Organics, 179

Butleigh, 120, 121, 122

—C—

C&C, 143, 163, 164, 166

Cambridge, 42, 103, 113, 121, 123

Cameron's of Hartlepool, 169, 172

Campaign for Real Ale, 13, 160, 186

Canada, 134, 140

cans, 150, 163

carbonation, 115, 125

Catal Huyuk, 13

Cato, 16, 17, 18, 19, 23, 40, 43

Caxton, 46

Celts, 24

cereals, 14, 39, 102

Chamlet, 144

Champagne, 76, 77, 111, 115, 144

Champney, Burnett, 138

Charlemagne, 21, 22, 24

Charles II, 57, 60, 64

Charrington's, 145

Chase, William, 183

Chaucer, 34, 41

cheese, 50, 55, 122

Cheltenham Brewery, 138, 146

Cherry B, 145

Cheshire, 89, 178

Chevallier, Clement, 66

China, 38, 162

chocolate, 71, 84

cicera, 34

cider brandy, 69, 71, 72, 73, 74, 75, 78, 83, 90, 182, 183

Cider De Luxe, 115

cider merchants, 63, 85, 86, 105, 111, 112, 129

Cider Museum, 10, 35, 68, 175, 183, 191

ciderkin, 55, 82, 86, 118, 119

cidermen, 93

cidre, 22

Cidre Artois, 165

cisera, 17, 34
Civil War, 56, 58
Clapp's, 129, 136, 138, 168
Clark, Peter, 9, 34, 49, 54, 56, 83, 84
clones, 92, 101
Clytha Arms, 179
Coate, 129, 130, 135, 136, 141, 144, 148, 158, 160
coffee, 71, 79, 84
Coles, Henry, 137
Columella, 18, 19
common cider, 82, 83, 86, 90, 99
Common Ground, 180
Compleat Planter and Cyderist, 74, 78
concentrate, 28, 29, 30, 63, 122, 134, 142, 147, 150, 151, 159, 172, 175, 180, 181, 189
Constellation Brands, 161, 166
contract growers, 120, 142, 143, 174, 180
Coombe's, 169
Corn Laws, 100, 121
Cornish, Rev Thomas, 97, 130, 131
Cornwall, 31, 88, 90, 177, 184
costard, 30, 33
Countryman, 169
Courage, 91, 145, 148, 157, 173
Cox, 103, 170
Credenhill, 105, 113
Crone, Robbie, 29
Crowden, James, 9, 54, 119
Crumpton Oaks, 174
Cumbria, 178
cyder, 54, 72, 75, 78, 79, 81, 82, 83, 85, 118, 171
cyder-royal, 71, 72, 75
Cydrax, 118, 150
—D—
Dabinett, 171
De Villis, 21, 22, 40
death duties, 129
Defoe, Daniel, 83, 84, 86, 90
DEFRA, 179
dégorgement, 77, 182

Dent & Reuss, 150
dépense, 36, 50
Derbyshire, 88, 178
Devon, 17, 29, 32, 34, 35, 47, 49, 53, 54, 62, 74, 84, 86, 87, 88, 90, 95, 105, 111, 117, 121, 128, 129, 132, 136, 138, 146, 158, 159, 177, 182, 183, 186, 192
Devonshire colic, 87
Diamond White, 153, 158, 159, 160
Digby, Sir Everard, 61
Digby, Sir Kenelm, 61, 75, 192
distillers, 70, 73, 74, 77, 82, 183
distilling, 28, 29, 69, 70, 71, 73, 74, 155, 177, 182
Domesday, 30, 31
Dorset, 60, 63, 83, 90
draught, 85, 87, 112, 126, 130, 135, 136, 138, 151, 160, 171
Dry Blackthorn, 152, 158, 161, 170
Duncumb, John, 97, 99, 100
Dunkerton's, 178, 180, 186, 189
duty, 56, 79, 126, 133, 141, 145, 146, 152, 153, 159, 160, 163, 165, 170, 172, 175, 176, 182, 184
duty-exempt, 153
—E—
East Malling Research Station, 124
eau de vie, 69
Elizabeth I, 49, 52, 70
Ellis, William, 74, 78, 106, 191
enclosure, 39, 40, 48, 58, 73, 84, 98
English Housewife, The, 70, 76
English Husbandman, The, 50, 53, 192
engrossment, 39, 40, 73, 98
estate management, 18, 22, 30, 40, 43, 57, 75, 104
Evelyn, John, 45, 56, 57, 59, 60, 61, 62, 63, 64, 65, 66, 71, 75, 78, 85, 192
excise, 56, 72, 74, 79, 152
Exeter, 52, 79, 87, 105, 118
—F—
farm gate sales, 167, 187

195

fermentation, 19, 28, 35, 36, 47, 55, 57, 63, 67, 68, 76, 81, 87, 93, 94, 95, 97, 101, 109, 115, 120, 123, 132, 151, 185

Fiennes, Celia, 66

Findlater Mackie Todd, 150

fine cider, 51, 77, 80, 81, 82, 83, 88, 97, 99, 135, 151, 190

Finland, 162

Fitzstephen, William, 41

Flying Firkin, 188

Foot, Mark, 130, 135, 137, 168

Foster's, 162

Foxwhelp, 115, 175

France, 16, 32, 59, 60, 61, 63, 73, 76, 77, 100, 106, 133, 134

Franks, 20, 22, 24, 25

French, Roger, 47, 53, 55, 67, 81, 91, 189

Frosty Jack, 159, 174

—G—

Gardener, Master Ion, 42

Gaymer, 96, 104, 105, 112, 116, 117, 124, 125, 128, 135, 136, 140, 141, 146, 148, 153, 158, 161, 166, 168, 170, 189

Gaymer's, 104, 105, 117, 124, 136, 146, 161, 166

General Views, 96, 99

Gennet-Moyles, 64

George's, 92, 138

Gerald de Barri, 33

Gerard, John, 43, 44, 45, 55, 118

Germany, 22, 23

gin, 70, 71, 73, 75, 77, 78, 84, 92, 184

glass, 57, 75, 76, 77, 134, 140, 141, 163

Glastonbury, 26, 120, 175

Gloucester, 31, 32, 48, 93

Gloucestershire, 32, 47, 49, 54, 57, 84, 89, 90, 92, 93, 95, 97, 121, 129, 132, 136, 146, 177, 179, 180

Godwin, 117, 143, 144

Good Cider Guide, 160, 169, 171, 172, 177, 178, 179, 186, 191

Gospel Green, 182

Gower, John, 41

grafting, 42, 43, 44, 58, 68, 92, 100, 101

Grand Metropolitan, 149

Grapes, 14, 23

Gray's, 105

Great Western Railway, 116, 121

Green Mountain Cider, 161

Greenall Whitley, 148, 155, 156, 157

Gregory of Tours, 20, 21

Guénolé, 20

Guinness, 125, 144, 148

Gutenberg, 18

Gwatkin, Dennis, 181

Gwent, 179

Gwynt y Draig, 179

—H—

Hagen, Ann, 26, 27, 28, 29, 34, 191

Haines,, 72

Haines, Richard, 65, 71, 72, 73, 74, 78

Hancock's, 169

Hardy, Thomas, 108, 115

Harris, Richard, 43, 44

Hartlib, Samuel, 57, 58, 59, 61

Hartpury, 180, 185

Harvest Wines, 161

Hatton, Ronald, 124

Healey, Dennis, 152

Healey's Cornish Cyder, 183

Heathfield, 97, 130, 131

Heck's, 169, 175

hedgerows, 44, 61, 66, 118

Henley's, 105, 117, 129

Henney, Mike, 175

Herbert Durham, 125

Hereford, 10, 34, 45, 47, 66, 68, 93, 102, 105, 106, 111, 113, 117, 118, 121, 124, 134, 140, 143, 144, 146, 147, 151, 162, 175, 183, 191

Hereford Times, 124

Herefordshire, 29, 45, 47, 48, 55, 56, 57, 59, 60, 66, 68, 74, 78, 83, 84, 87, 88, 90, 92, 93, 95, 96, 97, 99, 101, 105, 106, 107, 112, 116, 117, 120,

121, 124, 127, 129, 137, 147, 155, 174, 175, 177, 180, 181, 183, 189, 192

Hero of Alexandria, 17, 23

Hindlip Agricultural College, 184

Hogg, Robert, 68, 74, 86, 102, 106, 107, 108, 109, 111, 113, 120, 121, 192

hogshead, 48, 56, 63, 64, 67, 72, 73, 74, 79, 86, 97, 99

honey, 28, 29, 30, 86

Hooker, John, 54

Hooper's Hooch, 159, 173

Horrell's, 137, 148

Hughes, Mike, 161, 162

Hundred Years' War, 32

Hunt's, 105, 117, 138

hydraulic press, 104

—I—

import tax, 134

Inch's, 129, 159, 160, 161, 169

Ind Coope, 138, 145, 168

independents, 159, 161, 167, 168, 169, 170, 172, 176, 187

—J—

Jackson, Roger, 10, 164

Jamaica, 52, 74, 84, 150

JD Wetherspoon Organisation, 171

—K—

Katy, 170

keeve, 82

keeving, 63

keg, 147, 151, 152, 156, 160, 170, 182

Kent, 25, 29, 33, 41, 43, 44, 45, 57, 124, 144, 178

Kilvert, Francis, 179

King Offa, 183

King's Acre, 134

Kingston Black, 182

Knight, Keith, 174

Knight, Thomas Andrew, 67, 68, 100, 101, 102, 116, 118, 120, 121, 192

Knight's, 102, 172, 174

Kopparberg, 165

—L—

lager, 148, 150, 151, 152, 153, 159, 164

Lambrini, 182

Lang's, 129, 168

Lawson, Nigel, 152

Lea, Andrew, 185

lead poisoning, 88

leathercoat, 63

lees, 23, 63, 70, 74, 76, 89

Leicestershire, 178

lever press, 16, 17, 23, 35, 50, 95

Lincolnshire, 66, 178

Llanblethian Orchards, 179

Lloyd, Frederick, 121, 123

London, 32, 40, 43, 46, 47, 48, 56, 57, 60, 62, 70, 73, 77, 78, 79, 83, 84, 85, 87, 88, 90, 93, 101, 102, 111, 117, 118, 121, 122, 128, 136, 137, 138, 160

Long Ashton, 120, 123, 124, 125, 130, 134, 184, 185

—M—

Mac, Fiona, 9, 113, 128, 174, 177

maceration, 36, 49

Magna Cider, 145, 168

Magner's, 12, 142, 143, 163, 164, 165

malo-lactic fermentation, 67

malt, 12, 14, 28, 29, 30, 35, 70, 73, 97, 103, 180, 181

Mann Crossman & Paulin, 145

Mansell, Sir Robert, 75

Markham, Gervase, 50, 53, 55, 70, 76

Marshall, William, 17, 35, 74, 89, 91, 92, 94, 95, 96, 97, 98, 99, 119, 185, 191, 192

Matthew Clark, 158, 159, 161, 166

Matthews, Dave, 177, 179, 191

mechanisation, 104, 128

Médaille d'Or, 107

Merrydown, 159, 172, 173, 174

méthode champenoise, 77, 115, 126, 151, 182, 183, 189

Michelin, 107

mill, 13, 15, 16, 21, 31, 32, 33, 35, 36, 46, 47, 50, 62, 64, 67, 88, 95, 103, 104, 105, 108, 109, 112, 114, 115, 131, 135, 168, 174
Minchew, Kevin, 180
Mitchell, Peter, 185
MMC, 157, 158, 171
monasteries, 25, 30, 43
Monmouthshire, 90, 121
Monopolies & Mergers Commission, 148, 154, 155
Much Marcle, 112, 121

—N—
NACM, 134, 141, 142, 153, 177
Nailsea, 130, 138, 145
National Association of Cidermakers, 132
National Farmers' Union, 142
National Mark scheme, 133
Neile, Sir Paul, 56, 60, 62, 63, 67, 68, 75, 76, 77, 79, 83
Neville Grenville, Robert, 120, 121, 123, 124
Newburgh, John, 60, 62, 71, 75, 79, 83
Norden, John, 46, 47, 62
Norfolk, 29, 33, 34, 45, 84, 90, 96, 104, 108, 112, 135, 158, 168, 184, 187, 189
Normandy, 22, 23, 33, 35, 50, 72, 73, 106, 134, 140, 183
Normans, 27, 30, 32
Northamptonshire, 178
Northern Ireland, 145, 163, 173, 178
Northumberland, 178
Norton Fitzwarren, 131, 148
Nourse, Timothy, 65, 78

—O—
Old Hazy, 160
Old Rosie, 171
Olde English, 146, 148, 152, 161, 170
olives, 16, 17, 19, 44
olivess, 15
Once Upon A Tree, 189
Orangina, 150

Orchard Centre, 180, 185
orcharding, 41, 44, 48, 49, 93, 95, 97, 102, 120, 125
orchards, 3, 11, 30, 31, 33, 41, 44, 46, 47, 48, 49, 54, 55, 57, 62, 66, 69, 86, 89, 90, 91, 93, 96, 97, 99, 100, 102, 103, 106, 107, 110, 111, 116, 118, 119, 127, 130, 131, 133, 134, 140, 142, 144, 145, 146, 149, 153, 174, 179, 180, 181
Owen, Ralph, 179, 187

—P—
Palladius, 19, 42
panking pole, 36, 69
Parkinson, John, 53
Parliament, 56, 58, 61, 71, 124
pearmain, 30, 33
pectin, 115, 140, 147, 159
Penney, Michael, 179
Pepys, Samuel, 57, 60
Perrier, 150, 152
perry, 11, 17, 19, 20, 21, 22, 33, 45, 47, 48, 49, 51, 52, 53, 54, 55, 73, 74, 79, 85, 86, 87, 99, 105, 110, 111, 113, 115, 123, 134, 143, 144, 165, 175, 179, 180, 182, 183
Perry Brothers, 12, 129, 169, 175, 187
Pershore Horticultural College, 184
Phillips, John, 29, 68, 83
phylloxera, 106
pilage, 50
Pippin, 103
Pitt the Elder, 79
Plan of St Gall, 21, 22
Plantagenet, 32
Pliny, 16, 17, 18, 19, 20, 22, 40, 43
Plumpton College, 184
Plymouth, 52, 74, 89
pomace, 15, 16, 36, 50, 55, 86, 95, 108, 109, 115, 118, 123, 140, 159
Pomagne, 115, 135, 144, 151, 182, 183
pomatium, 21, 22
pommeau, 72

Pomona, 56, 59, 60, 61, 62, 63, 64, 66, 67, 71, 75, 78, 81, 83, 85, 92, 94, 106, 108, 189, 192

Pony, 144

Porter, 91

Portugal, 64, 72, 77, 100

pot still, 183

pounding, 95

Pratt, Maurice, 163, 165

press, 13, 15, 16, 17, 18, 22, 23, 26, 32, 33, 35, 36, 46, 50, 82, 88, 89, 93, 95, 96, 104, 105, 108, 109, 112, 114, 124, 129, 131, 141, 146, 168, 172, 181

Primarolo, Dawn, 182

pupîtres, 77, 182

purchase tax, 152

pyratium, 20, 21, 22

—R—

racking, 28, 63, 67, 76, 100

Radcliffe Cooke, Charles, 121, 124, 132

Radegund, St, 20, 21

Radnorshire, 179

railway, 105, 113, 117, 128, 135

raw materials, 91, 116, 126, 132, 151, 180

Red Stripe, 150, 152, 153

Redstreak, 12, 59, 60, 61, 66, 92, 100, 102

refermentation, 76, 86

Rekorderlig, 165

Ribston Pippin, 103, 117

Rich's, 177

Richards, 169

Ridlers of Clehonger, 117

Risdon, Tristram, 53, 54, 192

Robert de Evermere, 33

Robinson's Cider, 181

Roger of Wendover, 32

Romans, 18, 24, 112

Roseff, Rebecca, 31, 33, 36, 41, 47

Rouen, 106, 107

Rout's, 105, 117, 168

Royal Society, 57, 59, 61, 76, 88, 90, 101, 191

Rudgard, John, 153, 158, 161

Rudge, Thomas, 97, 99

rum, 11, 53, 74

Rural Economy of the West of England,, 74

Ryelands Street, 113, 114, 183

—S—

Salle, Robert, 42

Salzman, Louis Francis, 33

Saunders, William, 88

Savanna Dry, 165

Saxons, 25, 26

Schweppes, 136, 138, 147

Scotland, 70, 74, 113, 141, 145, 163, 178, 183

Scottish & Newcastle, 145, 148, 163, 165

scratter, 50, 64, 95

screw press, 17, 23, 32, 46, 105

scrumpy, 81, 176

Scrumpy Jack, 155

Scudamore, Viscount, 59, 60, 63, 92, 94, 102, 120

scurvy, 53

Seidr Dai, 179

Seven Years' War, 79

shekhar, 14, 17, 22, 34

Sheppy's, 169, 170, 171, 187

Shepton Mallet, 131, 143, 145, 161, 175

ships' stores, 52, 54

Showering's, 129, 131, 138, 143, 144, 146, 148, 149, 152, 154, 158, 160, 168, 175, 180

Showering's's Vine Products & Whiteways, 146

Shropshire, 90, 147

sidir, 34

Simmens, Alex, 179

Simond's Brewery, 138, 145, 148

Sipsmith's, 184

siþere, 30, 34

small cider, 55, 136

Snowball, 144

Society of Independent Brewers, 188
Somerset, 12, 48, 59, 90, 96, 102, 105, 114, 121, 122, 129, 130, 131, 136, 138, 143, 145, 146, 162, 168, 174, 175, 177, 180, 182, 183, 191
Somerset Royal Cider Brandy, 183
Speed, Adolphus, 58
spices, 63, 71, 83, 86
spirits, 30, 70, 71, 72, 131, 132, 189
Spurway, Edward, 131
St Helier, 164
Stafford, Hugh, 17, 35, 50, 67, 78, 79, 81, 82, 86, 135, 189, 192
Stassen, 159, 165
steam, 91, 105, 109, 112, 114, 117, 118, 121
Stire, 66
Stone, Alan, 10, 177
Stonehouse, 160
Stowford Press, 170, 172
Strongbow, 150, 152, 153, 158, 160, 162, 170
Stroud Brewery, 146, 147
Suffolk, 66, 90, 91, 102, 171, 172
sugar, 14, 28, 29, 36, 67, 71, 76, 115, 143, 150, 151
Sunshine Cider Mills, 169
Surveior's Discourse, 62
Sussex, 31, 33, 45, 71, 96, 172, 173, 182
Sylva, 59
Symonds, 117, 155, 159
—T—
Taunton, 97, 99, 129, 130, 131, 141, 148, 149, 152, 153, 154, 157, 158, 159, 161, 163, 166, 168, 170, 172
Taunton consortium, 158
Taunton Dry Blackthorn, 148
Taylor, Capt Silas, 60, 61, 62, 63, 67, 76
Taynton Squash, 115
tea, 71, 84, 119
Temperley, Julian, 183
Templeman, Miles, 163
Tewkesbury Cider, 147, 149
Teynham, 43

Thatcher's, 160, 170, 172, 187
Thatchers, 169
The Beer Seller, 162
The Pub and the People, 139, 144
Thorney, 31, 183
tied estates, 91, 130, 138, 143, 147, 158, 167
training, 61, 95, 122, 125, 178, 184, 185, 188
Treatise on Fruit Trees, 58
Treaty of Methuen, 77
Troggi, 179
truck, 55, 118, 119
Truck, 118, 119
tumping, 62, 67, 97
tumps, 67, 115
Tusser, Thomas, 43
Two Dogs, 159, 173
—U—
ukcider.co.uk, 176, 177, 178
Usk Valley, 179
—V—
Valognes, 35, 50
VAT, 152
Vigo, 182
Vine Products, 146, 150
Vinetum Britannicum, 64, 71
vineyards, 23, 25, 26, 30, 31, 32, 54, 178, 188
—W—
wash, 35, 73
wassailing, 45
Watney Combe Reid, 145
Welsh Perry & Cider Society, 177, 179
West Country Brewers, 137
West Sussex, 33, 99
Westcote, Thomas, 54
Weston's, 10, 105, 112, 113, 114, 116, 117, 120, 122, 125, 128, 129, 137, 141, 146, 147, 160, 164, 169, 170, 171, 187
Whimple, 117, 138, 158
Whin Hill, 187, 189
whisky, 19, 74, 184

Whisky, 70
Whitbread, 91, 138, 145, 146, 149, 154, 157, 163
white cider, 159, 160, 164, 170, 174
White Lightning, 159, 160
Whiteways, 117, 129, 136, 138, 140, 141, 142, 143, 144, 146, 150, 158, 168, 172
wholesalers, 63, 80, 85, 116, 167, 181, 187, 188
Wickwar Cider, 138
wildings, 19, 36, 102
Wilkins, 129, 169, 175, 177
William Evans, 117, 147
William of Malmesbury, 31
William of Shoreham, 34
Williams Brothers of Backwell, 130, 169
wine, 3, 11, 12, 17, 18, 19, 20, 21, 22, 23, 25, 26, 28, 29, 30, 32, 33, 34, 51, 53, 54, 55, 60, 62, 63, 64, 65, 67, 68, 70, 72, 73, 75, 76, 77, 78, 83, 85, 86, 92, 106, 111, 115, 135, 146, 150, 151, 152, 158, 159, 161, 172, 173, 182, 183, 189

Witheridge, 49
Woodcock, 66
Woodlanders, The, 108, 115
Woodpecker, 125, 136, 150, 152, 162
Woolhope Naturalists' Field Club, 105
Worcester, 45, 49, 74, 93, 184
Worcestershire, 49, 54, 57, 90, 119, 121, 161, 177, 181
World War I, 126, 128, 131, 132, 135, 140, 141
World War II, 38, 130, 137, 140, 167
Worlidge, John, 64, 65, 66, 71, 72, 78, 85
Worth, Robert, 114
—Y—
Yarde Farm, 183
Yarlington Mill, 102, 181
yeast, 13, 28, 29, 35, 63, 67, 68, 123, 150
Yorkshire, 26, 31, 84, 178, 183
Young, Arthur, 92, 96, 102
—Z—
zoning, 141, 168